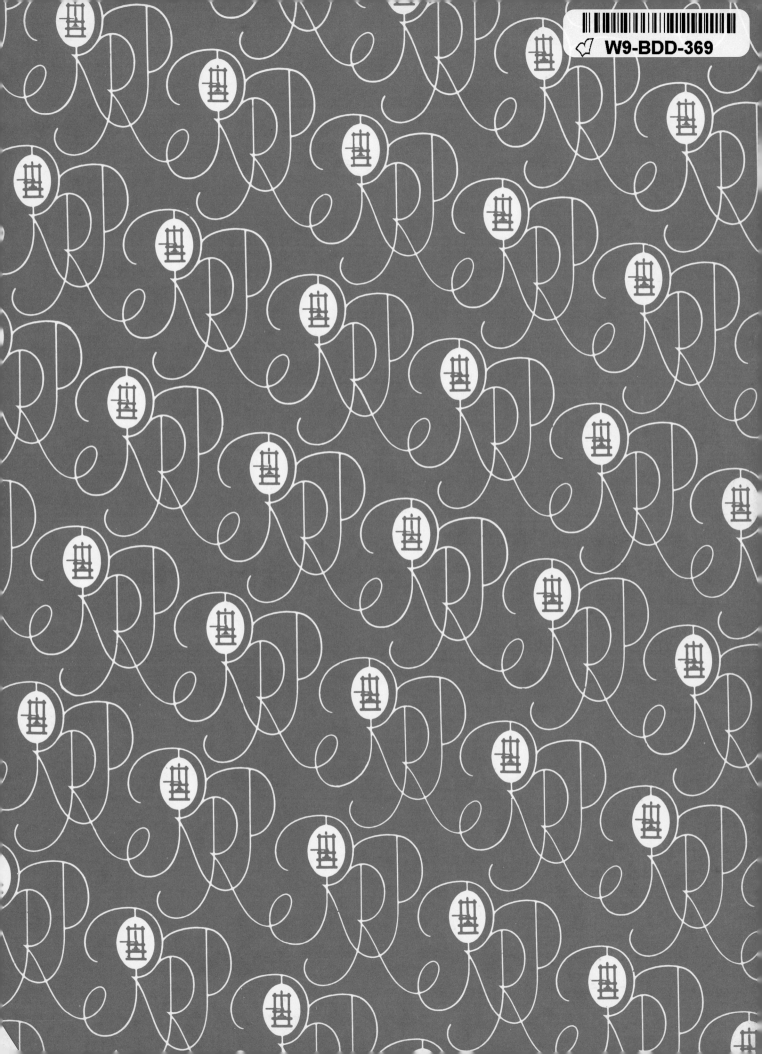

The Theatre Student

DIRECTING SHAKESPEARE
IN THE CONTEMPORARY THEATRE

The Theatre Student

DIRECTING SHAKESPEARE IN THE CONTEMPORARY THEATRE

Frank McMullan

PUBLISHED BY
RICHARDS ROSEN PRESS, INC.
NEW YORK, N.Y. 10010

Standard Book Number: 8239–0284–6
Library of Congress Catalog Card Number: 73–82374
Dewey Decimal Classification: 792

Published in 1974 by Richards Rosen Press, Inc.
29 East 21st Street, New York City, N.Y. 10010

First Edition

Manufactured in the United States of America

To Tommy
John and David

FRANK McMULLAN, Associate Professor of Play Production and former Head of the Directing Department of the School of Drama at Yale University, has some notable firsts in his theatrical career. He is the first of only two Americans to direct Shakespeare at Stratford-upon-Avon, England, where he directed a highly praised production of *Measure for Measure* in 1946. At the invitation of the University of Chile and Catholic University, he accepted a Fulbright grant to be the first American guest director and lecturer in theatre arts with the university-connected professional theatres Teatro del Instituto of the University of Chile and Teatro de Ensayo of Catholic University at Santiago, Chile. He directed the Latin American premiere of *Look Homeward, Angel* and a production of *The Taming of the Shrew,* both in Spanish, for which he was awarded a Chilean "Tony" in 1958. He established a theatre program at the University of Panama and directed *The Matchmaker* there. In 1962 he organized and headed a perform-

ing arts mission to the United Arab Republic (now the Arab Republic of Egypt), on behalf of the United States Department of State and the Egyptian government.

Mr. McMullan has distinguished himself in the educational as well as the professional theatre. He has served as guest director at the University of Arkansas Fine Arts Center, the Ohio State Summer Theatre, the San Diego Shakespeare Festival, the Champlain Shakespeare Festival, and numerous professional summer theatres; and he directed the summer drama school of the University of Vermont for several seasons. He has directed scores of plays —Broadway revivals, the classics, and many original scripts. He is the author of *One World in Drama, The Directorial Image, The Director's Handbook,* and numerous articles in *Theatre Arts, Players' Magazine,* and British and Spanish publications.

Mr. McMullan received a B.A. degree from the University of Georgia and an LL.B. from Georgia Law School. He then enrolled at Yale, where he received a Master of Fine Arts degree in drama.

CONTENTS

9

FOREWORD

The material in this book does not, by sequence of presentation, try to suggest a step-by-step procedure for the director. Procedural approach to a play and its production will vary according to the individual director, the play, and the conditions under which it is produced. However, the subject matter is discussed in a general order which implies the desirability of the director's possessing certain basic knowledge about Shakespearean productional and interpretive problems before beginning rehearsals and making production plans. The topics and sub-topics are intended as reference points of directorial consideration. Their synthesis can conceivably constitute an approach to Shakespearean production.

This book has been written for the director who already has some knowledge of the fundamentals of his craft but wishes to learn to handle special problems in putting Shakespeare's plays on the stage. No claim is made for original scholarly research into historical and critical material, but a wide range of sources and original thought have been used to build up a background and set forth in one book the salient features of the information and technique necessary for intelligent and imaginative Shakespearean productions.

The author, out of his own years of experience in directing Shakespeare, believes strongly in a director's need of understanding the theatre conditions for which Shakespeare wrote and the realization that those conditions must be reference points for contemporary production of his plays. Shakespeare's writing techniques bear a direct relationship to the physical means of audience communication. An equivalent relationship should be established by the modern stage and settings in order to allow the plays to express themselves in their own terms. The director's knowledge of Shakespeare's texts as they have come down to us and the preparation of his own working script are important. Aware of the mode and form which characterize the plays, the director can work effectively to accommodate them to our stage—proscenium, thrust, or in-the-round.

The cinematic nature of the plays' structure requires care in the choice and use of stage space in the placement of scenes, pictorial dramatization of scenes, and special attention to the need to establish and maintain the continuity of scenes throughout the performance. These are some of the particular problems encountered by the director in staging Shakespeare. A great problem involves the director's work with the actor, who is for the most part untrained and inexperienced in handling Shakespeare's archetypal characters. The difficulty of speaking blank verse, moving and behaving in the nonrealistic world of the play, which nevertheless must be real and truthful, can be overcome only by special acting and directing techniques.

Above all, the director standing between Shakespeare's world and ours must bridge the two by his view of the play and his means of expressing that view. New approaches and techniques as well as old are examined in the pages which follow. Today's theatre calls upon contemporary aesthetics and values proposed by today's critics and artists.

In an era in which innovation in the theatre often takes precedence over all other dramatic values, the director finds himself impelled to meet the demands of audiences satiated with entertainment provided by films and television as well as the stage and thus seeking new theatrical experiences. Innovative production stems from a desire to find the relevance of Shakespeare to contemporary society in revolutionary meaningfulness, in terms of either politics, sociology, or psychology. The result is often Shakespeare distorted or transmogrified to conform to the director's personal and timely concept and expression. The director's creativity or resourcefulness dominates that of the primordial creativity of the dramatist. The original is usually diminished in favor of a narrow vision, and the medium and point of view of the director become the focus of audience attention.

But how can the director be true to himself and to Shakespeare? The answer lies in his ability to find contemporaneity in the universal. If, as Stark Young asserted nearly half a century ago, a play is a work of art, it is "a living thing." As a living thing it speaks to a modern audience and evokes a vigorous response. In so doing it nourishes its own life, which "must be restated in every revival—." Life in a play "is not a fact, it is not a fixed and permanent statement; it is an ever changing reality, unconfinable, a ceaseless flux, but real." It is the director's "business as an artist . . . to discover a rendering of such a kind as will restate for the audience present the significance of the life of the play."* A director has many choices of interpretation and many ways and means to convey it in performance and production. The validity of his decisions can be measured only in their acceptance by enlightened critics and audiences interested in timeliness, which is timeless.

It is one of the purposes of this book to assist today's director of Shakespeare to make artistic choices which are illuminating and responsible, as well as creative and innovative.

———————

* Stark Young, *Theatre Practice* (New York, Charles Scribner's Sons, 1926), pp. 141–5.

ACKNOWLEDGMENTS

The author of a book is always beholden to a number of persons who helped him in diverse ways to achieve publication. I am no exception. I give grateful thanks to all. I appreciate particularly the secretarial assistance of Vera Deutsch and the verification of reference details by Judy Kopanic, Librarian of the Yale School of Drama. To Paul Kozelka, the editor of this series of books for the theatre student; and to Mrs. Ruth Rosen, Executive Editor of the Richards Rosen Press, Inc., my gratitude is due for invaluable editorial and publishing suggestions.

My many thanks to my wife cannot be counted. She has encouraged me; she has been patient; and she has been understanding. Her practical help in preparing the manuscript for publication has been immeasurable.

For permission to reproduce photographs used in this book I wish to thank the American Shakespeare Festival Theatre, Stratford, Connecticut; the Berliner Ensemble, Berlin, German Democratic Republic; the Champlain Shakespeare Festival, Burlington, Vermont; Coward, McCann & Geoghegan; the Guthrie Theater; Hofstra University; Macdonald and Company (Publishers) Limited; George E. Joseph, staff photographer for the New York Shakespeare Festival; the National Theatre Company of Great Britain; the Governors of the Royal Shakespeare Theatre; the Stratford Shakespearean Festival, Ontario, Canada; and the School of Drama, Yale University.

F. M.

Woodbridge, Connecticut
June 1, 1973

Chapter I

THE DIRECTOR'S DOUBLE VISION

Plays written in a historical period other than our own have built-in barriers between them and the reader or the audience. These must be removed or penetrated if the works are to become accessible to us in productions in the contemporary theatre. The question of thematic relevance must wait for a later discussion. (See Chapter V: "Making Shakespeare Contemporary.") We are concerned now with taking Shakespeare off the library shelf and evoking imaginatively the world of his plays for the stage.

Only a few people have read all thirty-seven plays attributed to Shakespeare. A director is usually reasonably familiar with the great tragedies and the most frequently performed comedies. The dramatic facts as to the characters and the through-line of the narrative are common knowledge to him. The language of the plays does not get in his way, the characters are distinguishable, and the main dramatic values often stand clear.

The plays unfamiliar to the director, on the other hand, may seem opaque and resistant to his artistically creative eyes. In the preliminary reading the director must learn the facts of the play: *who* the characters are and their relationships, *where* they are, *what* they are doing, and *why* they are doing it. To determine these facts the director may find himself constantly referring to the list of *dramatis personae* to sort out the characters. The language will require close and continual reference to the footnotes and glossary to determine meanings. Many readings are necessary before he can gain the basic knowledge he needs to make the play open up to him. The director of Shakespeare must be free to believe the fiction of the play just as though it were a modern play about modern people and their problems. He must be able to respond to the dramatic stimuli by making the imaginative leap over the centuries without being aware that he is doing so.

FREE IMAGERY

The actual approach to the interpretation of Shakespeare for the stage involves the director in a flow of spontaneous imagery which evokes a double vision. On one level he forms a concept of a play in terms of its emotional impact, subject, meaning, and structure. His vision of it from this point of view is derived from an attempt to apprehend it by submerging himself in the world of the play. On the second level the director has a vision of the play on the stage in terms of actors, scenery, costumes, lighting, and sound. These visions may occur separately or together. Yet they are dependent upon one another; interpretation and production must coexist. This process of double vision not only occurs in the study and planning stage of the director's work but also continues throughout rehearsal and the process of production. All the while the director revises and reshapes each vision, the interpretive and the productional. In the preliminary stages, however, the images constituting both visions should be welcomed in all formlessness, freedom, spontaneity, and novelty.

It will be noted that the imagery of the director at this stage of his preparation for production does not derive from a study of the language of the play in the manner followed by Caroline Spurgeon or other Shakespearean scholars who search for images and their recurrence to formulate an interpretation. Later, the director may very well consult such studies in imagery for stimulation and understanding. Now, however, he may consciously or unconsciously be influenced by his private and individual response to imagery in the words. But the words are mainly generative of nonliterary imagery like actor behavior to denote some revelation of character, the pictorial dramatization of a moment, etc. Or the imagery of words regularly recurring and

15

strongly stimulative may suggest purely interpretive concepts. In subsequent and deeper study of the play the director may consciously find "image hunting" and the words to be helpful in discovering patterns which will influence his approach to a play.

It is impossible for the director to come to a play of Shakespeare with a completely free mind. He has already formed some impression of the play from reading it, hearing about it, or seeing it in performance. He cannot approach the play as he would a new play which he reads for the first time. (Of course, even a new play comes to the director with some associations and even biases.) The director can only strive to wipe his mind and feelings clean and try to be positively receptive to new and different stimuli and images. Ideally, he should allow his images of the play, on the level of interpretation and on the level of production, to emerge by free association.

Such emergence is hindered not only by preconceived general notions about the play but by the Shakespearean language, which sets up a screen between the reader and the play. Nevertheless, it is advisable for the director on his first reading to read straight through, even though he may not be able to see through this screen of strange and obsolete words. On this first reading he should try to open himself to as much feeling and meaning as possible. He should try to grasp the overall sweep and impact. After the initial reading and response to the play he should read it a second time, this time stopping to learn the meaning of words and individual lines of dialogue. A director must absorb at least the outer meaning of the language of a play to permit even a limited number of images to emerge. Repeated readings and study will open up new sources of images. (Reading the play aloud and listening to recordings of performances of it can be helpful to the director. However, though his own reading of the dialogue and the readings of professional actors will naturally suggest approaches to character, they should not be thought of in those terms. Such readings should be considered as merely means of opening up the director's sensibilities to the play. They serve to start the flow of imagination.) Eventually the director will be able to penetrate the screen of language and will respond easily to the imagined stimuli of the play. In this first period of exposure, the director should be filled with images, but he should not yet allow them to form a definite

and unchanging pattern. This is the *open* period.

To put this to practical use we must select and examine a play. We might avoid some of the problems of overfamiliarity if we select *King Lear,* which is not usually studied in high school and often not deeply studied in college. It is a play which until the 1960s was not frequently performed in the United States. The only productions in the last two decades important enough to recall are John Houseman's with Louis Calhern in 1951, those of the American Shakespeare Theatre Festival with Maurice Carnovsky in 1963 and 1965, Peter Brook's with Paul Scofield in 1964, that of the Stratford, Ontario, festival with John Colicos in 1964, and the one at Lincoln Center with Lee J. Cobb in 1968. Four of these productions, it will be noted, were presented during a two-year period. Naturally, reviews and commentary have appeared in newspapers and magazines, and a great deal has been written about Brook's production in books on the avant-garde drama. General interest in the play has increased considerably. Nevertheless, compared to the other great tragedies, it is not well known, and it is possible to respond imaginatively to it without too many preconceived notions or too much bias.

In the first period of relatively uninhibited response to *King Lear* the director's images may be both fragmentary and complete and relate to a moment, scene, act, or even the entire play. For example, 1. 1 * can be imagined as a kind of Judgment Day trial taking place in a vast wasteland: Gloucester, Kent, and Edmund gossip and wait; then the sound of a horn, wild and primitive, reminding us of something associated with biblical days; the hurried and apprehensive entrance and huddled grouping of Regan, Cornwall, Goneril, and Albany; the slow and majestic entrance of King Lear, followed by Cordelia; the examination and the evidence; the judgments and sentencing; the defensive protestation of Kent as well as of Cordelia; the banishment; and the ominous plotting and threatening against the judge. Of course, these images might occur in or out of sequence at first and be organized later. Certain "moments" in this scene might stand out and special images might flash into one's mind. For example, the Regan-Goneril group, which was imagined in a hurried and apprehensive entrance, might

---

* Meaning Act 1, scene 1.

turn as a unit and simultaneously greet Lear —each one of the group suddenly and simultaneously smiling. Perhaps all could wear grinning masks—to be removed before their next appearance. Another "moment" might occur when the coronet, which Lear has given to Albany and Cornwall to "part between" them, is being borne out on a pillow, held by a court attendant. As he comes near Goneril and Regan they both reach for it, look at one another, smile, and allow the coronet to be taken out. A sequence of images possible from the opening scene of the play concerns the Fool. He can be visualized as the first character to come onstage as the lights come up. He might dawdle on, pass in front of the throne chair, bow to it absentmindedly, thinking the King is in it—and then go on a few steps before he realizes his foolish mistake. And then after he looks about furtively he might grinningly rush to the throne, plop into it, and go through an imaginary moment in which he pretends to be King Lear. When he hears the voices of Gloucester and Kent he could jump out of the throne and start out, but then could stop, look in the direction from which the voices are coming, and then hide behind the throne to see and overhear all that develops in scene 1. At the end of the scene he might jump into the throne chair for the ride as it is being pushed off by the court attendants.

As can be seen, interpretive and staging images intertwine and are mutually dependent. These images might emerge at random after repeated readings and take a considerable period of time to materialize. The lapse of time, however, becomes a period of gestation, and the images take on some kind of order. This does not mean, of course, that even though they have crystallized into some kind of order they will eventually be translated into actual performance and production. They, it must be repeated, are subject to revision and even to rejection.

Scenes 3, 4, and 5 of the first act take place in Goneril's house, which can be imagined as a house of mirrors. The mirrors are held by the Knight, Oswald, the Fool, and Goneril. Each one, in his own way, shows Lear what Lear has become. First of all, divested of his royal robes and now in hunting dress, he has changed from a *king* to a *man*. Roaring authority has become a spoiled old man calling for his dinner. And when no one answers, his Knight holds up his mirror to show Lear how much he has declined in esteem, affection, and

kindness in Goneril's household. Oswald, representing the servants, overtly mirrors the disrespect in which Lear is held. So vivid is the image Lear sees that he strikes Oswald—to destroy the mirror.

When Lear looks into the Fool's mirror he sees the grotesque face of another fool. Bewildered, Lear cries out (scene 4):

Does any here know me? This is not Lear.
. . . . .
Who is it can tell me who I am?

And the Fool answers, "Lear's shadow!" Continuing the discussion in search of his identity, Lear sarcastically asks Goneril to give her name to affirm that she is his daughter. She coldly replies that his behavior is affected and prankish and unbecoming to one who, "old and reverend, should be wise." She further mirrors the image of his knights who are

Men so disordered, so debauched and bold,
That this our court, infected with their manners,
Shows like a riotous inn. Epicurism and lust
Makes it more like a tavern or a brothel
Than a graced palace.

And she demands "instant remedy." His anger blurring his vision, he calls for his horses to make immediate departure from Goneril's house. But before he goes he turns the mirror for Goneril to see her own detested kite's form and calls upon the goddess Nature to "Dry up in her the organs of increase"; but

If she must teem,
. . . . .
Turn all her mother's pains and benefits
To laughter and contempt, that she may feel
How sharper than a serpent's tooth it is
To have a thankless child!

Then, his head swimming with vertigo, he overturns his chair and table, rushes out to his knights' quarters, and returns to exclaim that fifty of his knights have been dismissed. Ashamed of the hot tears streaming down his face, he implies he will go to another daughter who is "kind and comfortable." He then leaves Goneril's house of mirrors whose images crack and fragment his mind into oncoming madness.

Goneril's house may be identified for the audience by the use of one or more screens encrusted with broken mirrors. When Lear overturns his table and orders his knights away, whirling lights might catch these mirrors and turn his world into a grotesque nightmare of splintered light and darkness. This revolving light should be sudden and unexpected and should start slowly with Lear's "Darkness and devils!" and gradually increase in speed to his "To have a thankless child! Away, away!" The light should then pulsate until Lear departs. When he reappears in scene 5 with Kent and the Fool, two or three patches of light should slowly revolve to suggest the residual emotion in Lear. And when the Fool, who has been subtly goading Lear, says

> Thou should'st not have been old till thou hadst been wise

the lights should start pulsating again and continue until Lear and the Fool disappear in darkness.

The second act of the play constitutes a pattern of images of flights and pursuits, and arrivals and departures. First Edmund moves against Edgar, puts him to flight, and puts Gloucester in sworn pursuit. At this point Regan and Cornwall arrive from their castle, learn of Edgar's alleged treason against his father, and reward Edmund by accepting him in Cornwall's service. Kent and Oswald, messengers of Lear and Goneril, follow Regan to Gloucester's castle, become entangled in a quarrel, and Oswald calls for help against Kent, who is attacking him. This brings Edmund, Gloucester, Regan, and Cornwall to the scene. The result is the punishment of Kent by putting him into stocks. Lear's arrival and his discovery of the disrespectful use of his messenger eventually persuade Regan and Cornwall to appear to set Kent free. Lear's movement toward Regan for comfort and refuge is repulsed by Regan in sympathy with her sister. The arrival of Goneril and her alliance with Regan result in a rejection of Lear and Lear's flight into the impending storm. Gloucester out of sympathy rushes after him, only to return, and is ordered to shut his door against the storm—and Lear.

This pattern of movements resembles a spider's web woven by all. And all will be eventually entrapped by it, first Lear and Gloucester and afterward the rest. Weakened by a series of blows to his illusions about royal authority and filial gratitude, Lear becomes enmeshed as he struggles to disentangle himself. The spider's web is woven about his brain with such complexity and devilish artfulness that his mind slips into madness. The web spun of undeceptive-looking thread begins to harden into a torture rack of iron.

The spiders as well as the flies work in blindness. The images of seeing, blindness, appearance, and reality recur and add significance to the actions visualized in the director's mind's eye. Darkness and light are therefore most important to the staging of this act of the play. The area of light should always be small —just large enough to contain the action and suggest great and undefinable stretches of darkness. Gloucester's castle is a kind of link between the light of heaven and the pitch-blackness of hell. The characters suddenly appear and disappear. Their movements are short, quick, and strong. Lear moves forward only to retreat and ultimately paces around erratically. Regan, Cornwall, Goneril, and Oswald form a tight and solid wall against which Lear attacks and falls back. Gloucester stands between the two forces; Kent, the Fool, and the gentlemen stand silently on the sidelines, allied to Lear but helpless. When Lear leaves, they trail after him drooping and in disarray.

Act 3 is dominated by the storm, which sets up a dynamic field of imagery. Interactions in this field are the physical tempest, the tempest in Lear's mind, and the raging destruction and disorder of political and social life. Circumscribing all this is the chain of imagery of light and darkness. In the center is Lear "in his little world of man" (3. 1), scorning "The to-and-fro-conflicting wind and rain."

In the first scene Kent and the Gentleman play a sort of blindman's buff. Kent searches for Lear, who madly rushes out into the storm from Gloucester's castle, now ruled by Regan and Cornwall, and the Gentleman looks for Kent. Buffeted by the wind they stumble, get up, advance, retreat, spin, and finally see one another. And then clinging to one another they stand unsteadily in a flickering flame of light intermittently dashed to darkness. They picture the undaunted Lear "Contending with the fretful elements," while the division between Albany and Cornwall increases and the disturbing infiltration of spies from France undermines both parties.

Then Lear replaces Kent and the Gentleman in blinding light oscillating to the tune of his unstrung mind. He calls for the destruction of the world and the mold and seed of mankind. Ingratitude, unkindness, justice, mercy, and sin run like a thread in the tangled web of his thoughts. And as his "wits begin to turn" (3. 2) Kent and the Fool lead him toward dry shelter—a hovel instead of a castle.

Like a melodramatic film, alternating camera shots to pick up a parallel story and to increase suspense and tension, the cold wind-swept heath fades out and the camera in a flashback closes in on Gloucester and Edmund inside the castle. The storm, raging inside as well as out, is reflected in Gloucester's dismay at being dispossessed of his home and his wary resolution to side with the King. And nature rampages headlong in its path of destruction as Edmund plots to betray his father and hastens the ruin of family and home.

Again the scene fades and the eye of the camera focuses on Lear, Kent, and the Fool as they seek refuge from the storm inside the shelter. Entrance is delayed by Lear, who would rather endure the tempest outside than the stronger one beating in his weakening mind. Shunning madness by a show of compassion for the poor unsheltered Fool, he urges the boy in while he remains outside to pray. In the fiery light of the storm he peers into the dark corners of his mind and sees there the "Poor naked wretches" whose "houseless heads and unfed sides" the great like himself have neglected (3. 4).

> Take physic, pomp;
> Expose thyself to feel what wretches feel

he cries out in anguished sympathy and penance. The camera, now equipped with X-ray lens, has been focusing upon the inner world of Lear, and we see the blurred image of Edgar disguised as Poor Tom as he emerges from the hovel. The Fool's scream heralding Poor Tom's appearance shatters Lear's prayer and turns Lear's eyes upon the naked wretch. Like Lear, Edgar is "Unaccommodated man . . . no more but such a poor, bare, forked animal." Lear begins to tear off his clothes, to strip himself naked like his twin in misery. The king declines to the state of man. The madman and the other pretending madness mirror one another. At this stage of Lear's enlightenment Gloucester appears and looks upon a scene which illuminates his own state. Lear, Edgar, and Gloucester are a three-way mirror. Lear refuses Gloucester's offer of food and fire in order to talk first with Poor Tom the "philosopher," and then all seek refuge in Gloucester's farmhouse as the image fades from the screen.

The focus changes again to Gloucester's castle when the camera dollies in on Cornwall and Edmund in a flashback. Their demonic faces in torchlight, they resolve to apprehend Gloucester for alleged treason against his patron.

Now we cut back to the interior of the shelter where the image of Gloucester and Kent emerges. As Gloucester departs to his castle to prepare for the coming of Lear, an X-ray picture of Lear, the Fool, Edgar, and Kent is projected on the screen. Lear, tormented by his own friends, is chased by the Fool and Poor Tom covered in black diaphanous material to suggest the fiends, his daughters. He directs Edgar, whose foul fiend bites his back, to sit as "justice" in a mock trial of Goneril and Regan. The Fool and Kent are ordered also to sit in judgment. Two joint stools represent the "she-foxes." Lear, the prosecutor, makes the charges against the hard-hearted defendants. Three shafts of light from directly overhead encircle the justices, the prosecutor, and the defendants. After bursting out in anger against Regan, Lear appoints Edgar one of his hundred knights if he will change his garments; Lear does not like their "fashion." The old man stands and stares. Kent finally persuades him to lie down and rest, and he obeys, asking that the curtains of his imagined bed be drawn. The King stretches out at the feet of the justices, who are sitting in the center of the stage. The Fool, Edgar, and Kent stare straight ahead into nothingness. They sit motionless in silent grief over the body of their crucified lord and master. The three pools of light fade to one embracing golden light, which crowns their heads like a halo. The awesome image is held for the audience in silence. After a long pause a harp string snaps, the light changes and spreads across the stage, and the bleared image of the X-ray camera is replaced by the clear but bleak vision of Gloucester with two attendants carrying the white fire of torches. They lift up their master to take him in a litter toward Dover where welcome and protection await him. The lights dim as they slip away into the night; the Fool pauses to look sadly around and then sobbingly disappears in the opposite direction to "go to bed at noon" (3. 6). Shakespeare does not bring him back on the stage again. The mad Lear, the king, has lost his crown and wears the Fool's coxcomb. He is his own fool and needs no other.

Disorder reigns inside as well as out. Regan

and Cornwall, in Gloucester's castle, have displaced the owner and seek his apprehension for alleged treason. The army of France has landed, and Gloucester's letter stolen by Edmund is the incriminating evidence against Gloucester. The storm angrily reflects the inversions, the unnaturalness, and the discord between visitors and host, father and son, state and state, and thus sister against sister and brother against brother. Madness of passion riots in Cornwall, Regan, and Goneril as they scream for revenge upon Gloucester. Edmund, his son, appears in silence and departs with Goneril to Albany to urge his preparation for war with France. Then Gloucester is brought in and bound to face trial. The visitors become judges to accuse their host. Tied to the stake, Gloucester cries out to "the kind gods" for help as the foot of Cornwall stamps out his eyes. "All dark and comfortless," he calls (3. 7) upon Edmund to requite the "horrid act" but learns from Regan that his son was his informer. Eyeless and in blinding pain he realizes that Edgar was wronged. He is thrust out of his own gates to "smell/His way to Dover." He had sight but did not use it and now he must rely upon his other senses.

But Cornwall bleeds "apace" and calls for Regan's arm. She slowly comes toward him as though to help him and then suddenly turns away, leaving him to stagger out into the darkness. The victim of an attack by his servant, who said "I have served you ever since I was a child," the father-master is mortally wounded by his child-servant. Like Gloucester he is betrayed by his child and like Gloucester he bleeds. Betrayed by his wife, he bleeds to death alone.

This segment of action in the last scene of the third act parallels the mad trial of Lear's daughters. This cruel inquisition, unlike the grotesque hallucinatory arraignment of evil, punishes the defendant not with words but with horrifying torture. Thus we see two faces of justice. If the audience will look back on the first scene of the play, they will recall another "trial" scene and another face of justice. In the last scene of the play is a last trial and a final judgment. These thematic repetitions and parallels and contrasts form a sequence of images which can create a meaningful pattern.

The pictorial representations of these images are markedly different. The first and second have already been described. The image of the third, the inquisition and punishment of Gloucester, is intensified by a flaming brazier which projects the shadows of the predatory vultures as they hover over their prey. The lights from the brazier falling upon the bleeding eyes of Gloucester turn the world red. The vultures, Cornwall and Regan, circle their tortured and helpless quarry. They alternate in encircling movements of attack and braked stops as the "third-degree" investigation of Gloucester accelerates by questions and heightens in emotion. Gloucester, "tied to the stake," provided by a primitive rack wrought from rough tree trunks and vines, is gradually forced to his knees and then face up as he is thrust back on the rack. This whole nightmare action of the trial takes place in a well-like area of the stage. The stamping action of Cornwall is down toward the victim's face, which is hidden from the audience's view. However, when Gloucester raises his head into view the eye sockets should look as though they are oozing fountains of blood which has spilled over his hands as they come up slowly before he says, "All dark and comfortless! Where's my son Edmund?" The answer Regan gives him of Edmund's betrayal is followed by a long silence before he whispers in enlightened astonishment:

> O, my follies! Then Edgar is abused.
> Kind gods, forgive me that, and prosper him!

Then he is led out with the rack partially unfastened but still tied to him and trailing after him. Regan goes out in one direction and Cornwall lurches out in the opposite direction. The two servants remaining onstage look off at the drooping vultures and determine to help

> the old earl, and get the bedlam
> To lead him where he would;

and protect him from harm. One goes after Gloucester and the other to

> fetch some flax and whites of eggs
> To apply to his bleeding face.

These movements of Gloucester, Cornwall and Regan, and the servants originate out of disorder and should heighten the grotesqueness of the bloody events. And now we turn to Acts 4 and 5 to see the aftermath of the storm.

In the first scene of Act 4, when light licks across the stage with its narrow, long tongue, we see a bleak, dreary morning with no one in sight. After a silence two figures appear, moving painfully and slowly toward us. A streak of red light leaves a trail of blood behind them. One old man, with a gnarled walking stick for a third leg, moves forward uncertainly and holds the hand of the other and pulls him along. He, Gloucester, lagging behind, reaches out with his other hand to feel his way. These two in tandem come along in silence, and then, suddenly, Edgar appears and stops short on seeing them and turns to us with his question:

> But who comes here?
> My father, poorly eyed?

When he finishes saying "Life would not yield to age," Gloucester breaks away from the Old Man and, in despair, waves him away. Full of remorse he rejects help:

> I have no way, and therefore want no eyes;
> I stumbled when I saw.

The irony of Edgar's presence and his inability to reveal himself to his father cannot be lost on the audience. Too, Gloucester's loss of physical vision and his simultaneous acquisition of spiritual insight makes its dramatic impact. Though Gloucester is separated from Edgar physically and cannot recognize him though he is actually present, Gloucester's inner light leads him toward the "beggar-man" and "naked fellow." The blind father senses some kinship with the man and remarks that when he saw him in last night's storm he recalled that

> My son
> Came then into my mind,

Bitterly thinking of his blindness, Edmund's unnatural betrayal, and Edgar's suffering as well as his own, Gloucester considers man's condition:

> As flies to wanton boys are we to th' gods;
> They kill us for their sport.

Urging the Old Man to depart for clothing to cover "this naked soul," Gloucester decides to entreat the beggar to lead him to the cliffs of Dover. The Old Man's reply and Gloucester's answer extend the ironic absurdity of Gloucester's predicament—and man's: "Alack, sir, he is mad!" and " 'Tis the time's

plague when madmen lead the blind." Seeing no solution Gloucester urges Edgar, the child, to lead him, the father, to "the very brim of" the cliffs of Dover from which he will "no leading need." Gloucester thinks he can bring to an end his purgatorial journey through life.

At the Duke of Albany's palace (4. 2) we see the effect of Gloucester's and Lear's downfall. We know that the storm reaches inside as well as out. No one is safe from it. The injury done to the king can but hurt his subjects. Violence breeds violence. And so the marriage of Goneril and Albany is destroyed when news of the violence of Lear's and Gloucester's treatment reaches Albany and he realizes what a "monster" his wife is. The destruction of Albany's home by the storm is only the beginning of the whirlwind which gathers momentum with the landing of the French army and threatens his dukedom.

> No blown ambition doth our arms incite,
> But love, dear love, and our aged father's
> right. (4. 4)

is Cordelia's explanation of France's presence in Britain. Her holy crusade is expressed in

> O dear father,
> It is thy business that I go about!

with its biblical implications. Hers is a mission of mercy.

Near Dover (4. 6) Edgar and Gloucester play out their prologue to a grotesque comedy. Like minor clowns they go through the action of Gloucester's attempt at suicide. Edgar, pretending to set his father on the brim of the precipice to allow him to hurl himself to death on the rocks below, actually fools the old man, who merely falls to the smooth ground unhurt. Having experienced a symbolic death, Gloucester is cured of his death wish and thenceforth determines to

> bear
> Affliction till it do cry out itself
> "Enough, enough," and die.

Then the main comedy commences with the entrance of Lear fantastically bedecked with wild flowers.

Lear and Gloucester, the principal clowns, then enact their comic routine of questions and answers which paint the absurd picture of the world exhibited on this "great stage of fools." Exhausted, the leading clown sits down on the earth and his comic partner helps him to pull off his boots. They rest in silence and stare into the void.

The arrival of Cordelia's emissary breaks their silence. He comes to rescue the old clown from the circus of life and to take him into healing retirement. Lear playfully runs away, followed by the attendant who will take him to his nurse.

As Gloucester is being led away to refuge and comfort, Oswald enters, spies "A proclaimed prize," and unsheathes his sword to kill the "published traitor." But again Edgar rescues his father from death. He slays Oswald and leads Gloucester away to be protected by a friend, as the drums of war are heard in the distance. These are the counterpoint chords to the dissonant music made by God's buffoons playing sourly on unstrung instruments.

Looking back at the suicides and clown scenes we notice that they have a special quality. The light is cold and bleak but it is clear. The actors mime the action of suicides like two children naively but deeply and seriously involved in a world of make-believe. It is pitiful and amusing to see Edgar, who in one sense plays a trick upon his poor old blind father and takes a certain childish delight in it. Yet, underneath the apparent delight is a little boy who plays a game in dead earnest. He is playing "for real" the role of a doctor who deludes the patient into acceptance of a nasty-tasting medicine which will make him "all better." His playmate father is indeed sick of life but is cured of his illness—at least momentarily.

The game with Edgar over, Gloucester plays another with Lear the actor, who insists on a game of his own. It is a game of make-believe that creates the thin line between reality and illusion. It is a theatrical game of improvisation that is founded on truth. The dramatic event involves Lear the actor, who makes Gloucester alternate as actor and audience. Gloucester participates in the action and comments upon it. The play that Lear, completely immersed in his part, enacts is a morality. He peoples it with characters other than Gloucester, plays scenes with them, and points out the moral of each scene. At the end of the morality play, he turns to his partner to assure him that he knows he has been playing a part. As king-actor who has fashioned the script from the telescoped events of his life, Lear finishes the play to take off his pinching boots,

turns to Gloucester with "I know thee well enough; thy name is Gloucester," and then comforts his weeping audience with

Thou must be patient. We came crying hither;
Thou know'st the first time that we smell the
air
We wawl and cry.

This is the moral of this play. The world is a "great stage of fools" and "When we are born, we cry that we are come" to it. Then Lear's mind slips from the illusions of drama to the reality of his life and he cries out for revenge with "kill, kill, kill, kill, kill!" The appearance of the gentleman who would "lay hand upon him" becomes the image of an enemy who would make him prisoner and perhaps take his life, and Lear in playful madness runs away with the challenge: "Come, an you get it you shall get it by running." And he is off with "sa, sa, sa, sa," a hunting cry. This is black comedy indeed.

This demonic sound blends into soft music and we next see a sickroom with the Doctor and Cordelia as the nurse in attendance (4. 7). The Good Samaritan Kent is also at the bedside. The patient Lear is asleep at first but soon stirs in half-dreams and wakefulness. He does not know whether he is in heaven or hell, dead or alive. Though he is not in "perfect mind," yet he thinks this lady is his child Cordelia and knows she does not love him. Her sisters, he remembers, have done him wrong—but they had no cause. Cordelia has. "No cause, no cause," Cordelia protests. Though his "great rage . . . is killed in him," it is dangerous to make him try to recollect what has happened, the Doctor advises. And his nurse leads him gently away as he murmurs:

You must bear with me. Pray you now, forget
and forgive; I am old and foolish.

Then the ugly, insistent drums of war drown the plaintive music and we are jolted with the image of hate and evil contention.

The rest of the play, except for the very end, is a full spectrum of conflict, with final confrontations and judgment. We move from "domestic broils" to war and heraldic trial by sword—the doomsday settling of accounts between Good and Evil.

Sisters, impassioned by lust and jealousy, fight against one another for the love of the same man. Edmund, loving neither, devises strategies to keep each at the other's throat, to use the authority and power of Goneril's husband to win the battle and capture Lear and Cordelia, whom he plans to hold for his own ambitious purposes. Albany, conscience-stricken over the mistreatment of Lear and Gloucester, is torn between his allegiance to his wife, whom he no longer loves, and his devotion to the King. The two armies of Albany and Regan stand on opposite sides, poised to attack one another. Urged to "Combine together 'gainst the enemy" (5. 1), Albany agrees to consult the commanders as to a battle plan. The two leaders, allied in an uneasy truce, go to their tents. Albany is approached by a mysterious ragged stranger who presents a letter to him. The audience knows this is Edgar, who has given Albany Goneril's letter to Edmund. The stranger swears to present, after the battle, a champion to fight the one who may challenge the truth of the letter's contents. A new combatant is added who increases the intensity of the conflict.

Trumpets, drums, flags, and soldiers criss-cross in symbolic battle. Lear, Cordelia, and her forces appear and retreat before Edmund's forces. Then Edgar and Gloucester flee across the battlefield as the French soldiers are herded before the conquering Edmund, who has captured Lear and Cordelia. Rescue turned to defeat, Cordelia despairs for her father, but he, weary of life in the big world, joyfully looks forward to a happy life together with her in the small world of their prison cage where they can

> pray, and sing, and tell old tales and laugh
> At gilded butterflies, and hear poor rogues
> Talk of court news; and we'll talk with them too—
> Who loses and who wins, who's in, who's out—
> And take upon 's the mystery of things,
> As if we were God's spies;   (5. 3)

Happiness will come to them when they are no longer participants but are bystanders in the world. Withdrawal is better than commitment and involvement. Their strife is over in this discordant, absurd world. But the gods have decreed otherwise. Evil is still predatory—and contentious.

The arrival of Albany and Goneril with their forces, and Albany's demand that the captives be turned over to him for judgment precipitate a quarrel over Edmund's position in the new hierarchy. Albany accuses Edmund of treason and demands that he prove his innocence on the field of honor. If no one comes to challenge him, Albany will; he throws down his gauntlet. Edmund throws his down to maintain his "truth and honor." A herald is summoned to trumpet the call for a challenge to Edmund. In mortal agony from Goneril's poison, Regan slinks away to die.

Edgar, the challenger and "champion," now in magnificent knight's dress and masking helmet, confronts Edmund. The ritualistic ceremony of tournaments is observed, and the trial of Good and Evil begins as the trumpets speak. Albany stands in judgment between the combatants. When Edmund falls, Goneril, his accessory in crime, tries to save him but the judge proves her guilty too and she flees. Edgar reveals himself, as Edmund asks for forgiveness. For Edmund "The wheel is come full circle." Fortune's wheel, which turned and raised him high, has now turned again and dashed him to the earth. He is once more on the bottom where he began. Dust to dust.

Edgar, like a chorus in an ancient tragedy, narrates how he escaped from his father's wrath in "madman's rags," then met him "with his bleeding rings," saved him from despair, resolved himself before the trumpets called him to the field of honor, but his father's

> flawed heart
> (Alack, too weak the conflict to support)
> 'Twixt two extremes of passion, joy and grief,
> Burst smilingly.

A messenger brings the news that Goneril and Regan are dead—Goneril by her own hand and Regan from her sister's poison. Kent comes forth and demands the whereabouts of Lear. Edmund, commanded by Albany and meaning to do some good despite his own nature, begs that someone be sent to the castle to prevent the hanging of Cordelia, ordered by him and Goneril. He is borne out to die.

As the messenger approaches the castle, the prison gate slowly rises with a rattle of chains and a deafening clamor of iron scraping against the metal frame of the opening. The messenger enters in silence. After a long pause there is a shrill cry followed by sobs which get louder and louder, and then Lear appears with Cordelia in his arms. He stops, stifles his sobs, and then walks slowly in silence to the center of the stage—the center of his world. He places Cordelia gently upon the ground and asks for a looking glass to see if her breath will mist the mirror. Kent, Edgar, and Albany see the horrible image of the end of the world. When the mirror shows no sign of her breath, Lear catches a feather and thinks he sees it stir in response to Cordelia's breathing. Begging her to "stay a little," he thinks he hears her speak and bends over her to hear.

> What is't thou say'st?—Her voice was ever soft,
> Gentle and low, an excellent thing in a woman—

Turning to Kent he momentarily recognizes him and welcomes him. But Kent knows no man is welcome. Lear is all alone; he sees no one and knows no one, "All's cheerless, dark, and deadly." He sits and leans over Cordelia.

Albany, the reigning lord, hands back Lear's kingdom and reinstates Kent and Edgar, then turns to see the Fool brought in and thrown down like a sack of potatoes—dead by hanging. The grieving old man moans over his daughter and the Fool:

> Thou'lt come no more,
> Never, never, never, never, never!

Then once more he thinks Cordelia breathes, and in quiet joy he dies. Edgar thinks he has fainted but Kent knows he is at peace at last and says:

> Vex not his ghost: O, let him pass; he hates him,
> That would upon the rack of this tough world Stretch him out longer.

He is gone and

> The wonder is he hath endured so long;
> He but usurped his life.

Edgar is left to "Rule in this realm, and the gored state sustain." Age gives way to youth and a new order—which may come out of the world's disorder.

The images for the first scene of this last act of *King Lear* consist of hurried, fragmented movements stopped by sudden appearances which position the actors on the stage to show suspicion, questioning, and opposition. This static and irregular but temporarily balanced composition holds its shape uneasily and then the elements explode into the frantic action of the next scene of battle already described. This

montage of movement, color, and sound fades out and is succeeded by the image of spears encircling Lear and Cordelia like a cage. After Edmund gives his instructions for their death and is departing with satisfaction, he is stopped by the commanding voice of Albany. And once again the opposing figures are positioned in a static but volatile composition, which ultimately changes into the formal movement of the ritual of the trial between the two knights. This in turn changes into thrust and parry motions which end when one contestant drops wounded. In contrast are the blinking movements of first Regan and then Goneril as they go out of focus. We ultimately concentrate upon the avenging knight bending over his victim and ringed by the soldier-spectators. The spectators become audience at a storytelling, changing postures and attitudes as the narrative spins out but doing so in unison and thus giving the impression of manipulated puppets. This, too, is a kind of ritual interrupted only by the sudden cry and entrance of the Gentleman who tells of Goneril's death.

The image of this unexpected and broken movement is followed by a series of similar images: Kent's entrance, the bringing in of the bodies of Regan and Goneril, and the exit of the messenger. Then the rhythm sharply changes with the sound of the rising prison gate and the slow, painful movement of Lear holding Cordelia in his arms.

The next scene is pictured as one of penitents at a shrine. Lear and Cordelia form a cross, Lear dead across the body of his daughter; Albany, Edgar, and Kent are on their knees; the soldiers in the background kneel, lowering their flags; the bodies of Goneril and Regan lie in the shadows, one on either side of the central group. When Albany says "Our present business/Is general woe," all the flags form a curtain and shut the dead from our view. And the last picture of all is of this lowered curtain with Albany on one side, Kent on the other, and Edgar in front as he says the epitaph:

> Speak what we feel, not what we ought to say.
> The oldest hath borne most: we that are young
> Shall never see so much, nor live so long.

And the lights fade the image from the screen.

This was what has been called the "open period" of the director's procedure in double vision. It will be noted that certain scenes of the play are imagined in more detail than others. Too, the images are metaphoric, symbolic, and realistic, depicting concepts, staging, and production. Some are strongly envisioned and some are faint. Some are highly individualistic and private and cannot be communicated to an audience. They are primarily stimulative, to be rejected or accepted in the actual refining process of interpretation and rehearsal.

THE WORLD AND FOCUS OF THE PLAY

After the director has responded to individual scenes in terms of spontaneous imagery he will have a sense of the entire emotional world of *King Lear*. He will feel its dominant mood and its variants. His assessment of this pervading quality is important as a basis for his work with the actors and the entire production. It is also important as a key to how he wishes the audience to respond. A number of specific factors are responsible for evoking the tonal impression of *King Lear*.

First of all, the historical period in which the play is set conjures up feelings by association. Judging by the references to Greek gods, we can assume it to be a pre-Christian era. (Study of Shakespeare's sources for the story also indicates such an era.) Throughout the play are signs of a primitive society. Lear's court has only a thin patina of civilization over it. The simple ritual of assembling royal figures, their bowing and kneeling to their king, and Lear's own behavior bespeaking power and authority lend an air of false gentility and refinement at the beginning of the play. (Gloucester's attitude toward his bastard son, however, keys the audience to a society which, though wearing the mask of respectability, yet is tolerant of extramarital sexuality; and Edmund's presence at court seems acceptable.) The king's arbitrary and autocratic relationship to his children and the court, his violent anger against Cordelia, and his imprecation to the sun, to the goddess of the infernal world and witchcraft, and the heavenly bodies, which for him are omnipotent, tear away the thin layer of civilization and reveal a barbaric world. His threatening Kent with his sword is further evidence of behavior characteristic of such a world. Uncontrolled passion, abhorred by civilized persons, is illustrated throughout the play by Lear, Goneril, Regan, Gloucester, and Edmund. In Lear it is at first incipient madness, which grows to outright insanity, but in the others it is normal and intrinsic to their nature. Civilizing influences have been only superficial. Homage to the powers of the netherworld and witchcraft, attempted physical violence, and unbridled emotions are evidential signs of barbarism.

Cruelty grows naturally in such an ambience. Man's inhumanity to man is illustrated at the outset by Lear's treatment of his loyal subject Kent and his unreasonable and harsh rejection of Cordelia. The stocking of Kent by Cornwall, the driving of Lear out into the storm by his unfeeling older daughters, Gloucester's irrational threat against the life of his son Edgar, the torture of Gloucester by Cornwall and Regan, Goneril's poisoning of her sister, and the hanging of Cordelia and the Fool are barbaric outrages thought to be possible only in an uncivilized society.

Physical violence preoccupies life in such a society. A king draws his sword against his subject Kent; Kent challenges Oswald with his sword at the ready; Gloucester's eyes are put out; a servant kills Cornwall, his master; Regan kills the servant; Oswald attempts to murder Gloucester and is killed by Edgar; and Edgar kills his brother Edmund. Physical force and action form a background for the lust which overwhelms the sisters Goneril and Regan in their ultimately deadly conflict over the seductive and amoral Edmund. And the physical is naturally dominant in animalistic life.

Man as animal is illustrated not only by the dominance of the physical in emotions and action but by animal imagery pervading the language of the play. Lear in his quarrel with Kent refers to himself as the Dragon, which is the heraldic symbol of Britain. It is an image which is evoked continually by Lear throughout the play. Goneril, Regan, Edgar, and Albany allude to it frequently. It colors their thinking and constitutes a prevailing mode of expression. Man is often likened to a monster, a human being distorted into an animal, a lower form of life.

Related to this recurring theme is the image of man twisted into forms contrary to the mold of nature. Lear refers to Cordelia as "a wretch whom Nature is ashamed/ Almost t' acknowledge" (1. 1). Edgar is to Gloucester an "Abhorred villain! Unnatural" (1. 2), who "falls from bias of nature." Edmund, on the other hand, is to Gloucester a "Loyal and natural boy" (2. 1).

The world of *King Lear* is predominantly antispiritual and pervaded with the sense of things physical, the use of brute force, and the perception of the human inverted to the animalistic and the chaotic. Inversion is the prevailing mode of the life of the play.

The theme is sounded by Goneril after Lear's division of the kingdom when she says about her father, "Old fools are babes again" (1. 3). She and Regan proceed to treat Lear like a child, and their actions exemplify the shifting of roles whereby the children dominate the parent. Life is turned upside down repeatedly in the play. We see Oswald and other servants usurping the position of the master when they treat the king, at Goneril's prompting, like a lowly person when he calls for his dinner. Edmund, the bastard, tops the "legitimate" in his treachery toward Edgar; the low of birth rises above the high. In his treachery toward his father he gains his father's title and becomes Duke of Gloucester. Edmund, Goneril, and Regan, in their ascendancy over and replacement of their father, invert the roles of children and parents and exemplify generational cannibalism in its most abhorrent form. The Fool tries to point out to Lear what is happening between him and his daughters when in 1. 4 he replies:

> e'er since thou mad'st thy
> daughters thy mothers . . . thou gav'st them
> the
> rod and putt'st down thine own breeches,

He is even more specific when, after Goneril's appearance and complaints against him and the Knights, he says to Lear:

> For you know, nuncle,
> The hedge-sparrow fed the cuckoo so long
> That it had it head bit off by it young.

The principle of reversal in Lear's world operates vividly in the repeated references to mental states, for example, those who see are blind, and those who are blind see: Lear and Gloucester illustrate this, and the imagery of blindness and sight runs throughout the play and marks the ultimate development of character from ignorance to enlightenment. Closely related to this imagery is that of "reason in madness." Lear's fantastic arraignment of his daughters, with a fool, a madman-beggar, and an exiled subject as jury, has a special and sane logic which makes fantasy real. He achieves true rationality in his maddest behavior after he meets the blind Gloucester, led to Dover Cliff by his son Edgar. Here he sees most clearly into the paradoxes of society and probes into the meaning of man's existence.

The emotional and intellectual climate of *King Lear* is symbolized by the central image of the storm, which, in its terrible and brute force, reflects a world dominated by nature in its most primeval manifestations. It is a world in which stability and normality are uprooted, torn, and twisted inside out. Relationships, moral, ethical, and political values, modes of being, levels of reality, the family, and the state are all reversed and distorted. Though Lear journeys through stations of personal darkness to enlightenment and understanding through experiences of suffering, it is all useless. The equilibrium of his world seems transitory and achieved at a price incommensurate with its worth. The gods mock and laugh at the human condition. Man seems destined to live in tempest, chaos, and violence. Peace and enlightenment are temporary; cold and darkness are permanent. In his sermon to Gloucester (4. 6) Lear recognizes man's destiny:

> When we are born, we cry that we are come
> To this great stage of fools.

Kent describes Lear's world as "All's cheerless, dark and deadly" (5. 3) and, when he dies, urges Edgar not to trouble his departing spirit:

> O, let him pass; he hates him,
> That would upon the rack of this tough world
> Stretch him out longer.

This is the world and focus of *King Lear*.

Lear is the center of this world which his life illustrates. The characters around him augment the illustration. The play is a study not of their psychology but of their allegoric nature. Each one is a crystallization of characteristics. A clinical analysis reveals a syndrome symptomatic of a disease-ridden cosmos. Though the director and actors must speculate and make a diagnostic appraisal of each character to create living performances based on psychological tendencies and traits expressed in feeling and mental attitudes, the effect is artistic embodiment rather than lifelike representation. (Whereas the representational attempts to make the audience believe what takes place onstage is completely lifelike, the presentational candidly says to the audience that all it sees and hears is only suggestive of life—a reflection of it and not a duplication of it. The representational tries to make the audience believe it is seeing people in a room with the fourth wall removed, unaware of the audience watching. The presentational asks the audience to remember it is in a theatre and urges the audience to use its imagination to fill in elements of reality.) Their mode of communication is presentational. Details of character are less important than totality of character. Shakespeare gives the characters subtextual bases implied but not specified. They are introduced to the audience fully formed and fully revealed, without psychological antecedents, and their progression throughout the play fails to explain or show why they are as they are. Their portraits are defined by bold, hard, and definite lines which outline but do not detail their features. The imagination is invited to complete the picture. Personality may be devised from archetypal evidence.

Lear and Gloucester grow in insight and gain in stature without permitting us to see the causes of their blindness and weakness. We must rely upon speculation rather than specific data. Edgar and Albany undergo a change and development of character without revealing background or causal conditioning. Their growth seems almost gratuitous and requires considerable audience indulgence. The other characters of the play show little if any mental or spiritual movement and are consistently resistant to anatomization.

Character development in *King Lear* is prescribed by dramatic function rather than by psychology. Lear and Gloucester open their eyes to their mistakes and delusions in order to communicate to the audience a view of man in the special world of the play. Lear is continually urged to "see better," and only physical and mental suffering can sharpen his sensibilities to the point of awareness. The Fool and Edgar, however, play a considerable part in creating this awareness: the Fool by direct appeal and Edgar by his naked presence and mad behavior. Lear sees himself in his companions of the storm of the night and the storm of his mind: man as a fool. Of course, he realizes the hard-hearted ingratitude of his daughters but, most important, he sees with mad lucidity the kind of world of which man, the fool, is the center. His focus on man in such a world is, significantly, in response to the overruling poetic idea of the play. In the allegoric mode of *King Lear*, "the important fact is not that he [Lear] should open his

eyes but that, on opening them, he should react as he does." [1] His meeting the blinded Gloucester on the heath is the occasion for his most profound insight and the painting of the portrait of man in an absurd society. In his anatomization of society and his encapsulated sermon he sums up life on "this great stage of fools." The stage is obviously a metaphor for the universe and man is the tragic actor. This is what Shakespeare wanted the audience to understand.

CRITICAL OPINION AS A REFERENCE POINT

The interpretive phase discussed up to this point is characterized by comparatively few and highly subjective responses by the director himself, unlimited by the influence of specific and formal criticism. Such responses constitute a highly individualistic view of the play, and yet the director will find that some of the same aspects of this approach to *King Lear* have been used by scholarly critics. Shakespearean criticism is embodied in generally objective aesthetic concepts and historical investigation. The director of Shakespeare can objectify, supplement, or clarify his interpretive approach and views by reference to critical opinion. However, critical opinion usually varies about both approach and views, and the director has the awesome burden of reaching his own conclusions. Nevertheless, the director of any one of Shakespeare's plays should be acquainted with significant critical opinion published over the years. Nineteenth- and twentieth-century criticism is especially helpful to today's director. A survey here will point out a selected list of critics and their general approaches.

Prior to nineteenth-century criticism, the work of Samuel Johnson, his "Preface" and notes to his edition of the plays in 1765, is most valuable to a director. Johnson found fault with Shakespeare but attested to his greatness nevertheless. He praised him for his ability to arouse basic human emotions and to draw characters recognizable as common types: "they are the genuine progeny of common humanity, such as the world will always supply, and observation will always find. His persons act and speak by the influence of those general passions and principles by which all minds are agitated, and the whole system of life is continued in motion. In the writings of

---

[1] Henri Fluchère, *Shakespeare and the Elizabethans* (New York, Hill & Wang, 1956), p. 132.

other poets a character is too often an individual; in those of Shakespeare it is commonly a species." [2] Contrary to the neoclassical critics, he approved of Shakespeare's mixture of comedy and tragedy as defensible for the dramatic rewards of the total emotional and intellectual effect. He found censurable, however, Shakespeare's looseness of structure and his carelessness in not indicating time and place of scenes, and his use of puns and coarse humor. Above all, Johnson accused him of sacrificing "virtue to convenience, and [he] is so much more careful to please than to instruct, that he seems to write without any moral purpose." [3] This stricture is especially interesting to the modern director who is pulled between the desire to entertain the audience and the current critical insistence upon making Shakespeare didactically relevant.

Critical concern with character analysis may be said to have reached a high point in 1777 with Maurice Morgan's *Essay on the Dramatic Character of Sir John Falstaff.* Yet, though he treated each aspect of Sir John's character in an effort to acquit him of the charge of cowardice, he, according to Irving Ribner, really was not chiefly concerned with character itself but with demonstrating that Shakespeare's plays could be read to provide insight into "the understanding of philosophical and psychological issues . . . It was this philosophical approach to Shakespeare which was to dominate the criticism of the nineteenth century and which is still important today." [4]

In the nineteenth century Samuel Taylor Coleridge, a philosophical critic, gave lectures on Shakespeare between 1808 and 1819 that are a milestone in criticism. (For a compendium of his lectures and notes, and reports on his lectures, see T. M. Raysor's *Coleridge's Shakespearean Criticism,* published in 1930.) Though his insight into character is almost without equal, his criticism is not psychological but philosophical. Character is seen by him as a means for expressing universal philosophical truths. He was notably influenced by the view of tragedy held by Georg W. F. Hegel:

that tragedy results from the conflict of inner human qualities; for example, Hamlet is unable to achieve the necessary balance between the active and the contemplative. Of great interest to the modern director is his view that Shakespeare's plays, like all works of art, possess organic unity in which disparate parts are synthesized and subject to criticism only by internal references, external rules of drama being irrelevant. Thus he rejected strictures against loose plotting, incredibility, historical inconsistencies, and the mixture of comedy and tragedy. Moreover, he postulated that drama, like art, is dependent upon the truth only of imagination, which creates an illusion of life accepted in poetic faith by an audience's willing suspension of disbelief.

In 1875 Edward Dowden published *Shakespeare: A Critical Study of His Mind and Art,* which is a philosophical-biographical commentary. Although biographical criticism is no longer highly esteemed, Dowden suggested an interpretive approach that might be imaginatively stimulating to a director who is seeking to discover the world of Shakespeare through the plays. (*The Personality of Shakespeare,* by Edward G. McCurdy in 1953, was a biographical investigation through Freudian theory. Of course, another approach to Shakespeare the man is Caroline F. E. Spurgeon's analysis of imagery in the plays.)

At the beginning of the twentieth century A. C. Bradley's *Shakespearean Tragedy,* published in 1904 in the form of a series of lectures, is deeply insightful of character. So much emphasis on character, however, has caused a diminution of value in the view of contemporary critics. Yet it must be remembered that his analysis of tragic characters sought a design for Shakespeare's moral or philosophical world. Bradley sees this world in terms of good and evil, exemplified in *King Lear* and discussed in the pages that follow under the heading of "Shakespeare's Characters and the Modern Actor." Thus character is the medium for expressing thematic values. In addition to the value of this approach for the director is Bradley's stimulatingly vivid evocation of the emotional climate of each of the great tragedies. Here is rich creative food to be used for their actual production.

Harley Granville-Barker's *Prefaces to Shakespeare,* first published in two volumes in 1927, revised and enlarged in 1946, is probably the most practical body of research

---

[2] "Preface to Shakespeare," in D. Nichol Smith, ed., *Shakespeare Criticism* (London, Oxford University Press, 1936), pp. 92–3.

[3] P. 102.

[4] Irving Ribner, *William Shakespeare: An Introduction to His Life, Times, and Theatre* (Waltham, Mass., Blaisdell Publishing Co., 1969), p. 202.

and criticism yet available to the director. Written by an actor, director, playwright, and scholar, it may be directly translated not only into interpretation but also directing, acting, and production. Although he based his entire approach on Shakespeare's theatre conditions, the modern director can adapt many of them to the theatre as it exists today. Granville-Barker did not work on a reconstructed Elizabethan stage but he took advantage of the experience of William Poel (*Shakespeare in the Theatre,* 1913), whose pioneer thinking and practical staging of the plays proved conclusively that Shakespeare wrote for the stage of his day.

The studies of both Poel and Granville-Barker were continuations of earlier historical criticism. In 1907 Walter Raleigh made his contribution with the essay *The Influence of the Audience on Shakespeare's Drama.* He stressed that the plays were the product of Shakespeare's stage and designed by the demands and physical conditions of that stage. He found no evidence of a pervading philosophical vision of the author and opposed concern with character, insisting that the total effect of the drama was all important. Furthermore, he denied that Shakespeare's audience degraded his work but stated that it, rather, caused him to transcend their restraints.

George Lyman Kittredge's notes to his edition of sixteen of the plays and his *Shakespeare: An Address,* published in 1916, took the strong position that the purpose of criticism was to discover what Shakespeare meant to his Elizabethan audience.

E. E. Stoll, a student of Kittredge at Harvard, in *Shakespeare Studies* (1927) and *Art and Artifice in Shakespeare* (1933), also emphasized the physical conditions of Shakespeare's stage and insisted that his plays adhered to theatrical convention which was basically artificial and demanded an enlargement and even a distortion of reality. Plot, rather than a philosophical view of life, reality of character, or biographical revelations, was primary.

George Pierce Baker's *The Development of Shakespeare as a Dramatist* in 1907 and Brander Matthews' *Shakespeare as a Playwright* in 1913 are other important works based on theatrical considerations of the age of Shakespeare. More recent historical criticism includes Peter Alexander's *Hamlet, Father and Son* in 1955, Nevill Coghill's *Shake-

speare's Professional Skill* in 1964, and John Russell Brown's *Shakespeare's Plays in Performance* in 1967. These are valuable books for the director's orientation to Shakespeare in his own theatre.

A second approach to historical criticism was taken by those scholars interested in the social, political, and intellectual world of Shakespeare. Hardin Craig's *The Enchanted Glass* published in 1936 and E. M. W. Tillyard's *The Elizabethan World Picture* in 1943 are especially noteworthy and provocative.

The study of poetic imagery, though begun earlier, received great impetus in 1931 with the publication of Caroline Spurgeon's *Shakespeare's Iterative Imagery* and, in 1935, of her *Shakespeare's Imagery and What It Tells Us.* Though limited in value by her attempts to reveal Shakespeare's biography through his imagery, her work shows pervading imagery in the plays which points to thematic values and indicates the basis for what developed into a school of criticism which saw the plays as "dramatic poems" with little dependence upon the necessity to view Shakespeare as a dramatist subject to the requirements of the Elizabethan theatre.

Perhaps the chief or at least the most influential scholar in this approach to Shakespeare as a poetic dramatist is G. Wilson Knight, who in 1930 wrote *The Wheel of Fire,* whose introduction set forth his beliefs. He maintained that one must submerge oneself in the play to absorb the impact of the entire play in order to discover its mood or "music." Shakespeare, he insisted, demanded "poetic interpretation," which is highly subjective and is based upon internal, organic criteria, in contrast to "criticism," which is objective and stems from external canons. One cannot apprehend a play by concentrating on character or plot and cannot allow historical matters to distract from total attention to the poetry. Imagery and symbolism are for Knight the keys to integrating themes and patterns of meaning which are related to Christian belief and tradition, particularly to the mythical as represented by the death and resurrection of Christ.

Many Shakespearean critics have been influenced by Knight and agree with him in regard to the unity of the plays as works of art and to the importance of poetic imagery in understanding them. A few of the works of these critics are: L. C. Knights' *Explorations*

(1946), *Some Shakespearean Themes* (1959), and *Further Explorations* (1965); Derek Traversi's *An Approach to Shakespeare* (1938) and *Shakespeare: From Richard II to Henry V* (1957). Traversi sees plot as an instrument of poetry and seeks the symbolism of action. To him the play is a "dramatic poem" expressed in terms of "one large extended metaphor." [5] Robert B. Heilman's study of *King Lear* in *This Great Stage,* published in 1948, and his study of *Othello* in *Magic in the Web* in 1956 seek to find a central and unifying moral theme through imagery, action, and character in relation to one another; and Donald Stauffer's *Shakespeare's World of Images* in 1949 uses plot, character, and language to express Shakespeare's view of life.

This eclectic survey has been determined mainly by selection of critics and criticism which can be translated into practical theatrical production. Emphasis has been placed on the "historical" and the "imagery" schools because they are germane to the point of view of this book. Those scholars who find stage conditions of Shakespeare's theatre and the imagery of the plays important to interpretation can contribute richly to the perception and imagination of the director in today's theatre. A review of the sections on "Free Imagery" and "The World and Focus of the Play" will indicate subjective responses to *King Lear* which bear general similarity to those of critics who use imagery, symbolism, and metaphor to determine the total vision of the play.

PROBLEMS

Free Imagery

1. Three students should select a play to which they find they respond with strong feeling (serious or comic) and each should write single words or phrases to describe the free imagery evoked by moments and/or scenes of the first act. (They should use this book's description of the "double vision" of *King Lear* as an example.)

2. Each act of this play selected by the three students should be used as exercises in free imagery by three other students.

3. Out of the discussion of free imagery for the whole play the students should try to find a cohering overall image.

4. Several students should rehearse mo-

---

[5] Ribner, p. 222.

ments or scenes based on imagery. When the work is presented in class, students should try to cite movement, pictorial moments, and behavior which they think embody the director's imagery.

5. Find an image for each character in *The Tempest.* Consider flowers, animals, and birds as character images.

6. Direct scenes inspired by images.

7. Find an image for a thrust-stage set for *The Tempest, As You Like It,* and *Twelfth Night.*

The World and Focus of the Play

1. Select a play you consider to be a tragedy. Analyze it for its "world" or "tonal impression" and then discuss possible staging, the use of properties, scenery, costumes, character behavior, and sound effects to communicate this overall emotional quality. (The director's search for an overall image for a play after his response in free imagery may involve the discovery of the world or tonal impression.) Repeat for a comedy, a history, and a fantasy.

2. Select a scene from a play which you consider to be a key to the world of the play and direct it for its tonal quality. (For example, the second scene of Act 1 of *Richard III* between Ann and Richard is such a scene.)

Note: The focus of a play is the greatest point of interest for the audience. It may be that aspect of a play—its theme, characters, plot, or language—which the playwright has intended to emphasize above all others. Such emphasis is determined from his selection and arrangement of the materials of the play. The director usually supports the playwright's dramaturgic emphasis by direction and production. However, the director may so interpret and produce a play as to change the focus to an aspect not emphasized by the playwright. In any case, every production of a play should have a definite focus. It is the director's job to determine, establish, and maintain that focus.

3. What are the characteristics of organization of elements of a play whose focus is on the *theme* or thought of a play? On *character?* On *plot?* On *language?*

4. Cite a Shakespearean production which focused upon the meaning of the play. How did the director's work with the actors and the scenery, costumes, lighting, and sound effects help to point up the meaning?

5. Select a play, determine its focus, and describe how its production (directing, acting, scenery, costumes, lighting, and sound effects) can establish, support, and project that focus for the audience.

Critical Opinion as a Reference Point

Note: The interpretive process consists of the subjective experiencing of a play in terms of imagery and the objective analysis of the work in terms of critical opinion.

1. Discuss critical opinion which helped to organize your free imagery of a play into a more coherent and objective interpretation.

2. Compare A. C. Bradley's essay on *Othello* in *Shakespearian Tragedy* with Granville-Barker's in *Prefaces to Shakespeare*. Find a scene about which they offer opposing opinions. Direct the scene in two ways to illustrate these two views.

3. Base the direction of a scene from *King Lear* upon the interpretation of Robert Heilman in *This Great Stage*. Direct the same scene as interpreted by Jan Kott in *Shakespeare Our Contemporary*.

4. Stage *Hamlet,* 2. 2, in accordance with the ideas put forward by John Dover Wilson in *What Happened in Hamlet*. Begin the scene after Voltimand and Cornelius exit and end it with the entrance of Rosencrantz and Guildenstern.

5. Direct a scene from *Measure for Measure* as interpreted by G. Wilson Knight in his essay in *The Wheel of Fire*.

6. How does Caroline Spurgeon's *Shakespeare's Imagery and What It Tells Us* help the director to determine the meaning of a play?

Chapter II

ORIENTATION TO SHAKESPEARE

For many modern directors, staging a Shakespearean play is like a visit to a foreign country where the visitor knows neither the language, the people, their customs, nor their outlook on life. Only knowledge and true understanding can create a deep and sympathetic relationship between strangers. Shakespeare requires a lifetime of devoted study. Scholarship has created a great and forbidding literary-industrial complex based on all aspects of his life, times, and theatre. A director (or anyone else) can encompass only a limited amount of it. Yet he does need to know certain fundamentals which apply to the production of all Shakespeare's plays and special knowledge for the production of each individual play.

In acquiring the fundamentals it is important to point out that though a literary background is necessary it cannot substitute for actual experience in rehearsal and performance to find dramatic values which transcend the text. An actor's pause, look, vocal inflection, or smallest detail of behavior can suddenly light up a moment impossible for literary criticism to reveal. On the other hand, literary criticism has its own special revelatory powers. Yet it is Shakespeare as a man of the theatre with whom the director in today's theatre can most readily relate.

If the director wishes the past to speak to the present he must discover what in the past is different as well as what is not different from the present. Of great importance are the theatrical conditions under which Shakespeare's plays were placed on the stage for performance. The physical theatre, the actors, the texts of the plays, and theatre conventions governed the preparations for performances then just as they do now. The modern director's insight into the plays will be deepened by some basic knowledge of these aspects of Shakespearean production. This knowledge cannot be based solely upon fact: Facts are few about the stage of Shakespeare's day; conjecture abounds, and scholars sometimes mix fact with fiction. However, there is sufficient genuine evidence to help today's director.

His Stage and Ours

We know that the Shakespearean company performed at the Globe, its permanent home, at Blackfriars, at court, in innyards, manor houses, marketplaces, taverns, castles, gardens, and any other places large enough for an audience and the action of the play. Playing conditions were as varied and unpredictable as they are today when we find plays presented in · commercial theatres, schools, churches, old warehouses, halls, garages, barns, and abandoned cellars, to name only a few of the many likely and unlikely places. Shakespeare's actors, like today's, had to be adaptable and improvisatory. The plays, loose in structure and appealing strongly to the audience's willingness to make believe, lent themselves to the exigencies of place and time.

This means that there was no "typical" Elizabethan playhouse for which Shakespeare wrote his plays. Fewer than half the plays of the First Folio were first performed at the Globe, and more than twenty had their premieres at the Theatre and the Curtain Playhouse or Blackfriars and at court. When away from London the King's Men performed Shakespeare's plays under touring conditions and did not expect the standard facilities of the permanent theatres. Yet Shakespeare wrote his plays for conventional staging conditions. He took certain things for granted while maintaining his freedom as a creative artist. His style of writing varied throughout his career; he continued to be experimental and innovative.

Today's director must remember, however, that he wrote for the theatre and audiences of his age. Only in the last few decades has this fact been considered significant. It is now understood that the physical theatre influences playwriting and the audience's dramatic experience. A director can approach plays and their staging in modern theatres and before modern audiences with greater intelligence and sensitivity if he has some knowledge of Shakespearean staging conditions and practices.

J. L. Styan, in his chapter on "The Essential Elizabethan Stage" in *Shakespeare's Stagecraft,* insists that there is no proof that it consisted of more than four elements:

1. A tight, enclosing auditorium.
2. A projecting platform almost as deep as it was wide.
3. Two upstage entrances on to the platform.
4. At least one balcony.[1]

It is probable that this is the consensus among Elizabethan scholars. Various attempts have been made to reconstruct or restore the Globe as the typical or ideal playhouse.[2] Asserting that lack of evidence makes such attempts futile, Alois M. Nagler does present incisive and neat arguments for a Shakespearean stage, and I shall draw liberally from the information he provides because he combines a sense of practical theatre with scholarly research and evidence.

When Shakespeare came to London he found two playhouses, the Theatre and the Curtain Playhouse, both located in the North End of London. Little is known, however, about the physical appearance of these theatres. The "only pictorial record of an identifiable Elizabethan stage," Nagler reminds us, is the De Witt sketch of the Swan Theatre. In 1596 or thereabouts one "Johannes de Witt, a Dutchman, visited London and sketched the inside of the Swan." Although the original drawing was lost, a copy was made by "De Witt's friend, Arend van Buchel, presumably from the original," and found in the Utrecht University Library in 1888.

Nagler asks, "What was going on in the theatre while the wretched draftsman, who lacked an eye for perspective, was doing his sketch? I believe that a rehearsal was in progress." He conjectures that De Witt visited the theatre in the morning during a rehearsal, and this explains why no spectators are shown in

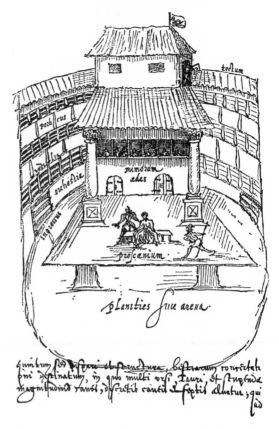

A drawing of the Swan Playhouse copied by Arend van Buchel, presumably from the original by Johannes de Witt.

the three galleries surrounding the stage. The eight people in the galleries above the stage are presumably actors or theatre personnel watching the rehearsal "and perhaps waiting for their cue."[3]

Another item of evidence is the contract for the building of the Fortune Playhouse, erected in 1600 by Peter Street, who was also the builder of the Globe. An acting troupe under the patronage of the Lord Admiral and headed by actor Edward Alleyn and Philip Henslowe, "shrewd theatrical investor," hired Street to build the Fortune "according to the manner and fashion of the said house called the Globe." Unfortunately, "the manner and fashion" of the Globe is not specified, and scholars speculate that any exact specifications for the Fortune must mean differences in these respects from those for the Globe. Precisely what the latter were no one really knows.

Scholars assume that Shakespeare's plays were performed on a platform stage. The

---

[1] Cambridge, Cambridge University Press, 1967, p. 12.

[2] J. C. Adams, *The Globe Playhouse* (2d ed. Cambridge, Harvard University Press, 1942). C. W. Hodges, *The Globe Restored* (2d ed. New York, Coward-McCann, 1968).

[3] A. M. Nagler, *Shakespeare's Stage* (New Haven and London, Yale University Press, 1958), pp. 9–10.

sketch of the Swan shows a platform; the contracts for the Fortune and the Hope both speak of a raised stage.[4] The action of various plays evidences the need of traps, one presumably large, supplemented by smaller ones. Nagler speculates that the larger one was used for the appearance of the cauldron at the beginning of the fourth act of *Macbeth,* and the smaller ones for the entrances of the three witches. Of course, the graveyard scene in *Hamlet* required the use of the larger one. In all probability, Barnardine in *Measure for Measure,* 4. 3, needs a smaller trap from which to enter after Pompey's

> He is coming, sir, he is coming . . . I hear his straw rustle.

Shakespeare's stage directions provide several examples of the need for two doors at the back of the platform. In *Richard III,* 2. 3 (F₁), there is the direction: "Enter one Citizen at one door, and another at the other"; in *King Richard II,* 1. 4 (Q₁), "Enter the King with Bagot and Green at one door, and the Lord Aumerle at another"; in *Coriolanus,* 1. 8 (F₁), Marcius and Aufidius enter "at several doors," and in 1. 9: "Enter, at one door, Cominius, with the Romans: At another door, Marcius, with his arm in a scarf"; in *A Midsummer Night's Dream,* 2. 1 (F₁), "Enter a Fairie at one door, and Robin Goodfellow at another."

Stage directions also indicate the need for some kind of upper platform or balcony. *Titus Andronicus* provides an example at the opening of 1. 1 (F₁): "Flourish. Enter the Tribunes and Senators aloft. And then enter Saturninus and his Followers at one door, and Bassianus and his Followers at the other, with Drum and Colours." (Two doors at opposite sides are also indicated.) Richard II's famous abdication speech is made after the direction (3. 3): "Enter on the walls, Richard, Carlisle, Aumerle, Scroop, Salisbury." And he obviously goes down after his

> Down, down I come, like glist'ring Phaethon:
> Wanting the manage of unruly jades.
> In the base court? Base court, where kings grow base.

"But," as Nagler points out, "Shakespeare required additional possibilities of entrances and exits . . ."[5]

[4] Nagler, p. 23.
[5] Pp. 25–6.

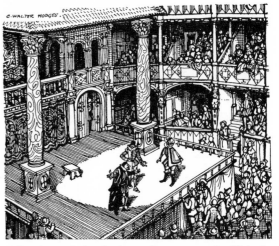

A "*conjectural sketch of a performance at the Globe.*" Reprinted by permission of Coward, McCann and Geoghegan, Inc., from The Globe Restored *by C. Walter Hodges.* ⓒ *1953 and 1968 by C. Walter Hodges.*

Following the lead of Hodges' *The Globe Restored,* in which he traces the development of the Elizabethan stage and conjectures the existence of a pavilion or booth, Nagler believes that this "booth served as an auxiliary stage, a potential scene of action, separated by curtains from the rest of the stage." Moreover, he thinks this stage was used when the stage directions called for a "discovery" like the Miranda-Ferdinand chess scene in *The Tempest.*

Nagler also points out that Ludwig Tieck arrived at the idea of a pavilion in the 1830s when, arguing that the actors should be as close as possible to the audience, he imagined a broad balcony supported by two pillars in the center of the Elizabethan platform stage. Under the balcony and "between the columns was a 'small inner stage', raised three steps high."[6] Nagler also agrees with Leslie Hotson's contention that "tent" means a "pavilion-like booth."[7] Moreover, this tent or pavilion, "related in function to the medieval common castle and essentially a neutral pavilion that could be localized at will, was assuredly the most important of the properties that the Elizabethan players took with them on their wanderings in England and on the Continent."[8]

The pavilion was placed against a curtain which served as a backcloth and in which

[6] P. 27.
[7] Pp. 30–1.
[8] P. 46.

were three slits, one in the center, one on the right, and one on the left, which could be used for entrances and exits to and from the pavilion. Hamlet's scene with his mother (*Hamlet,* 3. 4) and Imogen's bedchamber scene in *Cymbeline,* 2. 2, were doubtless played here.

The galleries of the public theatres and the top of the tent or pavilion, strongly constructed, were probably used for scenes with the stage directions "above" and "aloft." The *Romeo and Juliet* balcony scene, the monument scene in *Antony and Cleopatra,* 4. 15, Brabantio's appearance "at a window" in the opening scene of *Othello,* and the entrance of the two Volscian "Senators with others on the walls" in *Coriolanus,* 1. 4, are scenes which could be played on top of the pavilion.

Nagler proceeds, by following stage directions implicitly, to show how *Romeo and Juliet* might be staged on the platform, on top of and inside the pavilion. Scenes beginning in the pavilion spread over the platform. The tent (pavilion) closes when scenes are played on the platform alone. Stagehands place trees before the tent to represent Capulet's orchard. The wall over which Romeo leaps into the orchard is also placed in position by the stagehands. These properties, it is pointed out, have been mentioned in Henslowe's inventories. They are moved by the stagehands when no longer needed. Juliet's bed (Henslowe's "bedstead") is placed in the tent for Juliet to fall upon after drinking the potion and in accordance with the directions in the First Quarto version: "She falls upon her bed within the curtains." When Romeo arrives at Mantua, "a stagehand has fastened a board inscribed 'Mantua' over the entrance." [9] The scenes move rapidly from the platform to the top and inside of the tent in the order demanded by the text to insure continuity and rapidity.

In considering the problem of directing a play on his conjectural stage, Nagler asserts: "We have worked solely with Elizabethan elements: we have taken the frame from the Swan; we have borrowed the tent from Platter, the properties from Henslowe, and the backcloth from the Court performances." [10] His sources are evidential and his arguments are highly convincing. He takes issue with some Elizabethan scholars (an occupational habit) on certain points and is strongly supported by other authorities. He, with others, refuses to accept, in particular, John Cranford Adams' theories concerning the "upper stage" and "the study" or the "inner stage," put forward in his *The Globe Playhouse* and at first widely approved. Nagler's own theories stand up under practical application and appeal to the modern director.

The placement of the pavilion on the platform downstage of the actors' tiring-house, between the two pillars supporting the "shadow," gains an intimacy between the actors and audience not possible when an upper and an inner stage are located under a gallery like the one shown in the sketch of the Swan. Also, a pavilion with curtains on three sides, which can be raised to allow the audience standing and sitting on three sides to see the action of the play, is to be preferred to a recessed alcove which shuts off the view from the sides. The three entrances and exits to and from the pavilion and the acting space on the platform below allow flowing and continuous movement from one place of action to the other. Character movement can thus blend or dissolve smoothly without the abruptness which results from more constraining space and limited accessibility of ingress and egress.

DRAMATIC DYNAMICS OF SHAKESPEARE'S STAGE

The acting areas on Shakespeare's stage are related dynamically to one another when the dramatic action demands the use of two or three at the same time. When Richard speaks from the balcony to Bolingbroke on the platform below ("Down, down I come, like glist'ring Phaethon"), the relationship between the two men—psychologically, politically, and spiritually—is dramatized visually, and the words and the images are reinforced by spatial contrast.

The play-within-the-play scene in *Hamlet,* 3. 2, utilizes simultaneously the entire acting space provided by the Elizabethan stage. Four different groups of characters are held together by spatial relationships which help to dramatize the situation in which they find themselves. Hamlet, Ophelia, and Horatio constitute one group; Claudius, Gertrude, and Polonius a second; the Players a third; and the courtiers a fourth. The Hamlet-Claudius groups are in latent opposition, waiting for the Players group to awaken their hostilities into open conflict, and the courtiers react in

[9] Pp. 52–9.
[10] Pp. 60–1.

The model of the Globe Playhouse reconstructed by John Cranford Adams. Photo: Hofstra University.

embarrassment and surprise and shock to the other groups. Their placement onstage can tie them together in one locale while setting them off in dramatic opposition. On opposite sides of the platform may be placed the Hamlet-Claudius groups, with the Players in the middle in the pavilion. The courtiers may watch from the balcony and the outside edges of the platform. The dramatic dynamics of the scene, however, indicate to some directors that Claudius should be the main focal point and therefore seated on his throne in the central acting area, that is, in the pavilion-tent. The audience's main interest is in the King's reaction to the play being presented to the court. His elevation on the throne and his being framed by the tent opening emphasize him visually. The focus of audience attention could therefore oscillate easily among the three main groups: Claudius', Hamlet's, and the Players'. The neutral group of courtiers located on the balcony and on the platform

can be focused upon by the audience for short and quick intervals as they react to the main action. When the King calls for lights and Hamlet rushes forward with a candelabrum to peer into his face, Claudius' guilt and the court's confusion can have great impact upon the audience.

The use of the Elizabethan stage for soliloquies has obvious advantages. The greatest is its intimacy, when the platform rather than the inner or upper acting areas is used; the actor on the platform can walk to its edge at the center and at the sides to come closest to the audience when sharing with them the character's most secret and most private thoughts. Also, he can serve as chorus to comment on another character or the action upstage. Edmund in *King Lear* is both soliloquizer and commentator. Whether he speaks directly to the audience or, seemingly, thinks aloud, the actor makes intimate contact with the audience by coming downstage on the platform in a sort of cinematic close-up. Standing alone on the platform, he uses the space around him as well as his proximity to the audience to emphasize what he has to say. When the commentary is an "aside," the actor turns out toward the audience to show by face and suggestive tone of voice his attitude toward another character or an incident. Edmund, Iago, and Crookback Richard give the actor ample opportunity for such movement and behavior. Taking the audience into his confidence is a character's dramatic action. Directly involving the audience in the fiction of the play by making it an actor or character who becomes the confidant of a character, the drama takes on an extra dimension. The audience becomes a supercharacter who knows more than any character onstage. It is placed in a godlike position not only with powers of omniscience but possessing a perspective on characters and events. Too, this kind of audience involvement creates a special kind of theatrical experience. Shakespeare makes the audience aware of the frankly theatrical level of illusion, whereas the modern drama tries to make the audience accept the illusion as reality.

The platform of the Elizabethan stage is the main area for performances. This is so by virtue of its closeness to the audience and because it provides the largest free space for the greatest number of characters and the most possible movement by the characters. Even when the scene starts in the pavilion, it spills over onto the platform as it develops from static positions and exposition to action, reaction, and climax. More space and audience proximity are needed to enhance the dramatic progression and impact of a scene. From a technical point of view, action on the platform rather than within the pavilion with its obstructing framework permits better lines of sight for the audience.

Action on the balcony suffers from certain restrictions. It loses in dramatic pressure because of narrowness of space and increased distance between actor and audience. Too, the physical effort of looking up rather than at eye level can in itself be dramatic by sheer visual contrast, but an audience tires of protracted physical effort. When action on the balcony is joined with that on the platform the audience is presented with visual variety and permitted to rest its neck and eye muscles. On the other hand, an entrance onto the balcony can be in dramatic contrast to entrances made from upstage onto the platform. A position on an upper level can add authority to a figure by connotation; physical elevation reminds the audience of regal personages and others of status and power. This is a dramatic function of the balcony. When Richard appears on the balcony, flanked by two bishops, he has already elevated himself symbolically, and he forces the people to look up to him actually, even before he is elected king (*Richard III,* 3. 7).

Scenes take place on the balcony to achieve greater verisimilitude. (The Shakespearean theatre was a naive blend of actuality and imagination.) The upper level could suggest a speaker's podium or "pulpit," a hill, battlements, walls, or a window. In the forum scene of *Julius Caesar,* 3. 2, there is the stage direction "Brutus goes into the pulpit." Later, Antony "goes into the pulpit." They address the plebeians on the platform below.

It can be argued from an illusionistic point of view that the first scene from *Hamlet* should take place on the upper level of the stage. Here Francisco at his post can pace back and forth until he is challenged by Barnardo below on the platform (1. 1).

> *Barnardo.* Who's there?
> *Francisco.* Nay, answer me. Stand and unfold
> yourself.
> *Barnardo.* Long live the king!
> *Francisco.* Barnardo?
> *Barnardo.* He.

And as Francisco says, "You come most carefully upon your hour," Barnardo ascends the steps to the upper level. Francisco descends from the balcony as Barnardo says,

> If you do meet Horatio and Marcellus,
> The rivals of my watch, bid them make haste.

Then Francisco is on the platform and ready to challenge Horatio and Marcellus, who have just entered onto the platform. During this exchange below on the platform Barnardo is walking his post above. He obviously does not hear or see Horatio and Marcellus because Marcellus calls to him, "Holla, Barnardo!" And Barnardo replies, "Say,/What, is Horatio there?" Horatio, who has walked ahead of Marcellus and has already begun to ascend the stairs to the upper level, is then in view when he replies, "A piece of him." And Barnardo can salute or shake hands with Horatio and Marcellus on "Welcome Horatio, welcome good Marcellus." They then sit down on a bench on the balcony and Barnardo starts to tell the doubting Horatio of the appearance of the Ghost two nights in succession. The Ghost appears on another part of the balcony and "stalks away" when challenged by Horatio. When it reappears Horatio confronts it again, and Marcellus and Barnardo strike at it with their halberds, but the Ghost departs untouched. The balcony's limited space is sufficient for the restrained actions of the characters who appear on it. The awe and respect of Horatio, Marcellus, and Barnardo limit their reactions, and the dignity and majesty of the Ghost influence his behavior. His mysteriousness is enhanced by his appearance on the balcony. (His walking between heaven and earth—in limbo—is also suggested by his elevation.)

Contrast is fundamental to the nature of the dramatic. The two permanent doors on the Elizabethan stage are architectural features exemplifying this. They are used to show the audience by physical separation two different or opposing characters or groups of characters. In *Coriolanus*, 1. 8 (F_1), there is the stage direction: "Alarum, as in battle. Enter Marcius and Aufidius at several doors." This can only mean opposite doors. The dramatic moment demands a visual emphasis of the antagonism of these two warriors. Their almost simultaneous entrances through doors at opposite sides of the stage communicate their contrast and opposition in terms of nationality and personal antipathy.

Contrast in physical condition and attitudes is shown, as has already been cited for another reason, by the stage direction opening the ninth scene of this same act of *Coriolanus:* "Flourish. Alarum. A retreat is sounded. Enter at one door, Cominius with the Romans; at another door, Marcius, with his arm in a scarf." The appearance of Marcius immediately tells of his victory over Aufidius and the Antiates, the best of the Volscian army. Moreover, his entering alone signals to Cominius and the other Romans his singular heroism and strength. It is a prelude to his being proclaimed the savior of Rome and awarded the title of "Coriolanus." Marcius' entrance at the opposite door sets him apart from the other Romans and gives him special interest and audience focus. If he had entered with Cominius and the others, one of a crowd, he would have been of equal interest only. His separate entrance, set apart from the others by the door through which it is made, heightens the suspense of the audience and builds the dramatic moment, especially if Marcius delays coming onstage until after the others have entered. And surely there is a silent moment of surprise before the Romans react to his unexpected appearance with joyful shouts. It is a "moment" not to be slighted by the director, and the text assists him by specifying the kind of entrances the actors make at this particular juncture in the plot.

Most of the stage directions found in the First Folio edition of the plays indicate entrances and exits, but with the simple words "enter" or "exeunt" without specifying exactly where. Moreover, several apparently are meant to enter through one door as in the direction: "Enter Angelo, Escalus, and servants, Justice" at the beginning of *Measure for Measure*, 2. 1 (F_1). Of course, the director need not have all the characters enter through one door. It is obvious from the dialogue that Angelo enters first because of his position and because he is speaking. He is followed by Escalus, who is trying to persuade him of his point of view. He is in turn followed by the Justice, a lesser dignitary who does not speak until the very end of the scene. The servants, of course, might enter through the other door to bring on a desk for Angelo and the dock for Pompey, who is to enter later, to cite only one way of bringing them onstage.

The simultaneous entrances of two processions through these two doors, right and left, are enhanced ceremonially by the spatial relationship of the doors. The balancing of one door by the other, both located in the back wall of the pavilion or in the back wall of the actors' tiring-house, as shown in the sketch of the Swan, creates a formality in the architecture and in any action taking place at the same time through them both. Of course, parallelism is a favorite structural device of Shakespeare, and he could express it on the Elizabethan stage. J. L. Styan cites this direction, referring to both doors together, which helps "to formalize the stage"[11] in the third part of *Henry VI* (2. 5. 54, F_1): "Alarum. Enter a Son that hath killed his Father, at one door: and a Father that hath killed his Son at another door."

The two doors are referred to in order to indicate doors in a house and thus tend to increase audience belief in the reality of the

---

[11] Styan, p. 20.

moment. In the famous "brothel scene" in *Othello*, 4. 2, Othello tells Emilia to "Leave procreants alone, and shut the door"; and when she makes her exit she surely obeys him by going out through one of the permanent doors and closing it (or the curtains of the slits in the pavilion). It can be argued, of course, that this scene is purely symbolic fantasizing on the part of Othello and needs no actual door for Emilia to shut. Yet Othello does give her real money—or should—when he says, "We've done our course; there's money for your pains." The irony of the whole scene is increased if Emilia automatically—as though in a dream—obeys Othello, closes the door at the beginning of the scene, and then at the end of the scene enters when Othello calls her, takes the money he offers, and then throws it down in revulsion as she rushes to comfort Desdemona.

When Macbeth, Lady Macbeth, and the Porter hear a knocking (*Macbeth*, 2. 3), it must indeed come from a door, and the Porter opens the door to allow Macduff and Lennox to enter. Incidentally, the scene between Macbeth and Lady Macbeth, after the murder of Duncan, must have taken place on the balcony or on top of the pavilion to allow the Porter to enter at the door below, opposite the one where the knocking comes from. This staging assists Lady Macbeth when she refers to the knocking "At the south entry" and permits her and Macbeth to exit from the balcony as the Porter enters from the door below; thus the continuity from one scene to the next is unbroken.

Though a door may, in certain instances, localize by referring to a specific house or other place (Nagler uses the two doors to indicate the Montague manor house on the left and the Capulet home on the right in his staging of *Romeo and Juliet* [12]), it need not always indicate the same place throughout a performance. Literal localization from the point of view of geography and audience orientation are not as important as are dramatic values inherent in the scene. The director helps to dramatize a conflict by visual means by staging entrances on opposite sides of the stage for the two families, the Montagues and the Capulets; for two enemies, Coriolanus and Aufidius; and so forth. However, this does not mean that once having entered from one door a character must always enter and exit

[12] Nagler, pp. 52–65.

through it. This is not the kind of logic that should pervade a Shakespearean production. A director will find it impossible to adhere to it. The dramatic demands of a scene, the movement of its characters, and the sequence of scenes will not permit adherence to a realistic floor plan. (The localizing of the Montague and Capulet houses works particularly well through the scene of Tybalt's death, since the whole tragedy is founded on the rivalry between the two families.) An attempt to draw up a plan for the castle and its environs in *Hamlet* is bound to fail in terms of directionality of entrances and exits. Such a plan is unnecessary, anyway, and contrary to the conventions built into a Shakespearean play. The locale of a scene shifts in accordance with dramaturgic demands, the creative vision of the author, and the rules of the game established and accepted by Elizabethan audiences. Shakespeare's plays are not environmental; the *what* and *why* of the action of the plays are more important than the *where*. The characters of the plays tell us where they are, or their words and actions imply their whereabouts. The characters take their environment with them. And their creator continually asks the audience to use its imagination and make believe. The principle of "let's pretend" is basic to the writing and must be inherent in the staging.

The required overlapping of entrances and exits to maintain continuity and speed of performance often stretches everyday credibility. In a realistic play the audience would react with disbelief but in Shakespeare it makes allowances for the conventions of his stage. It is willing to accept the implausibility of people neither seeing nor hearing others when the playwright demands such actions. However, on a stage with doors on opposite sides, the director, not impeded by realistic localization, can move the departing characters through the door on the right while the arriving character enters at the left. Characters see only what is in front of them, if the dramatic fiction insists on it. Of course, the director may choose the stage area for the action that will aid the fiction. If, for example, the Polonius and Reynaldo scene (*Hamlet*, 2. 1) takes place on the platform, Reynaldo could exit right and Ophelia could enter left.

In these examples the director may see the dramatic dynamics of the physical characteristics of Shakespeare's stage illustrated by the use of playing areas and entrances and exits.

The play-within-the-play scene from Hamlet *as directed by Frank McMullan on a reconstructed Elizabethan stage at the Yale University Theatre, 1941. Set: Elizabeth Plehn; costumes: Frank Bevan. Photo: Commercial Photo Service.*

They are as apparent as they are on a modern stage. Shakespeare, like a modern playwright, wrote for the stage on which his plays were performed. Because Shakespeare wrote for the staging conditions of his theatre it is obvious that the modern proscenium stage, architecturally different from his, must be adapted physically by building out a forestage to project into the auditorium and/or using scenery which will accommodate to the demands of his plays. Let us cite some examples of the use of the proscenium stage for Shakespeare. The stage chosen for these examples is that of the Yale University Theatre.

Some years ago *Hamlet* was produced on a modified reconstructed Elizabethan stage. The proscenium opening at the Yale Theatre is 34 feet wide and 20 feet high. On either side of this opening, 5 feet 3 inches from the curtain line, are two permanent doors, 2 feet 11 inches wide, penetrating the two side walls of the auditorium. A forestage, 13 feet 1 inch deep and 46½ feet wide, was built to project into the auditorium. The audience sat only in front of this forestage. The designer created a setting with a painted façade of timbering and plaster characteristic of the Elizabethan innyard. Stage right and left there were two doors in the façade leading to steps on either side which permitted entrances and exits to and from the balcony. (The steps or stairs leading to the balcony were behind the façade, and characters could not be seen while climbing them.) The balcony was above an inner stage. The balcony had 3-foot entryways and opened to a depth of approximately 5 feet. The inner stage,[13] below and in the center of the set, had an opening of 13 feet and a depth of 6 feet. A traverse curtain was hung at the opening. In the center of the rear wall of this inner acting area were two doors which opened to a width of 5 feet. A trap, 6 feet by 3 feet 3 inches, was installed just behind the inner-stage curtain. The inner-stage opening was 17 feet 7 inches from the edge of the forestage. There were open archways suggesting windows above a railing at the balcony level, approximately 8 feet from the floor.

Thus the action of the play could flow over the forestage and be combined with action on the inner stage and balcony. Or action could take place in any one of these three areas and in combination with one or more areas. The director therefore chose where each scene should be located, and the action flowed with-

---

[13] The term "inner stage" will be used henceforth to mean an enclosed acting area equivalent to Nagler's pavilion.

out interruption from area to area. The inner stage was preset with the throne or other furniture props while the curtain was closed; such props were removed after the scene had ended and the curtain had been drawn. Action initiated in the inner stage could and did continue on the forestage because sight lines were poor except when the action took place in the center of the enclosure. This meant that the inner stage was merely a jumping-off place for action on the forestage. The King and Queen, of course, could sit on their thrones set just inside the inner stage and be in clear view of all members of the audience.

The forestage was bare except for two benches set right and left. There was also a bench permanently set in the center of the balcony.

This stage, therefore, approximated the conditions of Shakespeare's. (An important difference lay in the fact that this "reconstruction" did not permit the audience to sit or stand at the sides of the stage.) The permanent background, together with the three main acting areas, allowed the audience to concentrate on the words and action of the play without the possible distraction of constantly changing scenic devices. The colorful costumes in front of this neutral environment helped to project the characters. The forestage, of course, provided a sense of intimacy between actors and audience. The soliloquies, especially, gained in effectiveness through audience contact. The use of modern lighting served to enhance audience focus, wipe out parts of the background, and assist the actors in establishing the mood of each scene, especially the early morning and night scenes. The "mousetrap" scene depicted in the accompanying photograph shows the full stage in use. The mood of the scene is not strongly apparent because general illumination was necessary for the photograph.

The modern proscenium stage can be modified for a production of *The Taming of the Shrew.* In analyzing the play one finds that the three main acting areas of Shakespeare's stage are needed. To make Christopher Sly a prominent spectator of the play-within-the-play it is effective to follow the First Folio direction and allow to "Enter aloft the drunkard . . ." that is, on an upper stage. An inner stage below is convenient for the various indoor scenes at Baptista's, Petruchio's, and Lucentio's houses and, having established locale, to blend that acting area with that of the forestage. It will

be noted from the photograph of this production of *The Taming of the Shrew* that the shape of the inner stage opened it up on the sides and permitted better audience lines of sight than did the inner stage used for the production of *Hamlet.* The forestage for *The Shrew* was only 10 feet deep, but steps at the front edge led into the audience and permitted entrances and exits through the center aisle of the auditorium. The scenery extended onto the forestage and enclosed the side doors in the walls of the auditorium. Though the photograph was taken with general illumination, the performance took place in carefully designed lighting which suggested locale and mood. The set, with its stairways right and left leading to an upper level, with an inner stage and forestage, used the form of Shakespeare's stage, while stripes of green and white, together with colorful flags, arches, and swags, gave an overall feeling of a festival or circus and created an atmosphere to project the director's concept of the play.[14] The varied brilliant colors of the costumes contributed to this atmosphere.

Another variation on the form of Shakespeare's stage is demonstrated in the productions of *Measure for Measure* in 1946, one on the stage of the Yale University Theatre and the other at the Shakespeare Memorial Theatre, Stratford-upon-Avon, England. There is no need for an upper stage in this play. Therefore only two of the characteristic acting areas are suggested in the design: the inner stage and an outer stage—not really a forestage or even an apron stage, inasmuch as it did not extend beyond the proscenium arch into the auditorium (see photograph). On this two-area stage the scenes could alternate from the inner to the outer and vice versa without interruption of the flow of action. The action in one area overlapped that in the other. In fact, as the curtain to the inner stage was being closed, action could begin on the outer stage, and so characters moved from indoors to outdoors, and so forth. Of course, exits through the doors down right and left blended with the opening of the inner-stage curtain. The action of the play was "distanced" by the permanent outer proscenium and the false inner proscenium, and this was in keeping with the morality-play framework of the play as the director saw it. It is worth noting also that the two acting areas were not deep: the

[14] Referred to later in this chapter under "The Text and the Director's Working Script."

The Taming of the Shrew *at the Yale University Theatre, directed by Frank McMullan, 1955. Note the use of the three principal acting areas found in an Elizabethan theatre: the forestage, the pavilion-like inner stage, and the upper stage. Set: Jacqueline Beymer; costumes: Frank Bevan. Photo: Commercial Photo Service.*

The opening scene from Measure for Measure, *staged by Frank McMullan at Yale, 1946. Note the influence of the Elizabethan stage in the use of a shallow forestage and an inner stage behind the portal. An upper stage was not needed. The scenes alternated from forestage to inner stage. Set: Otis Riggs; costumes: Frank Bevan. Photo: Commercial Photo Service.*

The deputization of Angelo (Robert Harris) by the Duke (David King-Wood) from the production of Measure for Measure *by Frank McMullan at the Shakespeare Memorial Theatre, Stratford-upon-Avon, England, 1946. Set: Otis Riggs. Photo: Angus McBean.*

outer stage 11 feet and the inner stage 9 feet. This limitation of space served to concentrate audience attention on the few characters usually appearing in each scene. Only the scene of Claudio's arrest and the fifth act at the city gates called for a crowd of people.

Another example of use of the proscenium stage is the production of *Coriolanus* in 1956. That this is a play written for the use of an upper stage or balcony is evidenced by First Folio stage directions. The photograph of the setting for this production shows several stepped levels with a maximum height of only 42 inches from the stage floor. A center opening, representing the gates of Rome and Corioli, was designed for the topmost level. (This, as in the *Hamlet* and *The Taming of the Shrew* sets, was permanent. Different set pieces indicating the Duke's palace and the inside of the prison, to be used in the inner stage and set into position behind closed curtains, were designed for *Measure for Measure*.) The setting for *Coriolanus* was sculptured and formal in appearance. The stage floor space served as a forestage, and the uppermost level suggested the top of the Corioli walls when needed. However, such a level was symbolic, precluding the actual use of ladders called for by Titus Lartius, and necessitated the elimination of the line referring to ladders. Light changes suggested the shift of locale and allowed the audience to imagine the places of action. Imagination was spurred by the characters who announced where they were in Rome and in Corioli—indoors or outdoors. The action flowed over the levels and on the stage floor as needed and without a break in continuity. All action took place, of course, behind the proscenium arch. The setting met the demands of the play with only one line deletion made necessary for practical reasons. No real attempt was made to conform to the characteristic design of the Shakespearean stage. The relative lack of audience contact with the action of the play caused by the omission of a forestage piercing

Coriolanus as produced at Yale, directed by Frank McMullan, 1956. This play was staged behind the proscenium on a space stage, uninfluenced by the form of the Elizabethan theatre. Changes of locale were made by lights and dialogue. Set: Keith Cuerdon; costumes: Zelma Weisfeld. Photo: Commercial Photo Service.

"Coriolanus' Triumphant Arrival in Rome," from the Berliner Ensemble's Venice performance of Coriolanus, *directed by Manfred Wekwerth/Joachim Tenschert, 1966. Photo: Percy Paukschta.*

the proscenium arch did to some extent lessen the kind and amount of emotional impact of the play. However, the heightened emotional playing of the actors and the continuous physical action partly compensated for the absence of intimacy between the actors and the audience. The use of martial, discordant sound scored for the production also served to envelop the audience and establish and maintain a sense of immediacy of the theatrical event.

To see the Berliner Ensemble's production of *Coriolanus,* as adapted and staged by Bertolt Brecht and his colleagues Manfred Wekwerth and Joachim Tenschert, on a proscenium stage, with a white sheetlike half-curtain, in blazing white light from unmasked lighting equipment, is to question the need of a forestage or a three-sided thrust stage to achieve audience contact, the emotional and intellectual impact of the production is so overwhelming. Of course, Brecht was influenced by the structure of Shakespeare's plays and by Shakespeare's stage; yet, so far as I know, he never insisted upon or even suggested the use of a thrust stage, and certainly not a "reconstructed" Elizabethan stage.

Is a thrust or open stage necessary for Shakespeare? The distinguished former director of the Bristol Old Vic company and of the London Old Vic, Hugh Hunt, concedes that "Although a production of Shakespeare may have many advantages on an open stage, it is not the form of the stage which dictates the success of the performances." The success of the Chichester Festival, he notes, would not be less if it were housed in a theatre with a proscenium stage. Nor would Peter Brook's production of *King Lear* at the Aldwych behind a picture frame fail to attract audiences.[15] When this production was presented on the New York State Theater's stage, Peter Brook complained of its diminished effectiveness because of acoustical problems which may have emanated, in part at least, from the conditions of the open stage. Actually, it was not designed for the production of plays but for opera and ballet. Many successful productions of Shakespeare took place at the Shakespeare Memorial Theatre at Stratford-upon-Avon in spite of what was essentially a picture-frame stage, though the stage was later modified by adding a raked forestage. Peter Hall, appointed director in 1960, admitted three years later that the stage remained "an obstinate proscenium stage with pieces stuck on in the front." [16] Later, the stage was rebuilt and is now a thrust stage.

Shakespearean productions in Broadway theatres without forestages continue to be successful. Margaret Webster, noted American director of Shakespeare, sees "no value that we may derive from the actual reconstruction of an Elizabethan stage." Her experience of playing on one and of directing on a reproduction taught her "more about its disadvantages than its advantages." To group actors in-the-round is to work more as a sculptor than a painter and is a difficult technique. The "modern use of levels, rostra, and steps gives the director in many cases a more effective medium." A stage so used gives "approximately the same value for a spectator in any part of the theatre." She cites the problems of sight lines to the inner and upper stages. The inner stage, she argues, can be effectively used for intimate scenes and can best be used as a jumping-off place for action on the forestage. This forestage or apron does, she admits, "afford an invaluable degree of intimacy between actors and audience. An actor could really speak the 'To be or not to be' soliloquy

as if it were his thought made audible; the emotional contact he was able effortlessly to establish is at the very root of Shakespeare's writing." Though "it is often helpful to erect some kind of an apron stage; I do not myself think that it is essential. An actor can get intimacy without it." Great actors and great material can achieve it.[17]

Both Hugh Hunt and Margaret Webster rightly concede that an open stage has advantages for the production of Shakespeare but insist that it is not essential. Shakespeare on the modern picture-frame stage has succeeded under varying conditions of scene design, with and without a forestage or apron, raked stage, permanent sets, changing scenery *à vista,* revolving stage, tracked units, and so on. The caliber of the performances and the degree of imaginativeness of the staging have been primarily responsible for success or failure. The form of the stage and its scenic investiture and techniques have been only secondarily important. Yet it cannot be denied that the open stage and the intimate audience-actor relationship created for the Stratford, Ontario, Shakespearean Festival gave a new impetus to Shakespearean production in North America. Audiences were made aware of Shakespeare in new and stimulating ways. Shakespeare was no longer formal and distanced from the viewer—as though he were an exhibit of framed paintings hung in an art gallery or museum—but he was given the freedom of open space and he invited the spectator to occupy this space with him. The intimacy of audience contact and the continuously flowing action, speech, and character behavior created a series of visually stimulating images in filmic close-up. The pioneering accomplishments of the Canadian festival resulted in the building and establishment in Minneapolis of the outstanding Guthrie Theater and company originally dedicated primarily to Shakespearean production. So publicized have these two theatres become that the open stage was considered the panacea for all American theatre ills and the desirable form for staging all plays. Thus there was an explosion of theatre building throughout the country. Experience with the open stage, however, has taught some directors and audiences that certain environmental plays suffer when performed on such a stage, but in general Shakespeare gains.

---

[15] Hugh Hunt, "Theatre and Youth," in Stephen Joseph, ed., *Actor and Architect* (Manchester, Manchester University Press, 1964), pp. 72–3.

[16] Simon Trussler, "Shakespeare: The Greatest Whore of Them All—Peter Hall at Stratford 1960–1968," *The Drama Review, 13,* No. 2 (Winter 1968), 170.

[17] Margaret Webster, *Shakespeare without Tears* (New York, McGraw-Hill, 1942), pp. 54–6.

The Shakespearean Festival Theatre, Stratford, Ontario. Photo: Robert C. Ragsdale.

The Guthrie Theater stage in Minneapolis, showing a scene from Tyrone Guthrie's production of Chekhov's The Three Sisters, *1963. Designed by Tanya Moiseiwitsch.*

Theatre-in-the-round has also been used for Shakespeare but with widely varying results. Comedies, I believe, have in general lent themselves favorably to such staging. Though I am sure exceptions can be cited, the tragedies have worked less effectively in-the-round than on three-sided open stages. Much depends upon performances and directorial imagination and control. The arguments for and against theatre-in-the-round are well known and need not be repeated here. Its popularity as a theatre form seems now to be in the decline.

The modern director of Shakespeare has the benefit of recorded experience with many kinds of theatre and stage structure used for the production of Shakespeare. He must make his choice of stage form with the knowledge of this experience and he must bear in mind the demands of Shakespeare's plays in general and of an individual play in particular. His own concept of the play should be a strongly determining factor.

THE TEXT AND THE DIRECTOR'S WORKING SCRIPT

The director of modern plays written by American playwrights can be sure that the text, if published, is authentic. (Plays translated into English or adapted to English often present problems of meaning even if authorized for publication.) The playwright in this country today submits his own copy to the publisher. Sometimes it is different from the acting version performed on or off Broadway —Tennessee Williams' *Cat on a Hot Tin Roof,* for example. The copy represents the writer's preferred and authorized version. Moreover, he is able to insure the accurate publication of his play by proofreading the printer's copy. The publication of Shakespeare's plays was not authorized or supervised by the author even though sixteen of them were printed during his lifetime. Textual authenticity therefore is a director's nagging problem.

The conditions under which Elizabethan plays reached the reading public differed markedly from those obtaining today. First of all, plays were written not to be read but to be performed. Plays were not considered literature, anyway. And a playwright wrote a play especially for a particular company and sold the exclusive rights to that company. (Most writers today do not create their plays for a company—even for resident theatre companies very often—but for any producer, on Broadway, off-Broadway, or in any part of the country, who can organize companies for production. There are exceptions today and have been in the recent past. Certain off-Broadway groups produce plays written especially for them. The American Place Theatre, the LaMama Theatre, and a few others off-Broadway have their own playwrights. Clifford Odets used to write plays for the Group Theatre, and various playwrights wrote for the old Theatre Guild company.) In selling his play outright to an Elizabethan company the author could not resell it to a publisher. Besides, publication of a play made it available not only to the reader but also to theatrical companies.

A play was not protected by a copyright law and once published was open to plagiarism by other authors and production by any company at any time. Thus the playwright was unable to share in the proceeds from the sale of copies of his play to the public or from unauthorized performances. There was, therefore, reluctance on the part of the playwrights and the companies to permit publication.

However, companies did sell the "book of the play" to publishers when they did not wish to keep it in their repertory and when they dissolved as companies. When Pembroke's Men broke up in 1594 they sold their play books to publishers and divided the money among the actors. During the plagues of 1593–4 and 1603–4, when the actors could not perform, they needed money and evidently sold a large number of plays for publication. Sometimes plays were sold to the publisher to supplant pirated editions. Publication under these circumstances was legitimate.

Publishers often obtained copies of plays by illegitimate means. Knowing that there was a demand by the reading public for certain plays by the better-known playwrights, publishers would resort to several methods to secure the plays. One, it has been conjectured, was to send a stenographer to one or more performances to transcribe the play into shorthand. The margin for error was great when this method was used. First of all, the shorthand systems, as scholars have learned from studies of them, were quite inaccurate. Furthermore, the stenographers could not always hear the words correctly because of the actors' failure to articulate and project them. Noises from the audience and theatre vendors must have interfered with audibility. Too, it is reasonable to wonder whether stenographers could write down what they heard as rapidly as it was spoken. In fact, since a fairly accurate stenographic system was not invented until 1602, it is best to discount the accuracy of this method of transcribing plays from actual performance and submitting them for publication. Another consideration is that Shakespearean actors, like actors today, were not always accurate in quoting the author's words. Actors have always changed, added, or eliminated dialogue in performance, either intentionally or unintentionally.

Another way the publisher obtained the copy of a play was to send someone to the performances to memorize it. This was hardly reliable but enough of the play was captured to make up copy for the printer and to satisfy public interest and curiosity. A more practical method was to pay an actor of the company to write down his own part and to reconstruct the rest of the play from memorizing at rehearsal and performances the dialogue spoken by the other members of the company. He could also supply at least some of the stage directions. It is believed that the first editions of *Romeo and Juliet, The Merry Wives of Windsor, Henry V,* and *Hamlet* were published by this means.

Not only did the illegitimate practices of obtaining copy for publication contribute to the inaccuracy of the texts but so did printing methods. The procedure after securing the play for publication was to enter the title in the Stationers' Register on the payment of 6d. This was a record maintained by the corporation of printers and publishers to protect the publisher from infringement by other members of the corporation and from illicit publication by anyone. After the play was registered it was turned over to the printers. The compositor worked from the promptcopy which had been cut and changed by the Master of the Revels who had licensed the company to perform the play. This copy also contained the prompter's scrawled notes on stage directions, music, properties, actors' names, and so on. This was therefore not a very clean and fair copy. It is not surprising that the printed pages were full of errors. The author was not there to correct them —as Ben Jonson evidently was for the folio edition of his works. Even if someone checked the pages as they came off the press he was not able to keep up, and thus uncorrected pages were eventually bound up with the corrected ones. Few copies of the same edition are ex-

actly alike. The First Quarto version of *King Lear,* for example, differs one copy from another, corrected pages bound up with uncorrected ones. It is no wonder that the texts of Shakespeare's plays raise questions of authenticity. We cannot be sure that they accurately represent the playwright's creation.

Sixteen of Shakespeare's plays appeared in quarto form before his death and one, *Othello,* six years after his death, before the publication of the First Folio in 1623. These seventeen have been divided into so-called good and bad quartos. Ten or eleven of the good quartos were obtained legitimately, that is, with the consent of the companies to which Shakespeare had sold them.

The bad quartos are *Romeo and Juliet, The Merry Wives of Windsor, Henry V, Hamlet, Pericles,* and *Troilus and Cressida.*

The quarto editions up to 1623 and their dates of publication, according to Thomas Marc Parrott, are:

Titus Andronicus (1594, 1600, 1611)
Richard II (1597, 1598, 1608, 1615)
Richard III (1597, 1598, 1602, 1605, 1612, 1622)
Romeo and Juliet (1597, 1599, 1609, one undated quarto)
Henry IV, Part I (1598, 1599, 1604, 1608, 1613, 1622)
Love's Labour's Lost (1598)
The Merchant of Venice (1600, 1619)
Henry V (1600, 1602, 1619)
Much Ado About Nothing (1600)
Henry IV, Part II (1600)
A Midsummer Night's Dream (1600, 1619)
The Merry Wives of Windsor (1602, 1619)
Hamlet (1603, 1604, 1605, 1611)
King Lear (1608, 1619)
Troilus and Cressida (1609)
Pericles (1609: two editions; 1611, 1619)
Othello (1622) [18]

The remaining plays, nineteen or twenty, appeared originally in the First Folio, having been released for publication by the King's Men, the company to which Shakespeare had belonged.

When John Heminges and Henry Condell decided to publish all of Shakespeare's plays in the First Folio in 1623, it was, of course, necessary to secure the rights to the quarto editions. The cost of such rights, in addition

[18] *William Shakespeare: A Handbook* (New York, Charles Scribner's Sons, 1934), p. 201.

to that of printing, made the venture expensive, and a partnership consisting of Heminges, Condell, W. Jaggard, Ed. Blount, I. Smithweeke, and W. Aspley was formed to share the costs. (Being the only two surviving members of the original "housekeepers" of the Globe, Heminges and Condell were probably easily able to obtain the publication rights of the "play books" owned by the King's Men.)

There are thirty-six plays in the First Folio. (A thirty-seventh, *Pericles,* was added to the Third Folio, second edition.) Eighteen of these plays have no quarto editions, so the First Folio is their source. These, according to Heminges and Condell, were based on Shakespeare's own manuscripts. However, *Macbeth* is thought to be an acting version, with cuts and interpolations. The texts of *Measure for Measure* and *All's Well That Ends Well* are considered poor, deriving from a promptcopy, a transcript, or actors' scripts. Eighteen of the thirty-six have at least one quarto text. Two of these plays, *Romeo and Juliet* and *Hamlet,* had bad first quartos but good corrected second quartos, which the First Folio used for copy. The plays with bad quarto texts were presumably corrected for the Folio publication or the original manuscripts or transcripts were substituted for them. For the rest of the plays the versions of the latest published quartos were used. Some of the quarto texts are thought to be better than those of the First Folio because with more reprintings more errors occurred.

The Second Folio appeared in 1632, printed from the first with some errors corrected and some new ones added. The Third Folio followed in 1663, with a second edition in 1664; the Fourth Folio (the last), in 1685. Each was reprinted from the previous one. Corrections and improvements as well as mistakes occurred in successive publications.

The folios, unlike the quartos, divided some of the plays into acts and scenes. *Love's Labour's Lost* and *Henry V* are divided into acts; *Romeo and Juliet, Antony and Cleopatra,* and other plays have no divisions after preliminary announcements of "Actus Primus" and "Scoena Prima." *The Tempest* is not only consistently divided into acts and scenes but also has full stage directions. "The Actors Names," "The Names of all the Actors," and "The Names of the Actors," meaning the names of the characters, appear at the end of *Timon of Athens, Measure for Measure, The Winter's Tale,* and others. Consistency is not the out-

standing trait of the First Folio. The superiority of the folios over the quartos is a subject of debate among scholars. However, the First Folio is held in general esteem. Some quarto versions, the Second Quarto of *Hamlet,* printed in 1604, for example, may be in some ways superior to the First Folio edition. The modern director can compare the various folios and quartos and decide for himself which version he prefers, and he may compile his own acting edition of a play from the facsimile folios and quartos. Modern editions often include the First Folio version together with the nonpirated versions of the quartos, indicating which is which by special signs and notes. Heminges and Condell, Shakespeare's special friends to whom he bequeathed generous sums for the purchase of memorial rings, were neither scholars nor experienced editors and were the victims of their own ignorance and of slipshod printing methods, but they tried nevertheless to give us *Mr. William Shakespeares Comedies, Histories, and Tragedies,* "Published according to the True Original Copies." A note to the reader states: "to have publish'd them, as where (before) you were abus'd with diverse stolen, and surreptitious copies, maimed, and deformed by the frauds and stealths of injurious impostors, that expos'd them: even those, are now offer'd to your view cur'd, and perfect of their limbs; and all the rest, absolute in their numbers, as he [Shakespeare] conceived them." These claims have not been substantiated by subsequent editors, yet they may have been successful in persuading the reading public to buy copies of the First Folio. Ever since the publication of this edition of the plays and of the subsequent three folios, scholars have been trying to restore the texts to their "true original" state.

The first genuine attempt to edit the plays was made in 1709, twenty-four years after the Fourth Folio's publication, by Nicholas Rowe, dramatist and poet laureate. Unfortunately, he based his work upon the Fourth Folio, the most inaccurate of all. However, he did modernize the spelling, punctuation, and grammar, give a list of *dramatis personae* for each play, note the entrances and exits of characters, indicate location, and divide the plays into acts and scenes—a questionable contribution since the Elizabethans did not in general follow this practice. In a second edition in 1714 Rowe included the first biography of Shakespeare.

Alexander Pope, a highly respected scholar

and poet, was Shakespeare's second editor. His edition of the plays appeared in six quarto volumes in 1725. His copy was based upon Rowe's text and he occasionally consulted the earlier quartos and folios. His main contribution consisted of explaining obsolete words, further division and location of scenes, making arbitrary corrections in the language and meter to suit his own taste, and actually cutting many passages which he maintained were unworthy of Shakespeare and probably had been interpolated by the actors. He also excluded the seven plays added to the Third Folio in 1663, which Rowe had included in his edition. These were *The London Prodigal, Thomas Lord Cromwell, Sir John Oldcastle, The Puritan, A Yorkshire Tragedy, Locrine,* and *Pericles,* all plays attributed to Shakespeare but actually spurious except *Pericles.* Pope threw them all out. His work as editor hardly lived up to expectations.

The first editor of Shakespeare's plays now held in high esteem was Lewis Theobald, a fine classical scholar knowledgeable about Shakespeare and Elizabethan literature. His edition of the plays was brought out in 1726 under the title *Shakespeare Restored, or a specimen of the many errors as well committed as left unamended by Mr. Pope.* This was hardly tactful and he infuriated Pope, who subsequently took every opportunity to discredit him, but Theobald is today recognized as an inspired textual critic of Shakespeare. He showed meticulous care and great scholarly diligence in collating the various texts— though he used Pope's text as a basis—and made three hundred corrections and emendations which have been generally approved by editors who have followed him. He was the first to consult Shakespeare's sources, including Raphael Holinshed's *Chronicles* and Sir Thomas North's *Plutarch.*

Sir Thomas Hanmer, considered one of the worst of Shakespeare's editors, was responsible for an edition in 1744 based on Theobald's, which demonstrated in his cutting of scenes and emendations an appalling lack of judgment.

The next was Bishop Warburton, who also used Theobald's edition for his text but strongly criticized it in his preface and irresponsibly altered it.

Dr. Samuel Johnson's 1765 edition did little to restore the text, but his "Preface" is considered an important piece of criticism. Using Warburton's text, he wrote introductions to the plays and contributed numerous convincing explanations of difficult words and lines of dialogue.

Edward Capell and George Steevens were the first to draw attention to the importance of the quartos for textual study. Up to this time the folios had been considered the only authentic sources. Capell published his edition of Shakespeare's works in 1768. His study of the quartos and of the Elizabethan theatre was published after his death. Steevens reprinted twenty of the quartos in 1766 and supplemented Johnson's edition with his research. He reissued his edition in 1773 and revised it in 1778. This edition was the standard version of Shakespeare for many years, though he omitted the poems and sonnets and made many invalid alterations of the plays.

Edward Malone in 1790 included *Pericles* in his edition and also included the poems and sonnets and spurious plays of the Third Folio. His main contribution to scholarship was his *Attempt to ascertain the order in which the plays attributed to Shakespeare were written,* published in 1778. His research resulted in new knowledge of Shakespeare's life gleaned from records in Stratford and London; and he made further study of the sources of the plays and of the Elizabethan theatre.

The First Variorum edition, published by Isaac Reed in 1803, was based upon Steevens' work; the Second Variorum of 1813 was a reprint of the First Variorum; the Third Variorum, edited in 1821 by James Boswell the younger, was based on Malone's edition of the plays. The New Variorum was first published in 1871 by Dr. Howard Furness. The various editions contain complete collections of variant passages, emendations, and notes. They are now being published in paperback and are readily accessible and helpful to the director of Shakespeare.

The next important edition was called the Cambridge Shakespeare, published in 1863–6 and edited by W. G. Clark, J. Glover, and W. H. Wright; it was revised in 1891–3 by Wright. This edition became the standard and long remained so. Its text was reprinted in the Globe and the Temple editions. It contained all the textual variations and the most important conjectures by previous editors.

The New Shakespeare, published by the Cambridge University Press, edited originally by Sir Arthur Quiller-Couch and John Dover Wilson, now by Wilson alone, is a worthy successor to the Cambridge Shakespeare. It contains, in addition to highly esteemed texts of each play, introductions, commentary on the copy, notes, and a stage history. It is very informative.

The plays issued in convenient size and as inexpensive paperbacks, like the Bantam Classic series, the Folger Shakespeare, the Laurel Shakespeare, the Pelican Shakespeare, and the Signet Classic Shakespeare, contain critical commentaries on each play together with introduction, notes, references, and glossaries. These and other paperback editions make good rehearsal scripts for the director, actors, and designers. Most of these editions divide the plays into acts and scenes. (The Pelican Shakespeare does not, except marginally where it uses the act-scene division of the Globe text. A printer's ornament marks the point of division.) Lines of dialogue are numbered, a number occurring at the end of each fifth line. Lineation usually conforms to that of the Globe edition of 1864. (The Bantam Classic series numbers each tenth line after the first.) Words are glossed at the bottom, at the side of the page, or at the back of the volume. Editors differ markedly in their use of stage directions. Some include only those found in the folio or quarto texts or texts upon which the modern edition is based. Some editors conjecture fairly full interpretive stage directions in supplement to the ones found in the original texts. Scene locations as well as stage directions are described in full realistic detail in the New Shakespeare but are economically indicated in other editions. The Pelican edition does not indicate locale and, aside from entrances and exits, uses few stage directions.

Stage directions are included in the script of a modern play allegedly to help convey the author's intentions as to character, plot, and theme. Yet it may be argued that the dramatist who does his job in terms of dialogue reveals implicitly and/or explicitly his purpose and works in terms of drama, which is illustrated, rather than in terms of the novel, which is descriptive. Nevertheless, certain stage directions found in the folios and quartos can be, in spite of the Elizabethan staging conditions which are patently different from those of today, revelatory of Shakespeare's dramatic values. What could be more eloquent than the stage direction cited by scholars and found in the First Folio text of *Coriolanus* (5. 3. 183), in which Volumnia pleads that Rome be spared and kneels before her son together with Vir-

gilia, Valeria, and Coriolanus' son, and Coriolanus responds by the direction: "Holds her by the hand silent." This direction makes graphically clear the heart of the play: Coriolanus' relation to his mother. And there have been other citations of illuminating stage directions. For example, *The Tempest,* 3. 3. 17, indicates "Solemn and strange music: and Prospero on the top (invisible:)" The director is advised to have music, is told that Prospero is to be placed onstage on the highest level—probably the third level or the musicians' gallery in the Elizabethan playhouse—and significantly that Prospero is not seen by Alonso and his followers who watch "several strange shapes, bringing in a banquet; and dance about it with gentle actions of salutations . . ." And in *Richard III,* 1. 2, when Anne asks Richard where is one who loves her better than her husband whose corpse she accompanies to the tomb and Richard responds "Here," there is in the Folio the direction: "Spits at him." This is the beginning action in an outrageous sexual duel. Later, "She looks scornfully at him" and then with incredible daring and brazen confidence "He lays his breast open, she offers at with his sword" (which he had given her); and when the direction says "She falls the sword," we know Richard has won the duel. Surely these directions came from the original acting version of the play and tell the modern director just how the scene is to be performed to carry out the author's intentions.

The director in today's theatre, however, cannot expect to find such exact acting signals in many of Shakespeare's plays. The stage directions, for the most part, concern entrances and exits and musical cues. Modern plays are published with detailed stage directions. The plays published by Samuel French, the Dramatists' Play Service, and other drama publishing firms include complete directions as to movement and gestures, emotional attitudes, scenic descriptions, light, costume, and sound plots and attempt to present an exact production blueprint of the original professional production for the director, amateur or professional. These plays indicate what are presumably the author's intentions. Shakespeare's plays, because of the few directions that have come down to us—and we don't know whether these few represent his own shorthand of his intentions—leave themselves open to many creative interpretations. In fact, the paucity of stage directions and other evidence permits open investigation by each individual director who, according to his perception and imagination, will interpret the plays.

Of course, valuable keys to the values and meanings of Shakespeare's plays lie in the stage directions implied in text and subtext. Obviously the Duke in *Measure for Measure* gives Escalus a parchment that looks like a legal document when he says (1. 1):

> There is our commission,
> From which we would not have you warp.

And the actor will certainly have suited the action to the word when in *Macbeth,* 4. 3, Malcolm angrily admonishes Macduff:

> Merciful heaven!
> What, man! ne'er pull your hat upon your
>   brows;
> Give sorrow words: the grief that does not
>   speak
> Whispers the o'er-fraught heart and bids it
>   break.

A subtextual action can be found in *Measure for Measure,* 2. 4, just before Angelo stalks out leaving Isabella to deliver her soliloquy that begins with

> To whom should I complain? Did I tell this,
> Who would believe me?

In a passion of desire and frustration, completely exposed, Angelo demands that Isabella redeem her brother by giving herself to him. She must answer the next day or Claudio's life will be forfeit. He then starts out but returns to her on

> As for you,
> Say what you can; my false o'erweighs your
>   true.

Here he might take her by the shoulders on the first half of the second line, tear off the cross she wears around her neck, and throw it to the floor after he finishes the line (2. 4). This action or stage direction may be implied in Angelo's revolt against the recurring image of Isabella as saintly virtue in his soliliquy (2. 2), especially in the lines:

> O cunning enemy, that, to catch a saint,
> With saints dost bait thy hook: most dangerous
> Is that temptation that doth goad us on
> To sin, in loving virtue: never could the
>   strumpet,

> With all her double vigour, art, and nature,
> Once stir my temper: but this virtuous maid
> Subdues me quite.

This violent and shocking action by Angelo is, of course, permeated with symbolism which may be perceived consciously or unconsciously by the audience.

With the knowledge provided by the publication of Shakespeare's plays, from the earliest published editions to the most recent, the director may select his text and check it with the appropriate quarto and/or folio. He may consult the latest Variorum edition of a play for textual commentaries and select the emendations and meanings which reflect the best and most up-to-date authority and stageworthiness. He may, with extreme circumspection, cut questionable passages or passages noncommunicable to a modern audience. Conditions of production and playing time may sensibly dictate some cutting. G. Wilson Knight, noted scholar-critic-director of Shakespeare, who wrote such perceptive and imaginative interpretive works as *The Wheel of Fire, The Imperial Theme, The Crown of Life,* and *Principles of Shakespearian Production,* realizes the practical problems of getting a

> play from the text on to the living stage . . . The producer [director] should be able to hold the play in jig-saw bits in his mind, to sort them all out to build with them and recreate the whole from understanding of its nature. Such understanding gives him full powers to cut, adapt, even on rare occasions, transpose, according to circumstances; he has to consider his stage, his company, his audience. The feeling that cutting is sacrilegious derives from a totally false reasoning. The producer's business is not translation, but recreation. It is, however, true that nothing more swiftly and irrevocably gives a producer away than unenlightened cutting or iniquitous transpositions and additions. *You must by thought and intimate acquaintance acquire the right to do these things.*[19]

Granville-Barker in his "Introduction" to *Prefaces to Shakespeare* says "we cut and carve the body of a play to its peril." But he alleges that the exceptions to this rule involve the aesthetic problem of pornography: "Shakespeare's characters often make obscene jokes. The manners of his time permitted it. The

---

[19] G. Wilson Knight, *Principles of Shakespearian Production* (New York, Macmillan, 1936), pp. 51–2. Italics mine.

public manners of ours still do not." (He wrote this in 1945. The public today permits greater latitude.) "Now the dramatic value of a joke is to be measured by its effect upon an audience, and each is meant to make its own sort of effect. If then, instead of giving a passing moment's amusement, it makes a thousand people uncomfortable and for the next five minutes very self-conscious, it fails of its true effect." He does not urge this argument to include "turning 'God' into 'Heaven' or making Othello call Desdemona a 'wanton'" instead of whore or "deodorizing" *Measure for Measure* or making Beatrice "mealymouthed." "But," he says, "suppression of a few scabrous jokes will not leave a play the poorer . . ." Yet, he thinks "The blue pencil is a dangerous weapon; and its use grows on a man . . ." [20] This is the considered opinion of a man who was an actor, playwright, and director as well as a scholar of considerable standing. As director of the plays of Shakespeare he exerted significant influence on twentieth-century methods of Shakespearean production.

In discussing Brecht's version of *Coriolanus* as performed by the Berliner Ensemble, Peter Brook—probably the most brilliant director in the English-speaking world today, director of many notable productions of Shakespeare in America, England, and Europe—found that Brecht had rewritten the major confrontation scene between Coriolanus and Volumnia. "I do not for one moment question the principle of rewriting Shakespeare—after all, the texts do not get burned—each person can do what he thinks necessary with a text and still no one suffers," he wrote. But he objected to the shift in the play's emphasis resulting from the rewriting. Brecht did not consider the Coriolanus-Volumnia relationship central but wished to make the play more contemporary by pointing up "the theme that no leader is indispensable." Arguing that "any play of Shakespeare's has an organic sense," Brook contends that on paper it may "look as though the episode can reasonably be substituted for another, and certainly in many plays there are scenes and passages that can easily be cut or transposed. But if one has a knife in one hand, one needs a stethoscope in the other.

The scene between Coriolanus and his mother is close to the heart of the play." [21]

It will be worthwhile to select a modern edition of a Shakespearean play and prepare a working script of it. *Measure for Measure* is a good choice because of some textual difficulties and because of its relevance to the modern world.

Among modern texts that of the New Shakespeare series is recommended to the director. It is based upon the First Folio text. And it is corrupt, according to John Dover Wilson, one of the editors of the edition published by the Cambridge University Press in 1922. [22] (This edition is still held in high esteem, though some later ones have been published.) His charge of corruption is based upon evidences of abridgment and expansion of the text.

Abridgment is discerned in broken lines and irregularly arranged passages, abrupt changes in style, and cuts which leave the text obscure. In addition, abridgment is suspected because of the truncated characters of the Justice in 2. 1, Varrius in 4. 5, and, most importantly, Juliet in 2. 1 and 3, and in 5. 1. The latter is mute in her last two appearances, Varrius is silent in his only appearance, and the Justice has only ten lines of dialogue. Another indication of shortening is the five-and-a-half-line speech by the Duke in 4. 1, said probably to provide cover for the offstage conversation of Isabella and Mariana in which Mariana is persuaded to participate in the "bed-trick."

Wilson sees several signs of expansion of the text. One is a beefing up of the part of Lucio throughout the play but especially in Isabella's first interview with Angelo. The fact that speeches erratically and arbitrarily change from prose to verse is another sign. The hand of the adapter is seen here. Fault is found with 1. 2. 1–111, involving Lucio, the two gentlemen, Mistress Overdone, and Pompey. The dialogue fails to distinguish the characters in the first part of the scene, and there are contradictions in character knowledge of events when Mistress Overdone and Pompey talk in their scene. This seems to indicate writing at

[20] Harley Granville-Barker, *Prefaces to Shakespeare* (Princeton, Princeton University Press, 1946), *1*, 21–2.

[21] Peter Brook, *The Empty Space* (New York, Atheneum, 1968), p. 82.

[22] John Dover Wilson, "The Copy for *Measure for Measure,* 1623," *Measure for Measure,* Sir Arthur Quiller-Couch and John Dover Wilson, eds. (New Shakespeare ed. Cambridge, Cambridge University Press, 1922), pp. 97–113.

different times by different authors. Another bit of evidence of corruption is the carelessness of time sequences illustrated by the Provost's ordering Abhorson to prepare for the execution of Claudio and Barnardine at "four o'clock" tomorrow and some lines later the Provost's telling Claudio that he will be executed "by eight tomorrow" (4. 2. 52, 63). Wilson believes that the revisions of the play —abridgment and expansion—took place several years apart and "possibly by different dramatists."[23]

The abridgment probably took place for the court performance December 26, 1604 ("The evidence for this date is an entry in the Account Books of the Revels office").[24] The expansion, Wilson conjectures, took place later. The reference to the King of Hungary in 1. 2 is historically relevant and leads Wilson to believe that the lengthened version of the play appeared sometime after November 11, 1606, which coincides with the peace treaty alluded to in the play. He supposes that the play underwent two more revisions between its presentation before King James in 1604 and publication in the Folio in 1623. Though Shakespeare is believed to have participated in the 1604 abridgment, he did contribute three speeches in compliment to King James and his consort, but he had no hand in further revisions. Wilson states that the present edition of *Measure for Measure* contains 2,705 lines. He thinks more than 700 were contributed by the reviser and less than 2,000 were written by Shakespeare. Of the reviser's lines, 256 were "pure additions": 1. 2. 1–79; 2. 1. 188–280; 4. 2. 1–58; and 4. 3. 149–77. The rest of the more than 700 lines contributed by the reviser were "little prose-patches embedded in verse-dialogue," most of which "are connected with the reviser's favorite character, Lucio," and "strange prose, full of circumlocutions and verse scraps, which we regard as the reviser's attempt to expand 135 lines of Shakespearian verse to more than three times their original length."[25]

In his last paragraph Wilson points out another bit of evidence of corrupt copy for the play by mentioning the fact that the Folio "Beyond the necessary entries and exits, which are often lacking . . . contains no stage-directions of any kind, except at the beginning

of acts 4 and 5."[26] And he concludes that the manuscript used for the publication of the First Folio was made up of players' parts which the prose adapter transcribed, filling out the play "with additions of his own."

The modern director is justified in basing his cutting of some of the suspected passages of the play upon these scholarly assumptions. If he accepts all the assumptions of John Dover Wilson and cuts the play accordingly, he may need to do some revising of his own to suture the editorial wounds. Let us look at the text and consider some of the outstanding examples of passages allegedly written by someone other than Shakespeare and considered "pure additions."

The first occurs in 1. 2, and, as Wilson suggests, these additions can be considered in three parts. The first includes the dialogue between the two gentlemen and Lucio up to the entrance of Mistress Overdone. And, considering its dramatic quality, "It is sheer mud, dreary, dead; not even a maggot stirs."[27] It is undramatic in terms of plot, character, dialogue, and theme. The actors could clown around but it would be forced and unintelligible to an audience today. The second part of the scene, beginning when Mistress Overdone is seen approaching, does serve as a slightly amusing introduction to her and her profession. Upon her entrance she also furthers the plot by telling us about Claudio's arrest, the reason for his arrest, when he is to be executed, and about a proclamation. The third part, between Mistress Overdone and Pompey, presents a problem: Mistress Overdone contradicts her knowledge of events by asking Pompey questions about Claudio which she could answer. Obviously, the text has been tampered with.

For the reasons cited the director is justified in cutting the first 79 lines. He can begin 1. 2 with the entrance of Mistress Overdone, who introduces herself amusingly and accurately with

> Thus, what with the war, what with the
> sweat, what with the gallows, and what with
>   poverty,
> I am custom-shrunk.

This little scene, continuing with the excited

---

[23] P. 101.
[24] *Ibid.*
[25] P. 112.

[26] *Ibid.*
[27] P. 99.

entrance of the pimp Pompey, is amusing and establishes vice-ridden Vienna and the ambience of the whole play. Plotwise, this third part of the section of the play, from line 80 to line 111, is not necessary and may indeed have been added by someone other than Shakespeare. Yet it has dramatic value and is not without quality. In addition to its comic and atmospheric value it introduces the theme that though bawdy houses will be torn down their keeper will always have clients; sexual instinct will not be restrained.

Next, considering the trial of Pompey and Froth, arrested by Elbow and brought before Angelo and Escalus, in 2. 1, the director can tighten the scene and eliminate some of Pompey's tangential and not very amusing testimony by cutting lines after Escalus' "Go to: go to: no matter for the dish, sir" and continuing with his "Come; you are a tedious fool: to the purpose." Another cut can be made from Pompey's "He,/ sir, sitting, as I say, in a lower chair, sir" through his "Why, very well then: I hope here be truths." Another advisable cut can profitably be made after Escalus' "Why, no" and continuing with his line to Froth, "Where were you born, friend?"

Though Wilson asserts that lines 188–280 of 2. 1 have been added, they should be retained to wind up the trial of Froth and to allow Escalus to dismiss him. The subsequent testimony of Pompey is not only stageworthy in its clear humor but it furthers the theme of sexual instinct and legal strictures.

The question of the dramatic usefulness of the Justice can be resolved by considering him as one of the "officers" who enter with Elbow, Pompey, and Froth at the beginning of the trial. The director can employ the Justice as the court's scribe. He is also needed at the end of the scene for Escalus to address when he speaks of the sentence of Claudio, the severity of Angelo, and the role of mercy and the law.

The third "pure addition" cited by Wilson, 4. 2. 1–58, can be cut by the director without much loss, though its inclusion helps the actor who is to play Abhorson and provides some comic material.

Lines 149–77 in 4. 3, though an example of the expansion of Lucio's part, do provide more comedy and foreshadow the Duke's arrival the next day and his punishment of the jackanapes. It would also be too bad to lose the memorable description of the Duke as

"the old fantastical duke of dark corners." It is worth retaining in the script.

The problem of the presence of two friars in the play can be solved by eliminating Thomas from the *dramatis personae*. He is not referred to by name in 1. 3, and it makes dramatic sense to use friar Peter in this scene, in 4. 5, and in Act 5.

In 4. 5 the Duke's lines, beginning with line 39, serve no purpose and should be cut. The character Varrius seems unnecessary, and the Duke's speech to him should be excised.

These are the glaring textual problems, though they account for considerably less than the more than 700 lines attributed to non-Shakespearean hands. Most of these problems have been solved by cutting a number of the offending passages, but some lines have been retained because of their dramatic values and stageworthiness. Throughout the play the director will find, upon thoughtful study, many more blocks of dialogue which probably comprise the rest of the adapter's revisions and which he will wish to eliminate because they are awkward in expression, unclear, or undramatic. Prerehearsal cuts of this material can be made. Rehearsals of certain scenes will indicate the further need of the blue pencil; though actors are usually loath to have any of their dialogue cut, their inability to make it come alive in rehearsal can persuade them as well as the director of the need for cutting.

The director's concept of a play's focus can dictate cutting, emending, and transposition of scenes. And such editorial work by the director may not distort the play in the sense that the play takes on a meaning not organic to it. The fact is that Shakespeare's plays invite prismatic viewing; they can be seen from different points of view because they contain more than one meaning; and herein lies an aspect of the greatness of his plays. It is possible to see *Measure for Measure,* for instance, as a play of several meanings. It is about appearance versus reality, authority versus justice, wrong-doing versus forgiveness, and instinct versus restraint (law). These subjects constitute a single kaleidoscopic meaning. Seen in a morality or allegorical play framework, each then can be projected.

If, for example, the director transposes 3. 1 to the end of 1. 1 and thus makes two scenes into one, we use the longer scene as a prologue upon which the rest of the play is based. We learn at the outset the Duke's reason for his flight from his office, his assuming the role of a friar, his deputizing another, and, very important, his reason for selecting Angelo. And when the Duke ends the scene by saying

> Lord Angelo is precise;
> Stands at a guard with envy; scarce confesses
> That his blood flows; or that his appetite
> Is more to bread than stone: hence shall we see,
> If power change purpose, what our seemers be.

we are introduced to the theme of rigidity of authority and the implied theme of mercy naturally associated with power, the conflict between instinct and self-imposed and unnatural restraint, and the theme of appearance and reality. The thematic premise of the play is pointedly projected in this elongated scene. The audience is ready for the proclamation and the arrest of Claudio and the vivid picture of sexual license of the dukedom. The audience also knows that the Duke is the mainspring of the play—the supreme *animateur* of a manipulated show.

By transposing 2. 3 to the end of 1. 2, the director introduces the Duke, disguised as a friar, into the main action early and emphasizes his supervisory function in the play. And the Duke sees at once the results of Angelo's exercise of power.

Transposition of these two scenes and tying them to other scenes forward the main plot line: Angelo is deputized, and the audience learns that the Duke has been permissive in his rule and now wishes to bring about restraint of the licentious behavior of his subjects but considers it best to do so through someone else whose appearance of Puritanism he suspects, and thus the Duke becomes an observer of his deputy's rigid authority. By placing the "nunnery" scene (1. 4) next, Lucio goes to call upon Isabella immediately after Claudio's arrest and pushes her, one of the central characters, into the main stream of the play. The arrest of Elbow and Froth (2. 1) follows and further illustrates Angelo's determination to restrain the licentious citizenry. Coming next, 2. 2 brings the two central characters, Isabella and Angelo, together in direct confrontation and poses the main problem of the play. The arrest of Pompey again in 3. 2, this time together with Mistress Overdone, interweaves the subsidiary characters into the patterning of the play's general theme and sets the scene in contrast to the previous Angelo-Isabella scene and to the next meeting between the two (2. 4). This climactic scene, involving the chief protagonist and the antagonist, brings the play to such a high emotional peak that an intermission for the audience is suggested. (These seven scenes, in actual performance, consume approximately one hour and nine minutes of playing time, and the intermission at this point divides the play into two more or less equal parts.)

The second part of the play continues in causal progression with 3. 1, the scene of the confrontation between Isabella and Claudio and the intercession of the Duke. The scenes then follow as in the Folio text.

This example of cutting and transposition of scenes for the director's working script is predicated upon a definite point of view toward *Measure for Measure*. The play is restructured in terms of scene sequence in order to focus upon the Duke as a "power divine" who controls the world of the play and thus demonstrates for the audience in parable form the lesson of sovereign laxity, identity ignorance, tyrannical authority and power, repentance, mercy, and forgiveness.

It must be pointed out most emphatically that any other point of view of the play demands a different approach to problems of structure and cutting. The approach outlined for *Measure for Measure,* it must also be pointed out, is only one example. Each play presents its own problems. In all cases the director should be warned that restructuring Shakespeare by changing the order of scenes can be hazardous. The alternation of scenes is usually designed for dramatic parallelism, contrast, and juxtaposition, and changes can diminish the total effectiveness of the play. Restructuring and cutting are instruments of the adapter whose purpose is to use the play to fit purposes and conditions different from those of the author. The director should think twice before assuming two creative roles, though it is fashionable in today's theatre for him to consider himself the dominant creative force. Very few directors are good playwrights. (There are playwrights who also direct—and direct very well.)

One final note about the text and the director's working script. In the process of rehearsal certain of Shakespeare's words may be found incomprehensible to actor and probably to audience. Practicality must dictate substitution of another word or excision. The problem of sheer weight of verbiage and performance time too must be considered. At the risk of opposition it can be argued that *Coriolanus,* for example, should be edited for a modern audience. Coriolanus is not only a prig but can be a bore. *Timon of Athens* and *Titus Andronicus* are other plays which might gain by judicious surgery. Yet in general, trust in Granville-Barker's advice is not misplaced.

FORM

The form of the realistic play is well known mainly for its tightness of structure, its causal progression of action, its unity of action, and the everyday psychology of its characters. These characteristics are, of course, the opposite of those found in the Shakespearean play. The structure in Shakespeare is narrational and panoramic; it is not linear: The incidents are linked without seemingly apparent cause and effect and are in alternating scenes rather than successive ones. There is a prevailing sense of scene independence and "a tendency to episodic intensification." [28] As Bernard Beckerman asserts in his *Shakespeare at the Globe,* where he, as scholar-director, discusses the structure of those plays presented at Shakespeare's Globe and also on the reconstructed Globe stage of Hofstra College, the scenes cluster about the story line and suggest the "image of a grapevine . . . for the scenes often appear to be hanging from a thread of narrative." [29] (This is the structure typical of motion pictures and many novels. Both these media, like the Shakespearean drama, are also characterized by a frequent shift of locale.)

Nevertheless, this clustering of scenes results in patterns. (The total structure impresses the mind after the director obtains a firm grasp of the play as a whole.) Beckerman identifies the structural patterns. One he calls the "episodic," which he finds in the historical or biographical plays. In them a series of events is arranged in succession on the thread of the story. He cites *Macbeth, Hamlet, Coriolanus,* and *Julius Caesar* as examples, though they demonstrate some differences in form. There is foreshadowing of future events by brief earlier scenes which make the progression of events plausible. In illustration, the witches forewarn Macbeth of the danger of Banquo, but this information does not strongly affect the action until after Duncan's murder. Allusions are made early in the play to Macduff's

defection, but action involving Macduff does not achieve prominence until after Banquo's death. Thus the lack of direct and immediate cause and effect accentuates the episodic nature of the play. The episodic pattern becomes more obvious, Beckerman notes, after Macbeth's visit to the witches. He also points out that Macbeth's attempt to reach only "the immediate goal" rather than an "ultimate point in the universe" [30] emphasizes the episodic.

The second pattern he calls the "river pattern" because there are various tributary scenes flowing into one dramatic stream. As an example, *Twelfth Night* presents the grouping of characters who create the tributary scenes. Orsino, Olivia, and Viola constitute one group; Malvolio, Sir Toby, and Sir Andrew another; and Antonio and Sebastian a third. Eventually their activity is blended into one combined movement. *The Merry Wives of Windsor* is another illustration. It is also divided into scenes between various sets of characters: Mistress Ford and Mistress Page; Falstaff and the Garter Inn group; and Ford, Page, Shallow, Slender, Caius, and Evans. Though they go their separate directions, quarreling, seeking to win the hand of Anne Page or the favor of the "merry wives," all eventually come together to teach Falstaff a lesson and to win Anne Page.

The "mirror pattern" presents two stories equal in emphasis. The Lear-Gloucester stories in *King Lear* and the Orlando-Rosalind stories in *As You Like It* mirror the dramatic similarity and contrast for the audience.

The structure of the individual scenes making up the overall dramatic pattern of each play consists of "a portion of one action or story [and] is not followed by an advance or counteraction, but by a new line of development, often containing completely different characters." While some scenes, as Beckerman points out, end with "a strong emotional lift," like Hamlet's

> —the play's the thing
> Wherein I'll catch the conscience of the king.
> (*Hamlet,* 2. 2)

others contain a "leading" scene in the action that propels the play forward like the one in *As You Like It* when Duke Frederick banishes Oliver from court until he finds Celia, but most scenes "are rounded off, relaxed, brought to a subdued end." [31]

---

[28] L. L. Schucking, *Character Problems in Shakespeare's Plays* (London, Harrap, 1922), p. 114.
[29] New York, Macmillan, 1962, p. 46.

[30] P. 49.
[31] P. 54.

In moving from a consideration of the totality of a Shakespearean play in terms of its structural pattern the director must grasp the recurrent technique for the shaping of scenes. He then becomes aware of the plot and thematic premises constructed by the first group of scenes. The introduction of characters and the setting forth of relationships and actions inciting conflict and drama lead the audience from a state of balance to one of imbalance, which is the basis for the development of the play. Shakespeare, unlike the Greeks and many modern playwrights, usually begins his plays near the start of their action. Little exposition is needed because little has happened before the play begins. *Macbeth, King Lear,* and *Othello* are good examples of this structure. (*Hamlet* has a little more antecedent action than the two other tragedies, I think.) The premise of *Macbeth* extends over the seven scenes of Act I before Macbeth makes up his mind to murder Duncan, whose death and the witches' predictions form the basis of action for the rest of the play. Shakespeare structures the premise by establishing the witches' waiting for Macbeth in scene 1; following this with the presentation of Duncan and the progress of the war, featuring the accomplishments of Macbeth and Banquo; returning to the witches and the appearance of Macbeth and Banquo; the prophecy and the fulfillment of part of the prophecy by the messages of Ross and Angus in scene 3; the welcoming of Macbeth and Banquo by Duncan, his naming of Malcolm as the next in line for the throne, his decision to visit Macbeth at Inverness, and Macbeth's growing ambition together with his thoughts of desperate action in scene 4; scene 5, which presents Lady Macbeth with Macbeth's letter reiterating the prophecy, her determination that Macbeth shall have the crown, Macbeth's arrival home announcing Duncan's visit, and her demand that he

> shall put
> This night's great business into my dispatch

showing Duncan's arrival and welcome at Inverness; and in scene 7 presenting Macbeth's meditation upon Duncan's murder, his indecision, Lady Macbeth's insistence and plan of action, and his decision to go through with the murder. Though the scenes alternate in locale and characters until the sixth and seventh scenes, the development, though epi-sodic, is straight and linear and deals with a single plot.

Crises develop in Shakespeare, as in present-day drama, which lead to a climax. But this climax is not the climax of modern drama, which in Beckerman's view is "a single point of extreme intensity where the conflicting forces come to a final, irreconcilable opposition. At that point a dramatic explosion, leading to the denouement, is the direct outcome of the climactic release." [32] Rather, "we find," he says, not a climactic point in the center of a Shakespearean play but a climactic plateau, a "coordination of intense moments sustained for a surprisingly extended period." [33] *Lear* and *Hamlet* illustrate this in their long plateaus of intensity, *Lear* in 3. 2, 3, 4, 5, 6, and 7, and *Hamlet* in 3. 2, 3, and 4.

These plateaus, incidentally, pose a problem in determining intermissions desired by audiences today. The one intermission for *King Lear* decreed by the director of the play in the summer of 1965 at the American Shakespeare Festival came at the end of 3. 4. This meant that the first part ran approximately one hour and fifty minutes—a long, long time for an audience required to pay concentrated attention to some of the most complex poetry ever written for the theatre. The intermission at this point also broke the curve of intensity of the play which rises through 3. 7. This is the point for an intermission according to Granville-Barker, who prefers a single intermission during the play. "To this point the play is carried by one great impetus of inspiration, and there will be great gain in its acting being unchecked." [34] If there must be two intermissions, he suggests one after 1. 2, and the other at the end of Act 3. His suggestions stem from his study of the rhythmic pattern of the play and the time sequence. The presentation of the trial scene (3. 6) after an intermission and a short scene (3. 5) to reorient the audience to the Gloucester story makes for difficulties for the audience and the actors. The audience finds it hard to reenter the fantastic world of Lear's mind, and the actors struggle to return to the mental and emotional pitch of intensity of the scene. It seems to be an interpolation of a fragment broken off from another element. The scene loses some of its effectiveness because it is a

---

[32] P. 40.

[33] P. 42.

[34] Granville-Barker, *1,* 271.

part of the extended climactic plateau of the play.

Finding places for intermissions in Shakespeare is troublesome for the director of any one of the plays. The problem arises, of course, out of the modern audience's conditioning to the realistic theatre, which allows two intermissions. Intermissions are expected, and audiences are usually irritated if they don't get them. It has been argued that audiences will sit continuously for three hours at motion pictures without irritation and therefore should be willing and able to remain in their seats for Shakespeare in the theatre. It is easier for audiences to sit a long time watching a film because it is not as demanding as a Shakespearean production on a stage. Listening continuously for nearly two hours to *Lear* is a tiring experience even for the most knowledgeable and responsive members of the audience. What is the director to do about *Lear?* The director of the 1964 Shakespeare Festival at Stratford, Ontario, found an effective solution by giving the audience two intermissions. One was at the end of the first act, which ran about fifty minutes and constituted a curve which was the basis for the arch of extended emotional intensity formed in the third act. The second intermission came at the end of Act 3. This plan of sequencing the scenes and intermissions helped to make the "trial" scene more effective in Canada than in Connecticut even though Morris Carnovsky, the American actor, was, in my opinion, a more moving and impressive Lear than John Colicos, the Canadian one.

The Shakespearean climactic plateau, unlike the tight climax of the realistic play, is a natural result of general rather than specific or detailed motivation and scene intensification and independence. The extended climax leads gradually to an unraveling of all of the play's dramatic knots in what Beckerman calls the "finale" or Shakespearean denouement. It is the completion of the narrative line, which holds as much interest for the modern audience as for the Elizabethan one. The finales, which are a sort of "public" resolution, trial, or discovery, possess these characteristics:

1. a means for bringing about justice or of winning love [and usually consisting of the] discovery of the identity of disguised persons, trial, execution, repentance, single combat, suicide;
2. a judge-figure who pronounces judgment . . .

3. a ranking figure who reasserts order [and who usually speaks the last lines of the play unless they are] epilogues and songs . . .[35]

The Duke in the long finale of *Measure for Measure* is the judge-figure who brings about justice and offers marriage to Isabella. In a shorter finale, Fortinbras brings *Hamlet* to a close. Malcolm presides over the finale of *Macbeth,* and Lodovico performs a similar function in *Othello.* In some plays the judge-figure is represented by more than one character. In the finale of *The Merry Wives of Windsor,* justice and love triumph, with Page, Mrs. Page, and Ford making the pronouncements. Ford has the last lines. The lords assume the function of the judge-figure in *Coriolanus.*

The resolution of *King Lear,* let it be noted, is presented in illustrative action which is suspenseful in an overtly dramatic sense. *Hamlet, Macbeth,* and *Othello* demonstrate similar characteristics in their last scenes. In some of the plays the conclusion is almost entirely narrational and is without very much action. This is more likely in the comedies, light or dark, than in the serious plays. *Measure for Measure,* for example, is a play with an ending primarily expository. It is a set piece as arbitrary in a realistic sense as the resolution of a medieval morality play or a detective story.

Shakespeare's treatment of the conclusion of his plays is so consistent that it amounts to a convention and, as such, is difficult for many members of today's audiences. This is particularly true when the finale is extended and complicated in its unveiling of the narrational details leading to the judgment. The last scene of *Measure for Measure* can be especially trying for the audience—and the director. This convention, like the others discussed, is best understood and used in production for its nonillusionistic characteristics. The director can emphasize the ceremonial pageantry of the finale when all characters gather for the occasion—and a theatrical occasion it must be. Processions, banners, music, ritual, and protocol lend the color and elevation that the occasion demands. The resultant theatricality can so appeal to the imagination and emotions that audiences willingly relinquish thoughts of reality for poetic license.

---

[35] Beckerman, p. 36.

When we come to the end of a Shakespearean play do we sense not only a completion but also a unity? Is there a satisfying totality about it? At first thought Shakespeare's meandering main plot line, interrupted by or paralleled by one or more subplots, the multiplicity of characters, their arbitrary behavior, the mixtures of humor and seriousness, and the continuous shift in time and place seem to create amorphousness. Yet there is a unity in disparity and oppositeness.

Unity is achieved, as we have already seen, in a perceptive general structural pattern in which the order and arrangement of scenes obey some central referent. This is particularly apparent in the mirroring of contrasting situations to communicate a significant similarity: Hamlet's indecisiveness about avenging his father contrasted with Laertes, actively trying to avenge his father[36]; Lear's spiritual blindness contrasted with Gloucester's actual blindness; Prince Hal's roistering compared with Hotspur's triumph in battle; Falstaff's foolish courting of Mistress Ford and Mistress Page opposed to Fenton's youthful, romantic wooing of Anne. Audience perception of the continuous turning of the mirror to reflect now this side and then that results in a coherence of feeling and thought. Even when the audience responds in terms of causation the resolution and conclusion seemingly spring from a premise, even though thorny and sometimes incomprehensible complications arise in the process.

Out of the welter of a full stage of characters a single character may emerge to bring order and tie together the disparate parts of a play. Such a character not only has the largest share of the speeches to say and participates in the greatest number of scenes but he sets the tone of the play and influences the thoughts and actions of the other characters. In fact, the scenes involving other characters are merely dramatic ramifications of his career.[37] This central character gives focus to a play. This is obviously true of Lear, Hamlet, Othello, and Macbeth.

The poetic diction of a play individualizes and integrates it. First of all, this element is responsible for the origin and establishment of all the other elements: character, plot, and theme. It also circumscribes the play as a unifying envelope enclosing an audience and projects meaning more often felt than articulately perceived. Word imagery emphasized through placement and repetition achieves coherence and meaningfulness. Effusiveness and language color affect the dramatic form in its degree of tightness and compactness. The arialike flight of the soliloquy or even such stylistic characteristics as alliteration and double meaning indicate a freedom of poetic expression and are plastic. The form achieves totality and unity through metaphor suggested by the poetry.

Although the plot and characters may overtly express the theme in some of the plays, Shakespeare characteristically relies upon implication. The theme informs each aspect of a play but its presentation is oblique. Perhaps it can most easily be apprehended if the play is seen "as an expanded metaphor."[38] A play is a harmonious poetic vision to be beheld on a level of illusion above that of actuality. The theme usually cannot be reduced to a concise statement because of its subtextual expression, its magnitude, and its universality. So much is suggested without limitation. Shakespeare's habit of mirroring the different aspects of his subject permits us to see it in parallels and contrasts. ". . . the Shakespearean play [is] a manifold reflection of a theme irreducible and unseen. Yet every element in a great Shakespeare play—character, structure, speech—individually and collectively, is brought into an artistic unity through a structural and poetic expression of an unseen referent at its centre."[39]

A sense of the unity of the play comes to the director when he feels the totality of the play. This may be instilled in the mind by analyzing the play for what may be called the curve of intensity of the play. It results from the emotional and mental graph of the play's ebb and flow, which compels audience attention, interest, and involvement from the beginning of the play to the end.

The initial scene of *King Lear,* which is between Gloucester and Kent, with Edmund a peripheral figure, is quietly jocular as Shakespeare introduces these three characters. Their conversation is interrupted by the baleful sound of a horn announcing the arrival of

---

[36] Beckerman, pp. 58–9.

[37] Cleanth Brooks and Robert B. Heilman, *Understanding Drama* (New York, Henry Holt, 1948), pp. 180–1.

[38] G. Wilson Knight, *The Wheel of Fire* (London, Methuen, 1949), p. 15.

[39] Beckerman, p. 62.

Lear and the rest of his court. The sound and majestic arrival change the emotional climate and create a certain amount of apprehension. However, the scene maintains an emotional level or balance, though precarious, until Cordelia opposes Lear. The status quo is upset and the emotional pressures begin to register and the curve of intensity begins its ascent. As scene follows scene, the red line of emotion ascends and declines as temperature is registered on a thermometer. The curve of intensity of a play, however, may be described more accurately as a graph of peaks and valleys, with the high points becoming higher and the valleys becoming progressively less pronounced. That is, the general rising surge of emotional pressure is reflected in both peaks and valleys: The level of the valleys rises with the level of the peaks. In performances the curve of intensity is a chart of tempo and beat —a rhythmic graph. The falling action, it must be noted, does not descend to a level below the bottom of the first valley of the curve of intensity. The descending line on the emotional graph is approximately one third as long as the ascending one. The director must keep a picture of this curve of intensity in his mind as he directs each scene of the play and relates its comparative intensity to the overall emotional line. He consciously paces the performance, accelerating, decelerating, intensifying, and relaxing the various elements constituting a rhythmic pattern.

The rhythmic pattern of a play is based not only on the curve of intensity but also on the internal and external structure of the play. Externally, it is expressed by plot, which is the result of progression, causal or episodic. Let us look at some of the plot characteristics of *King Lear.*

"*King Lear,*" says Granville-Barker, "alone among the great tragedies, adds to its plot a subplot fully developed." [40] Bradley points out that the "chief value" of the double action "is not merely dramatic. It lies in the fact—in Shakespeare without a parallel—that the subplot simply repeats the theme of the main story." [41] These two actions create what Beckerman calls the "mirror pattern," the individual scenes polarizing around a single unifying subject.

The premise of *King Lear* is established by

the first two scenes of the play and forms "a sort of double dramatic prologue . . ." [42] The premise of a Shakespearean play, also called the Induction or preamble by critics, is often a basic improbability, in a realistic sense, upon which the entire structure of the play is built. It demands faith on the part of the audience. Often this faith is part of the heritage of the audience. Henri Fluchère notes the flouting of credibility in the preamble to *Lear.* An aged king who decides to rid himself of the burden of power calls before him his three daughters and divides his kingdom in proportion to their filial love. This Fluchère calls "a first absurdity: has so grave a political decision ever been taken so frivolously, has a father ever subjected his daughters to such a ridiculous test?" He further asks how "an old man could have remained all his life ignorant of the qualities and feelings of his daughters, brought up by him and designated his heiresses? How can Lear be so deceived by the obvious deceit of Goneril and Regan and fail to understand the reliance of Cordelia in expressing her true love for him? What is the psychological explanation for his blindness? The ease with which Edmund dupes Edgar is indeed comic. The play is throughout full of commonsense improbabilities." [43] Yet Fluchère believes Coleridge is right in his comment: "Improbable as the conduct of Lear is, in the first scene, yet it was an old story, rooted in the popular faith—a thing taken for granted already, and consequently without any of the *effects* of improbability." [44] The Elizabethans, it seems, did not hold the law of causality in great respect as we moderns of the realistic era do. Yet modern audiences have been seen to accept the absurdities and improbabilities of Shakespeare because of his appeal to their imaginations and the tacit understanding that they are not witnessing life but are participating in the theatrical event. They, no less than the Elizabethans, accept the plays on the faith of the genius of Shakespeare who transmutes life into art.

It will be noted that Lear, Cordelia, and Edmund are the catalytic agents who upset the equilibrium and instigate the actions resulting in imbalance. Shakespeare's technique in the use of such agents is similar to that of modern playwrights. Granville-Barker, commenting

---

[40] Granville-Barker, *1,* 270.
[41] A. C. Bradley, *Shakespearean Tragedy* (London, Macmillan, 1926), p. 262.

[42] Granville-Barker, *1,* 270.
[43] Henri Fluchère, *Shakespeare and the Elizabethans* (New York, Hill & Wang, 1956), pp. 109–10.
[44] Fluchère, p. 117.

upon the first scene, says, "Its improbabilities are neither here nor there. A dramatist may postulate any situation he has the means to interpret, if he will abide by the logic of it after." [45] Later in his book he elaborates that "We must not . . . appraise either his [Gloucester's] simplicity or Edgar's . . . with detachment—for by that light, no human being it would seem, between infancy and dotage, could be so gullible. Shakespeare asks us to allow him the fact of deception, even as we have allowed him Lear's partition of the kingdom. It is his starting point, the dramatist's let's pretend, which is as essential to the beginning of a play as a 'let it be granted' to a proposition of Euclid." [46] Russell Fraser echoes this view, when speaking of the symbolic rather than the realistic concept of Cordelia's role and character, in saying that "The first principle of good dramatic manners is to concede to the dramatist his given, so long as he is able to exploit it." [47] In my view, though, the willingness of audiences to accept an improbable premise of a play does not depend entirely upon the wish to "let's pretend" or upon "good dramatic manners" but also upon the provocative ingredients of the premise, which seduce and persuade by their very appeal to the imagination, presaging the fun and emotional and intellectual possibilities of the dramatic game to be played.

The double action of *Lear* intertwines from the beginning of the play by virtue of Gloucester's relationship to his king and becomes a single action controlled by an integrating theme when Gloucester in 3. 3 decides that his "old master must be relieved." Edmund, Cornwall, Goneril, Regan, and Albany become increasingly tied to the main action in their dealings with Gloucester, in their relationship to Lear, and in their own relationships as they bind together and are split apart in the aftermath of events culminating from their actions. The turning point of the play is in 3. 4, when Lear says his great "Poor naked wretches" speech. This is "The supreme moment for Lear himself, the turning point, therefore, of the play's main theme . . ." [48] (Granville-Barker explains that the turning point for Gloucester is his decision to "incline to the King" in the

previous scene. It does not make the dramatic impression that Lear's does, occurring in just a short scene transitional to the main action, but it seems to give Gloucester's character a new and definite direction and parallels Lear's spiritual progression.) As has been pointed out, *King Lear* has a long plateau of climactic intensity. There is no one moment which can be said to be the highest emotional peak marking the final and irreversible confrontation of the opposing forces. Conventionally, in realistic drama, the faltering action of a play begins after the climax. And plotwise—with Lear and Gloucester as the centers—*King Lear's* action turns downward, but, as Fraser has asserted, "the declining action, which is the dogging of the hero to death, is complemented by a rising action which is the hero's regeneration . . . As the one wanes to nothing, the other, which lives within it, emerges . . . The play fools us. Its primary story is not the descent of the King into Hell, but the ascent of the King as he climbs the Mountain of Purgatory and is fulfilled. . . . The rising and falling curves, the hero tasting his folly, the hero triumphing over it, intersect in the center of the play, in the fourth scene of Act III." [49] Actually, Fraser is making a distinction between the outer action of plot and the inner action of character and thematic development. The emotional tensions of the two simply differ; one is not necessarily better than the other. Yet the perceptive director should be aware of these two kinds of action.

The fourth and fifth acts of *King Lear* constitute an extended denouement that comes to a head with the last scene. The doomsday character of the scene, pointed by Kent's "Is this the promised end?" Edgar's "image of that horror?" and Albany's "Fall and cease" (i.e., let Heaven fall and all things end) in 5. 3, cannot but be noticed. This typical Shakespearean finale begins with the entrance of Albany with Goneril, Regan, and their soldiers. Albany is the "ranking figure" of justice before whom Edmund is arrested "on capital treason" and challenged to combat with a champion who will prove his villainy; Regan and Goneril declare their love for Edmund and exit to die, one by poisoning and the other by her own hand; Edgar appears, fights Edmund to the death, tells of his disguise as Tom o'Bedlam and his saving of his father from

[45] Vol. 1, 271–2.
[46] Vol. 1, 313.
[47] Introduction to *The Tragedy of King Lear* (New York and Toronto, The New American Library, 1963), pp. xxx–xxxi.
[48] Granville-Barker, *1*, 274.

[49] Fraser, p. xxii.

despair, and at the last reveals himself and tells (5. 3) of their "pilgrimage" before Gloucester's "flawed heart . . . Burst smilingly"; and then Lear enters with the dead Cordelia and dies. Then Albany resigns his "absolute power" to Kent and Edgar to rule in the realm "and the gored state sustain," but Kent rejects the offer in order to make a last journey to join his master, and Edgar, in the last speech of the play, takes up the royal reins to obey "The weight of this sad time" and to

> Speak what we feel, not what we ought to say.
> The oldest hath borne most: we that are young
> Shall never see so much, nor live so long.

The internal structure of the play supports and is contained by the external plot structure. It consists of the recurring correspondences, contrasts, and linkages of incident, image, character, and theme. The immediately apparent correspondence of the Lear and Gloucester plots has already been pointed out as basic to the play: Both fathers banish a child; both place their faith in illusion and duplicity; both are blind and fail to separate truth from falsehood; and both travel a purgatorial journey of suffering. The action of the play shuttles back and forth to carry forward both stories. The locales shift from Lear's palace to Gloucester's castle, to Goneril's, to Gloucester's, to the heath, to the environs of Gloucester's castle, to Gloucester's castle, to the countryside, and finally to a wasteland. The action moves from indoors to outdoors, symbolizing a movement from the appearance of civilization to the naked realities of primitive nature, from order to chaos. Environment thus seems to complement the mental and spiritual progression of Lear and Gloucester and to chart the fortunes of the other characters. From 4. 3 to the end of the play the action takes place outdoors near Dover, the rough and open boundary land between England and France which drops off from the cruel, rocky cliffs to the abyss below. This is the Golgotha of all who participate in this journey to Calvary.

The play also sets forth a series of character compositions which constitute a dramatic mural, telling a story of character relationships which allegorize a picture of humanity. Each composition is a panel in the mural. The first panel contains all of the figures. The following panels show various groupings of selected figures extrapolated from the total group. Shakespeare, the master painter, depicts fragments of the group in succeeding panels until he reaches the last, which brings together the whole group again. By dramatic color, line, and form he focuses our attention on the principal characters in the foreground while forcing the minor characters into the background. His mastery of perspective illuminates the narrative, character, and thematic progression and development.

The period of free imagery makes the director aware of many thematic threads. The "trial" image is evoked repeatedly throughout the play. And, in fact, it can serve as an overall dominating image for *King Lear*. The father-child relationship is paralleled and contrasted to demonstrate the generation gap and in various ways comment on the narration. Good and evil are set in opposition by character and action. Madness and reason are counterpoised. Blindness and sight are juxtaposed in character and event to reveal illusion and reality; darkness and light are extensions of the theme. Appearance and truth run in ironic parallel under the surface of words and deeds. Clothes and nakedness evoke recurring images to illuminate meaning. Order and disorder serve a similar function. Acts of violence forge a continuous chain which binds the world of Lear to the twentieth century. Irony of events mirrors the absurdity of life. The stage becomes a metaphor for the world.

This objective study of this aspect of the structure of the play will help the director to fix its totality in his mind and will furnish some guidelines for both his interpretive and productional visions. As he works with the actors on characterization moment by moment he will be able to relate character, event, language—everything—to the foundation and the building of the play into a coherent dramatic design. He will be aware of the importance and relationship of the pieces to one another and to the whole. He will recognize and underscore exposition, character revelations and developments, conflicts, crises, climax, and even be alert to parallel opposites. These aspects of the order and plan of the play constitute the director's reference points, which have a degree of tangibility and permanence. They give him perspective.

MODE

T. S. Eliot, in describing the qualifications of the ideal Shakespearean critic, might well have been referring in many respects to the Shakespearean director, who, among the many things he is, is also a critic. As a critic whose main function is interpretation, he must orient himself to the social, political, economic, religious, and theatrical conditions of the Elizabethan world in which Shakespeare wrote while remaining aware of the modern world. "To understand Shakespeare he [the critic] must understand the theatre of his own time— but also the differences between the theatre of his own time and that of Shakespeare's time . . . he needs also to understand the special conditions of the stage, the peculiar kind of reality manifested by those personages of the stage who strike us as most 'real', if he is to avoid the error of analysing dramatic characters as if they were living men and women, or figures from the historical past." [50] Understanding Shakespeare's peculiar kind of reality is the crux of the problem for the director.

He is conditioned in thinking and in practice by modern realism, not by Shakespeare's. "The so-called drama of 'Realism' which flourished at the end of the nineteenth century and the beginning of the twentieth [and continues to be the prevailing mode today in spite of attempts to break away from it] . . . wanted the spectator to forget, on entering the theatre, that he was going to see a play *acted*. Everything contributed to take away dramatic illusion or, it might be said, everything contributed to strengthen it. A 'slice of life in the raw' was offered in its most objective details; the characters were 'real', the story was 'true', the incidents 'authentic', the language appropriate in the mouths of the characters." [51] The director is naturally oriented toward this kind of realism. Most of the plays he directs are written in this mode. He is familiar with its structure. He is also familiar with the physical theatre for which realistic drama is composed. The drama of the past and the stage for which it was written are usually known to the director only in theory, and he has limited practical experience with them.

Shakespeare's dramatic mode must be understood if he is to be interpreted with some degree of fidelity to his intentions. How can the director orient himself toward this mode as well as the conditions of production? First of all, by the recognition of the main differences between the present-day realism of the theatre and the dramatic conventions of Shakespeare's

theatre. This is important for the director because these differences influence audience response and create distinct theatrical experiences. And the director is, above all, concerned with how the play and its production move the emotions and thoughts of the audience. The nature of their response results in a specific degree of interest, belief, and imaginative participation in a production.

Depending on the individual concerned, such participation will vary in proportion to the power of the emotional and intellectual appeal. An illusion of actuality created by a performance tends to affect one because of the factors of recognition and identification with characters, events, and thought. A performance removed to some extent from verisimilitude tends to lessen subjectivity and increase objectivity. One's theatrical experience is thereby affected. The naturalism of Chekhov or Williams can be deeply moving and thought provoking but no more so than the poetic theatricality of Shakespeare. Whether Shakespeare *is* deeply moving and thought provoking depends upon audiences' knowledge of the dramatic conventions of the Elizabethan theatre.

Audiences know that theatre is an art and not life. Only the most ignorant or childlike will mistake the make-believe of a stage performance for actuality. Yet the different genres and modes of drama present pictures of life in varying degrees of resemblance to life. Shakespearean drama is in mode or style altered somewhat but similar to that of the medieval miracle, morality, and interlude. It is narrative and pageantlike and depends predominantly upon the tradition and conventions of that drama. Elizabethan and Shakespearean drama is influenced by the conventional structure, depiction of character and events, and multiplace nature of the medieval drama. The Elizabethans often continued the tradition of storytelling in allegory and symbolism. The characters are essentially personalizations of abstractions rather than psychological. Many modern critics and scholars, in contrast to the psychologically minded of the nineteenth century, interpret the plays in light of this. G. Wilson Knight, in following one of his principles of Shakespearean interpretation, analyzes the plays in terms of "the use and meaning of direct poetic symbolism—that is, events whose significance can hardly be related to the normal process of actual life . . ." [52] In his essay

---

[50] T. S. Eliot, Foreword to Henri Fluchère, *Shakespeare and the Elizabethans* (New York, Hill & Wang, 1956), p. 6.
[51] Fluchère, p. 108.
[52] Knight, *The Wheel of Fire*, p. 15.

on *Measure for Measure* he explains the play in terms of allegory or symbolism. "The persons of the play tend to illustrate certain human qualities chosen with careful reference to the main theme. Thus Isabella stands for sainted purity, Angelo for Pharisaical righteousness, the Duke for a psychologically sound and enlightened ethic. Lucio represents indecent wit, Pompey and Mistress Overdone professional immorality. Barnardine is hardheaded, criminal, insensitiveness. Each person illumines some facet of the central theme: man's moral nature." [53] In his view the play is a morality play with obvious relation to the Gospels. *The Tempest* and other plays can be seen in a similar symbolic and allegoric light.

But as Henri Fluchère reminds us, "It would be absurd to maintain that the personages of the Elizabethan Drama resembled the Morality figures, feature by feature." Though playwrights borrowed the mold of the morality they "filled it with flesh and blood." And "within his own category each character, according to the talent or genius of each dramatist, according to his environment and to the adventures on which he embarks is particularized more or less clearly, picturesquely, profoundly, while each preserves his own idiom and function." [54] Note the individualizing traits of the Machiavellian villains Edmund, Don John, and Richard; yet they can be seen as representations of Vice. Shakespeare sees to it that the audience is not deceived by the details of character. They are villains in a play and often tell the audience so in asides and soliloquies. The level of dramatic illusion is that of the morality plays. Shakespeare makes no effort to establish or sustain an illusion of actuality. The level of illusion of Shakespeare's conventional drama is established and maintained by playwriting techniques which distance the audience and objectify their reactions. The audience for Shakespeare's plays is not asked to suspend disbelief to delude itself that the theatrical performance is life rather than fiction. In the realistic theatre the audience tends to forget it is in the theatre and is caught up in the illusion of life.

The theatre of Shakespeare continually reminds the audience that it is in the theatre and is observing a suggestion or reflection of life or a comment on it. It, unlike realism, does not represent life but presents it. These two kinds of theatre are, in general, at opposite poles on an imagined scale of drama. Yet neither is completely realistic or theatrical. And each possesses qualities typical of the other: The realistic is often theatrical and the theatrical lifelike. Lapses into naturalism are especially frequent in Shakespeare: "they are probably a major cause of his continuous popularity on the stage, and provide color for a psychological approach . . . " [55] Desdemona, as Bethel points out, breaks the conventional framework of Elizabethan poetic drama with her naturalistic reply to Emilia's "How do you, madam? how do you, my good lady?" by saying, "Faith, half asleep" (*Othello,* 4. 2). This sort of transition into naturalism is frequently made by Shakespeare, who like his contemporaries wrote to conform to no rigidly thought-out system. They oscillate between conventionalism and naturalism even in an individual play. This is characteristic of Elizabethan playwriting, which, in the hands of Shakespeare especially, continued what Bethel calls the "popular dramatic tradition." In addition to Shakespeare's revelation of his intuitive understanding of human nature in flashes of natural dialogue, he allows characters to reveal their human psychology by what they say about themselves or by what others say. Their words even in verse are revelatory. This is surely true even for a play as symbolical as *Measure for Measure.* All the characters in it possess clearly recognizable psychological traits which make them interesting human beings as well as symbolical representations. The humanity of Angelo is readily perceived. Isabella in love with purity is as understandable and as irritating as any adolescent going through a period of fanaticism. The Duke has often been called a lifeless character, in fact "a tall dark dummy," [56] more fantastical than human. Yet, when explaining to Angelo (1. 1) why he is going away secretly, he shows a shyness and a modesty becoming a sincere man:

> I love the people,
> But do not like to stage me to their eyes:
> Though it do well, I do not relish well
> Their loud applause and 'aves' vehement:
> Nor do I think the man of safe discretion
> That does affect it.

---

[53] Pp. 73–4.
[54] Fluchère, pp. 136–7.

[55] S. L. Bethel, *Shakespeare and the Popular Tradition* (Westminster, P. S. King and Staples, 1944), p. 17.
[56] Mark Van Doren, *Shakespeare* (New York, Doubleday, 1953), p. 187.

The realistic drama is not always true to its mode either. The conversational prose of Chekhov or Tennessee Williams is charged with poetically theatrical imagery and symbolism. Their plays possess moments of heightened reality which are characteristic of the conventional drama. The dissimilarity of the two modes is demonstrated, however, in their different ways of creating theatrical experiences.

The realistic theatre's demand that audiences yield themselves completely to the dramatic illusion of actuality results in their awareness of a single plane of existence: the reality of what they see and hear on the stage.

The conventional theatre of Shakespeare, on the other hand, constantly urges upon audiences the necessity of dual awareness of the play world and the actual world. In performance this duality is apparent the moment actors come onstage in their costumes, whether Elizabethan or of some other period. Costumes, unlike everyday dress, immediately call attention to their theatricality and distance the audience. (Of course, modern playwrights writing plays which take place in the past overcome the distancing effect of historical characters and events by attention to historical accuracy and detail in order to make their plays seem completely realistic. They wish to make the audience believe completely in the actuality of the performance. They attempt to hold the audience on one plane of reality by avoiding any devices which would cause awareness of any other.) The names of the characters, whether unknown, strange and antique, or known as historical or theatrical (Hamlet, Macbeth, Lear), are distancing.

If members of the audience are acquainted with the plays as dramatic literature they are conscious of the convention of theatre. In this case the plays, like the stories and characters of a Greek play, have become legendary and mythical to audiences. These factors are the result of time and theatrical vintage and must be considered in connection with all drama of the past. The Elizabethan drama in continuing the tradition of the medieval may be distinguished from the Restoration drama, for example, by its technical and structural characteristics utilized to affect audience multi-consciousness. These two periods of conventional drama are similar in the use of symbolical characters—the Elizabethan, allegorical and abstractions of the universal in mankind; the Restoration, abstractions of period "humors" prevalent in the upper stratum of society. They are similar, too, in their relative independence of causality of plot development and in their tendency to employ complexities of plot and subplot. Thus artificial, epigrammatic language of the Restoration alerted the audience to the theatricality of what was onstage. The audience knew that the characters were speaking with the wit and sophistication manufactured by the playwright. There was no effort on the part of playwrights to pretend that here was anything but a heightened if not distorted view of society or the legendary past. Elizabethan dramatists used blank verse, which represented for every member of the audience idealized speech which no one spoke in everyday conversation. The language characteristic of both the Restoration and the Elizabethan drama created a recognized and accepted convention. Both the aside and the soliloquy served to amuse an audience's double consciousness. Shakespeare, however, deliberately broke any possible realistic illusion by calling attention to the stage as such. The prologue in *Henry V* is well known. And Jaques' famous "All the world's a stage" speech in *As You Like It* broadens the image and its implications. The technique of employing a character to comment on the similarity of action to something the audience might see on a stage is illustrated by Fabian's observation when Malvolio appears to Olivia and her household in crossgartered stockings:

> If this were played upon a stage now, I could condemn it as an improbable fiction.
>
> *(Twelfth Night, 3. 4)*

Edmund in *King Lear* arouses the audience to laughter and reminds them of the conventionalism of the theatre when he says of Edgar (1. 2):

> Pat! he comes, like the catastrophe of the old comedy.
> My cue is villainous melancholy, with a sigh like Tom
> o'Bedlam.—

(It is interesting to note that this device is used today even in realistic drama.) One of Shakespeare's favored devices for reminding the audience of the coexistence of the play world and the real is his use of the play-within-the-play as exemplified in *The Taming of the Shrew, Hamlet, The Tempest, Henry IV, Part I, A Midsummer Night's Dream,* and *Love's*

Labour's Lost. Music is often used to mark the transition to and establishment of another world within the overall world of the play. Whether the change is to the make-believe of a play or masque or a different atmosphere, it is usually to a world of fantasy or the supernatural. Song in the plays, like song in the modern musical, changes the level of illusion and requires audience awareness of duality. The use of the chorus, a vestigial device from the morality plays, plainly told Shakespeare's audience they were in a theatre and must use their imaginations to believe in his fictional world.

Disguises in Shakespeare are purely conventional. The Duke in the habit of a friar moves through *Measure for Measure* without being recognized until he raises his cowl at the end of the play. Even those who know him intimately in everyday life fail to recognize him until the play demands it. Rosalind, like many other women characters, dresses as a boy and neither her female anatomy nor her voice betrays her in *As You Like It*. She reveals herself only at the proper dramatic moment. All these devices are employed to give the audience superior knowledge over the characters of the play and add a level of reality. Bethel points out these various conventional techniques. He goes on to argue convincingly that Shakespeare's anachronisms may indicate his ignorance of certain historical details of dress, furnishings, and habits but "he must have been aware of dealing, in the historical plays, with two ages, his own and some other." [57] The porter's reference to Jesuit equivocators in *Macbeth* was not accidental but to make the audience laugh by referring to an event of common knowledge. (It was not as frequently thought of by scholars as a "contemporary reference," Bethel notes, but "an ignorant anti-dating of St. Ignatius Loyola." [58]) This kind of breaking of illusion evidently was not considered jarringly incongruous but was accepted as part of the theatre convention of the time. In this case the reference had a double dramatic value: The equivocators had conspired to kill the king and as a serious subject treated lightly it was intended to amuse; the contemporary event paralleled Macbeth's own conspiracy to kill the king and thus tinged the moment with irony and a flood of excitingly dramatic connotations. "The co-

presence of such contrasting elements renders doubly impossible any mere illusion of actuality: once again, the audience must necessarily remain critically alert, whilst at the same time the historical element distances and objectifies what is contemporary, and the contemporary element gains current significance to an historical situation." [59]

In both parts of *Henry IV* Shakespeare treats the political events with some degree of historical accuracy and then, parallel with the historical, he presents Falstaff, Bardolph, Pistol, Nym, and Mistress Quickly right out of the contemporary life of London and the countryside. The scenes involving these characters cover a wide range of Elizabethan subjects, including the theatre, army recruiting, the dangers of travel, the kingship, and the practical view of honor versus the romantic. This contrast of history with current life served to illuminate by perspective and objectivity.

Shakespeare's treatment of characters, more than any other technique perhaps, interests the director because of the primacy of characters to modern audiences and actors. Yet his first consideration must, of course, be the poetic language which interposes itself between the audience and the play. It is a distancing element until the audience understands it, consciously or unconsciously, and is able to become caught up in it. Experience in seeing Shakespeare performed on the stage, without formal knowledge of the technical elements of poetry, will usually result in a natural audience accommodation. The audience must, however, be willing to give it the kind of thoughtful attention required by poetry. ". . . in poetic drama, verse form constitutes a convention of fundamental importance, demanding a mode of attention quite different from that appropriate to naturalistic drama. Whereas [it] requires the same sort of attention as is given to happenings in ordinary life, poetic drama requires the same sort of attention as is necessary in reading lyric poetry." [60]

The major part of the audience's attention should be given to the purely auditory and less to character. This, no doubt, was understood by the Elizabethan audience. The modern audience, conditioned by the realistic theatre techniques, is occupied unconsciously with thoughts about psychological motivation for character remarks and actions. And, un-

---

[57] Bethel, p. 45.
[58] P. 43.

[59] P. 46.
[60] P. 64.

less the poetic world of the play has seduced it to accept the proper level of illusion, disbelief and rejection will appear in laughter when laughter is not intended by Shakespeare.

The director, at least, must understand that motive and psychology are submerged in favor of the total theatrical effect. Viola in *Twelfth Night* does not tell Orsino or Olivia that she is a girl until the denouement demands it. She allows herself and others to become involved in a series of predicaments which, from a life-like point of view, hardly justify her delay. The same is true of Rosalind in *As You Like It*. In part, her motive in remaining disguised is less justifiable on a realistic basis than is Viola's. When she sees her father why doesn't she tell him who she is? Edgar in *King Lear* is forced, against nature, to endure the painful encounters with his father without revealing himself. The Duke in *Measure for Measure* allows Isabella to think that her brother Claudio has received the death penalty and forces her to wait until the grand finale of the play before he discloses his true identity. Surely these instances cannot be accepted by the audience as plausible except in terms of the imagination and on the heightened level of illusion demanded by the playwright.

Othello's trust in Iago, in spite of the obviousness to the audience of his villainy, is another problem in plausibility for the realistically minded. Othello's ignorance of civil life on a purely social or personal level is often advanced as explanation for his apparent gullibility. The modern actor who plays Iago usually tries to solve the problem by presenting him as "honest" Iago who, in only absolutely necessary instances, is the villain Iago.

A classic example of a character problem is the one faced by the actor who plays Prince Hal in *Henry IV, Part I*, 1. 2. Here he must appear hypocritical and scheming when he addresses the audience directly to tell them that he will play along awhile with Falstaff, Peto, and Poins in their wild escapades but he will throw them off in order that such an action will show even more highly in his favor than if he never appeared to need reforming. But Bethel argues that an Elizabethan audience would understand that Hal is merely foretelling what will happen and not to worry, that a prince who will become king is allowing himself to be besmirched by evil companions, and "that all will work out in accordance with the highest moral precepts." [61] Obviously this ex-

planation will not serve to allay the suspicion of most members of an audience today. Yet Bethel is right in using this to illustrate another example of technique common to the Shakespearean conventionalism. The author's purposes and design are obviously more important than the realistic psychology of character. The telling of a story in the narrative method also keeps the emphasis on the words in verse form and maintains the author's dominance over character.

Shakespeare thus seems primarily interested in holding up his characters as recognizable, traditional stage types. His "concern is mainly with the stage types held as common property among Elizabethan writers: Jaques, the melancholy man; Sir Andrew, the 'natural'; Parolles, the cowardly braggart. The only psychology conceivably applied in Shakespeare is that advocated by Ben Jonson, which differentiates human types according to their 'humours' (passions or, perhaps, attitudes) . . ." [62]

If the characters are recognized as stage types they should not be expected to reveal the minutiae of detailed realistic character or to show much development. The characters in the great tragedies do change, but this is not typical. Lear, Macbeth, Antony, Cleopatra, and even Angelo in a purely symbolical play show changes and yet they can be understood as stage types in a large sense because they represent man in relation to the universe and God. Theirs is a metaphysical world. Typically, characters do not often show calculated direct influence upon one another. Exceptions are Iago in his influence on Othello, Cassius on Brutus, and Lady Macbeth on Macbeth.

The soliloquies and asides are prominent conventionalizing techniques which alert the "multiconsciousness" of the audience. Prince Hal's "I know you all" speech in *Henry IV, Part I* illustrates what Bethel calls "direct address," which is one kind of soliloquy. (He uses Iago's speech in *Othello*, 1. 3, as an example.) His "thinking-aloud" soliloquy is exemplified clearly by Hamlet's "To be or not to be" speech. Asides are of two kinds. One is instanced by Bethel, who uses the box-tree scene in *Twelfth Night*, 2. 5, in which Sir Toby, Sir Andrew, and Fabian speak to one another unheard by Malvolio. Another by Hamlet's "A little more than kin, and less than kind." This is an aside for the audience only. [63]

---

[61] P. 69.

[62] P. 78.

[63] P. 88.

"Depersonalization" and the "double nature of characters" are further examples of Shakespeare's nonrealistic conventions. Depersonalization, a term originated by Muriel Bradbrook in her *Themes and Conventions of Elizabethan Tragedy,* consists of a speech which is more narrational than revelatory of character. Gertrude in *Hamlet* is used to describe Ophelia's drowning and actually loses her identity to become Shakespeare's "messenger." The principle of the double nature of characters is demonstrated by showing Claudius, the villain, turning hero when he speaks of the divinity of a king in his speech to Laertes in 4. 4. This nevertheless can, I think, be a psychological reference made by Claudius in order to win over Laertes in a moment of crisis. A more convincing example is Bethel's pointing to the character of Touchstone, who like most court jesters can *act* like a "fool" and *speak* wittily.[64] Again, it might be argued that the capacity for foolish actions and clever speech often resides in one person. Yet Shakespeare's use of such approach to character does become a convention.

Fluchère also discusses character from a point of view of Elizabethan convention. He asserts that "the characters are situated *outside* all realism . . . beyond the psychological determination governed by the chain of normal cause and effect . . . The character generally comes on cast in a simple mould, and we are not allowed to dispute or assess the motives of his behaviour."[65] A character is a "role" stipulated for him by the playwright. He must act and react in accordance with his creator's purposes. "Proteus in *The Two Gentlemen of Verona* abandons Julia for Silvia, betrays his friend and tries to steal his mistress, and then returns to his own first love; and all ends in a general reconciliation which the baseness of his treacherous conduct makes very improbable."[66] It might be agreed that a character in a romantic comedy is not expected to behave consistently like more normal, rational, moral, responsible human beings. In *Romeo and Juliet,* however, Romeo is hopelessly in love with Helena before he meets Juliet. But at first sight of Juliet, he forgets entirely about Helena and has no troubling thoughts about his inconstancy. He is, of course, only obeying his fate as a dramatic hero in an Eliza-

bethan play. The audiences then, like audiences today, were transported to an actual plane of illusion by the power of poetry and imagination. They do not think of motives—the whys and wherefores of behavior. Furthermore, if the characters believe what they are doing, so will the audience.

One of the most difficult scenes in all of Shakespeare to believe is the Lady Anne–Richard scene in *Richard III,* 1. 2. And how can actors justify the behavior of these two characters? How can the audience be made to believe that a noblewoman following her husband's coffin in deep sorrow can yield to the detested and despised Richard who has killed her husband? Fluchère says "it is not the evolution of feeling that attracts the dramatist and gives the scene its exceptional interest, but the ritual verbal fencing . . . the rhetoric of hatred, of invective and cynicism."[67] Sir Laurence Olivier emphasized this verbal fencing in his television and film performances of this play and turned Richard into an amusing, charming Mephistopheles. The audience no less than Lady Anne yields to Richard when he is presented in this way. Laughter at what amounts to a comic sex duel obliterates the audience's possible aversion and objectifies the scene. Amazing character behavior within this framework is theatrically acceptable. "Motives and reason are of merely secondary interest. The exigencies of the conduct of the plot, of the moral purpose, of the poetry, even of the verbal rhetoric are more imperative than those of the characters . . ."[68] Characters play their role. Sudden changes of attitude may upset psychological probability but obey the scheme of the play. Of course the very lack of predictability of character in accordance with a concept of psychological determinism creates surprises within the essence of the theatrical.

The modern director of Shakespeare can be aided by Bethel's categorization and definitions of typification:

[1.] A type presents in abstract certain features common to a class

[2.] a humour is a human being reduced to a dominant principle

[3.] an allegorical figure personalises an abstraction [and signifies the] representation of a virtue or vice or of some other abstraction

[4. a symbolic character] permanently em-

---

[64] Pp. 92–5.
[65] Fluchère, p. 131.
[66] P. 132.

[67] P. 133.
[68] *Ibid.*

bodies some great truth of human experience, or . . . expresses some aspect or aspects of the Deity in His relations with mankind.[69]

In his chapters on character Bethel reiterates that Shakespeare's mode is mixed and is not always one of pure convention. In it can be found many instances of naturalism. He often lapses into colorful and memorable flashes of human psychology. His dramaturgic system is not precise and frozen but is traditional and intuitive, pragmatic, and creative. The director of his plays for modern audiences interprets him most faithfully and illuminatingly when his staging reflects Shakespeare's insight into human nature, though Shakespeare obeys the signposts of conventionalism.

PROBLEMS

His Stage and Ours

1. Assuming that the Elizabethan theatre has a stage which includes a large platform, an inner stage, and an upper stage with one door right and another left of the inner stage (and that the audience sits on three sides of the platform), plot the placement of scenes for *Love's Labour's Lost* or a play of your choice which demands the use of these three acting areas. (Some of Shakespeare's plays do not demand three such areas.)

2. Select a Shakespearean play for production on a proscenium stage and describe or sketch a setting for it which utilizes the acting areas or stages of an Elizabethan theatre.

3. Select a play for presentation in a college dining hall. Work out a floor plan to scale which suggests a thrust stage permitting entrances and exits for rapid flow of action. It is assumed that the audience will sit on three sides of the stage, which may or may not be raised.

4. Devise a floor plan to scale for the production of a play in a room large enough to seat at least one hundred and not more than two hundred members of an audience. Show plan of seating. Keep in mind the need of three stages or acting areas.

5. Select an actual courtyard and plot scene placement for a production of *A Midsummer Night's Dream*. Show the position of shrubbery and other planting on ground plan. Indicate places of entrances and exits. Describe lighting scheme.

---

[69] Bethel, pp. 79, 98.

6. Imagine or select a real formal ballroom with a double stairway leading to a landing which can be used as an upper stage. Place doors for entrances and exits. Draw a ground plan to scale showing stairs and landing, doorways, and inner stage and/or main acting area together with aisles and audience seating arrangement. Indicate position of chandeliers which could be used for lighting the stage.

7. Select a play for an in-the-round production. Explain why you think this play would be effective in this kind of presentation. Draw a floor plan to scale showing the shape of the acting area, places of entrances, positions of furniture properties to use throughout the performance, and the seating arrangement for the audience. Indicate whether the stage is to be elevated.

8. Plot the scene placement of a play on the altar and in the aisles of a church. Explain why this play could be effectively staged in this environment.

Note: In all these problems consider the demands of the scenes in terms of space, spatial relationship as a reflection of the dramatic dynamics, and the establishment and maintenance of continuity of scenes. The use and placement of furniture properties and their removal without interrupting the flow of action must also be considered. Stage directions in the folio and quarto versions of the plays may be useful references.

The Text and the Director's Working Script

1. What are the advantages and disadvantages of dividing the plays into acts and scenes? (Examine the First Folio for act and scene divisions.)

2. Cite ten examples of stage directions implied in the dialogue of a play.

3. Cite ten examples of character behavior or "business" which by their appropriateness and dynamics may aid in dramatizing the text.

4. Compare the 1604 quarto version of *Hamlet* with the First Folio version. Cite main differences.

5. Prepare a working script of *The Taming of the Shrew* based on the directorial concept that Christopher Sly dreams that he is Petruchio and thus participates in the main action of the play. Work out theatrically convincing staging which will show Sly sleepwalking out of his bedroom aloft, becoming Petruchio, and, at the end of the play, returning to his bed as Sly. Cut and change the play as necessary.

6. Select a play for which you have a di-

rectorial concept and cut and change as necessary.

7. Select one of the history plays and cut passages which are unintelligible and/or over-elaborated for a modern audience.

8. Select a comedy and cut lines and situations which you think are unamusing to today's audience.

Form

1. Select plays not cited in this section which will each exemplify a type of structural pattern described by Bernard Beckerman.

2. Is Cymbeline the central character (the most fully developed, the most theatrically important, most active in the plot) in the play of that name? Why is it called *Cymbeline?*

3. Analyze *Cymbeline* from the point of view of its organizing principle. Does a shaping pattern emerge?

4. Where is the climax of *Cymbeline?* What directorial problems does it present?

5. What is the premise of *The Winter's Tale?* Who is the catalytic agent who starts the forward action of the play? Discuss its finale.

6. Does *The Winter's Tale* have both internal and external structure? Does it have unity?

7. Where would you place an intermission in *As You Like It?* Describe its curve of intensity.

8. Select a play and analyze it for its parallels and correspondences in plot and character.

9. As a group, study and discuss the influence and effect of structural elements of *premise, crisis, climax, intermission, finale, unity,* and *curve of intensity* on staging and the director's work with the actor.

10. Agree upon the selection of a particular play, analyze it for structural elements, and discuss possible directorial approaches to each element in this particular play.

11. Select a scene from one of the plays and improvise it in today's language and behavior.

Mode

1. Analyze *Love's Labour's Lost* for its recognizable real and human values in contrast with its implausibilities, dramatic conventions and artificialities, and aesthetically "distancing" values.

2. What dramatic conventions of writing and performance tend to objectify an audience's response to *Much Ado About Nothing?*

3. Select a Shakespearean play with characters without names—who are simply called "Gentleman," "Old Man," "Herald," "Knight," etc.—and discuss such generic characters' effect on audience believability of the play.

4. Find examples of plays within plays not cited in this section. How does such a dramaturgic device affect the level of illusion of such plays?

5. Discuss the psychological nature of the principal characters of *Measure for Measure,* though they can at the same time be viewed as allegorical. (Familiarize yourself with G. Wilson Knight's essay on the play.)

6. Which characters in *Henry IV, Part I* can be viewed as traditional stage types conforming to the theory of humours?

7. Select a play and discuss its elements which demand audience "dual awareness."

8. Cite examples of Shakespeare's combining naturalism with conventionalism.

9. Is there a Shakespearean "mode" for all his plays or does each play have its own particular mode?

10. Discuss the Shakespearean mode in terms of your understanding of "theatricalism." Cite examples of theatricalism in directing, acting, scenery, costumes, lighting, and sound.

Chapter III

SHAKESPEARE'S CHARACTERS AND THE MODERN ACTOR

Having established guidelines to the whole play through a study of its mode, form, free imagery, and the world and focus of the play, the director may then concentrate his attention on Shakespeare's characters. In separating character from the other play elements we must remind ourselves that all elements are interanimating parts of a whole. Yet each element is partially independent. At least, each can be temporarily and arbitrarily separated for study and visualization. The interconnections of the parts must be seen in relationship to the dominating and cohering influences. Because of the overlapping of subject matter there is bound to be some repetition in this discussion, but the very repetition will show more clearly how the various elements are related.

THE LEVEL OF BEING

Character must be studied in relation to its context especially in terms of its level of being. (See section on "Mode.") The interanimating parts of the context show a permeating and integrating quality which indicates this level. *King Lear* is strongly marked, from the beginning, by an aura of unreality and surreality. The action played by Lear in dividing his kingdom and then calling together the court to announce the divisions formally to test the love of his daughters jolts the sensibilities to an awareness of the eccentricity of the action. The unusualness to the point of strangeness automatically raises questions of plausibility. Lear's action, however, appears no more unreal than the protestations of filial love expressed by Goneril and Regan. Their artificiality in language and excessiveness in emotion can only mean pretense. Lear's two daughters seem to be playing roles or hiding behind masks at some charade. Cordelia's asides during her sisters' testimonials alert the audience to the falsity of Lear's actions and theirs. The audience watches with double vi-

sion. Cordelia's refusal to compete with her sisters for her father's love may seem perverse. Her love is deeper than her sisters', yet she refuses to express it to compete with them. She even seems hard and unaffectionate to her old father. Her conduct of the moment cannot be explained on realistic grounds. Her behavior seems above reality. The sequence of events —the banishment of Cordelia and Kent— challenges credibility. The refusal of Cordelia by Burgundy and the acceptance of her by France reminds one of a fairy tale or a story from the *Arabian Nights*. Kent not only protests Lear's actions, points out the flattery of Goneril and Regan, and vouches for the sincerity of Cordelia but asserts his duty to speak "When power to flattery bows" (1. 1) and challenges Goneril and Regan with

And your large speeches may your deeds approve,
That good effects may spring from words of love.

He acts as chorus and prophet and sets the rule of the game of make-believe and allegory.

As Russell Fraser points out, "the opening scenes have not to do with realism but with ritual and romance . . . They do not wear the aspects of life so much as the aspect of art. Kent, lapsing into rude rhymes as he takes his departure, catches and communicates that aspect. His language is admonitory, and simple—not naively but consciously simple: 'artificial'." And Fraser thinks the language of the other protagonists "is of a piece with his." It is filled with "legal and fiscal metaphors" appropriate for "the ceremonious (the other worldly!) business of proceedings at law and finance." [1] The use of such metaphors to mask the human qualities of love—to suggest

---

[1] Russell Fraser, Introduction to *The Tragedy of King Lear* (New York and Toronto, The New American Library, 1963), pp. xxvi–xxvii.

love as a commodity to be measured, weighed, bought, and sold—is both ironical and a sign of double levels of import. The prevalence of animal imagery in the likening of lower animals to man by Lear, Gloucester, and Albany, especially, suggests the allegoric. The continuous questioning and references to the religious and metaphysical focus attention on the supernatural and serve to alert the audience to a plane higher than the literal. Lear's use of language with a double meaning coincides with his developing insight into his own situation and is relevant to man in general. It is surely another sign of the surrealistic world of the play. The metaphoric comments of Kent, Edgar, and Albany—"Is this the promised end?" "Or image of that horror." "Fall and cease" (5. 3)—point up the doomsday nature of the scene in which Lear holds the dead Cordelia in his arms. It is a scene that transcends the particular and realistic and says something significant and meaningful about the capricious cruelty of life.

The repetition of episodes of trial, with defendants, prosecutors, and judges, cannot be overlooked, and their symbolic nature must register in the minds of the audience. They start with the first scene of the play and include Lear's confrontations with Goneril and Regan over the issue of the number of knights to be retained by Lear; Lear's mental and spiritual trial in the storm scenes; Lear's fantastic arraignment of his daughters before the hovel; Lear's trial of the sinners of the world when he meets Gloucester at Dover; Gloucester's inquisitional trial by Regan and Cornwall; Gloucester's attempted suicide and rescue by Edgar; and Lear's and Cordelia's arrest and imprisonment by Edmund (the trial by combat between Edgar and Edmund); and Lear's last trial of his reason and spirit at the death of Cordelia.

The vein of irony which runs through the whole play is overruling evidence of the heightened reality of the world depicted by the play. The characters are contradicted by fortune at every turn. Albany's "The gods defend her!" (5. 3) after he sends a messenger with a token of reprieve to the prison to halt her execution serves as prelude to the ironic sight of Lear's entrance with the dead Cordelia. The implausible and fairy-tale disguises of Kent and Edgar are never questioned by those who know them intimately and they heighten the irony of the situations in which the two find themselves with Gloucester, the

Fool, Edmund, the dukes of Albany and Cornwall, Regan, Goneril, and Lear. Such disguises may stretch credibility mightily but they enhance the dramatic effect brilliantly.

Symbolic implications and action, grounded in the realistic, create a consistent and ever recurring double image of life. The characters are intensified and crystallized—essences of psychology—into what Bradley called members of two groups of "Love and Hate . . . the two ultimate forces of the universe." [2] (Yet Bradley refuses to view the characters as symbolic or allegorical, or as abstractions.) Other critics saw the two in terms of Good and Evil. Their words and deeds are not melodramatic but are larger than life. Shakespeare was familiar with the morality plays and subtly adopted their modes as a convention in the popular tradition of drama. *King Lear* is one of his greatest accomplishments in this mode. This allegoric mode, however, presents the director and actor with certain practical problems.

Though the characters must be studied on the symbolic level and seen mentally as personifications of good and evil, love and hate, dictated by the ordering force of the play's meaning, the realistic basis for characters must be investigated and established. In fact, the symbolic becomes meaningful for the actor only when grounded in realism.

Modern literary criticism approaches the matter from a different point of view. In discussing the character of Cordelia, Russell Fraser rightly asserts that, "Less real than symbolic, her affinity is more to a creature of fairy tale like Cinderella than to a heroine of the realistic drama like Blanche DuBois. In delineating her behavior the playwright may be, psychologically, so penetrating and exact as really to catch the manners living as they rise: that is partly a gratuity." The playwright's intention, more importantly, is not to portray a "veritable woman" [3] but to symbolize a particular kind of woman. And, of course, Fraser is right too about the other characters of the play. He notes the stylized quality of the first scene but points out that "though *Lear* is essentially representational drama, though realism very quickly takes precedence over ritual, the element of the symbolic is never dissipated altogether but figures in important ways until

[2] A. C. Bradley, *Shakespearean Tragedy* (London, Macmillan, 1926), p. 263.
[3] Fraser, p. xxxi.

the end . . . It persists, not to give substance to the real, which is substantial enough—

> Out, vile jelly!
> Where is thy luster now?

—but to order the real and make it meaningful . . ." [4]

This ordering function of the symbolic creates a special world for the play, and the impersonation of character is achieved by an actor's awareness of it: An intensification is demanded of characterization. But first the actor must find a psychological basis; the symbolical and the archetypal must be embedded in realism. He must translate literary analysis into practical acting terms. Let us turn to several of Shakespeare's plays for examples, leaving *King Lear* for a detailed study of character.

PSYCHOLOGICAL BASIS FOR CHARACTER

Katharina, the shrew of *The Taming of the Shrew,* a clear example of an archetypal character, can be easily analyzed psychologically. An examination of what is said about her and what she says and does in her very first scene will indicate the kind of person she apparently is. When her father invites Gremio and Hortensio to "court her at your pleasure" (1. 1) Gremio replies, "To cart her rather: she's too rough for me," and gives Hortensio leave to woo her. But Kate turns on her father to ask if he will make a laughingstock of her "amongst these mates?" Hortensio answers:

> Mates, maid! how mean you that? no mates
>   for you,
> Unless you were of gentler, milder mould.

And she threatens

> To comb your noddle wth a three-legged stool,
> And paint your face, and use you like a fool.

Hortensio and Gremio remove themselves from her with

> *Hortensio.* From all such devils, good Lord
>   deliver us!
> *Gremio.* And me too, good Lord!

In these few lines of dialogue Kate establishes her fiery temper and her capability to resort to violent physical action. When she speaks of her sister as "A pretty peat!" she

shows her jealousy of Bianca. Her father has clearly demonstrated his partiality for his younger daughter. Baptista's

> Katharina you may stay,
> For I have more to commune with Bianca.

is also evidence of her rebellious nature. The audience is given a vivid portrait of a hot-tempered, strong-willed, rebellious, and jealous creature.

In 2. 1 Kate beats her sister for not telling her which of her suitors she loves best. Bianca protests she does not love one more than the other, but Kate thinks she jests. She can get no satisfaction out of her sister. When her father rescues Bianca and shows his sympathy for her, Kate is convinced that her father loves her sister more than her:

> She is your treasure, she must have a husband,
> I must dance bare-foot on her wedding-day
> And for your love to her lead apes in hell.
> Talk not to me, I will go sit and weep,
> Till I can find occasion of revenge.

Katharina is a completely frustrated girl. She is rejected by her sister and father—and she feels doomed to be an old maid. She seeks love and can find it nowhere. She can only seek revenge by seeming to be a shrew.

When she meets Petruchio, sent by her father, she is naturally antagonistic toward a suitor preferred by him. His familiarity in calling her Kate, his flattery and boldness can but put her on the offensive. Their conversation develops into a battle of wits and then becomes a sex duel, mentally and physically. It is a classic example of a comic dramatization of characters caught in a love-hate situation. Petruchio is obviously a match for her—a match in will, wit, vitality, and love. Petruchio understands her psychology:

> Father, 'tis thus—yourself and all the world,
> That talked of her, have talked amiss of her:
> If she be curst, it is for policy:
> For she's not froward, but modest as the dove,
> She is not hot, but temperate as the morn,

And Kate's last speech in the play proves Petruchio to be right. Like many of Shakespeare's characters, Katharina plays a role through the course of the play until the ultimate discovery of identity. Her words and actions belie her true self; her search for love and affection, frustrated at every turn, causes

---

[4] Pp. xxix–xxx.

her to seem to be what she is not. She finally sees the ridiculousness of her waywardness and stubbornness. Her complete enlightenment is evident in the journey to Padua, in 4. 5, and her transformation is obvious when she says to Petruchio:

> Then, God be blessed, it is the blesséd sun—
> But sun it is not, when you say it is not,
> And the moon changes even as your mind:
> What you will have it named, even that it is,
> And so it shall be so, for Katharine.

She has seen in Petruchio's arbitrary behavior toward her a burlesqued picture of herself. In the next scene she calls him "husband" for the first time; she is a new person who has found love and the truth about herself.

CHARACTER OBJECTIVE

The discovery of one's identity is often the character's objective in the plays of Shakespeare. This is true of Kate in *The Taming of the Shrew*. Her objective or goal in life is to be loved. Specifically, she wants a husband. His love is of primary importance to her, but the love of her father and sister is desirable too. Of course, she may not have articulated her life objective; she does not speak of it in the play, but her behavior implies it. She may be entirely unconscious of it or only partially aware of it, but the actress playing Kate must know what her objective is. This objective is what she *wants,* an all-enveloping *desire* which motivates and gives a central purpose to her life. Her every movement constitutes a unit of this objective. Her violent anger and her threatening Gremio and Hortensio in her first scene onstage is a unit related to her main objective. Kate's attitude and action are, of course, the opposite of what they should be; she cannot expect to be loved when behaving this way. Her behavior is attention-getting and a demand for love, even from two such unlikely suitors as Hortensio and Gremio. Kate's perversity is a result of her motive force: She wants to be loved and, though she does not succeed in achieving the warmth, comfort, sympathy, understanding, and the satisfaction of complete love, she is the recipient of attention and complaints and the object of fear and rejection. There is some satisfaction in this to her ego or self-love. If the love of others is denied her she achieves love of self. This is a need coming out of her overruling desire. So far in her life this is the only kind of love she

has been permitted. Her objective, therefore, includes self-love, and she is willing to go to any lengths to obtain even this version of love.

The actress personifying Kate must, therefore, select an objective to play which is based on these special circumstances of character. This means that the objective must be specific and not general. An actress cannot play "I want to be loved." This is too general; she would not have any definite actions to play. An objective must be expressed in the form of a transitive verb and lead to specific action and behavior. Kate's objective could be: "I want to be thought a shrew in order to obtain love." This will lead to actions, physical and mental, which will achieve her goal: She can throw a three-legged stool at Gremio and Hortensio; she can try to scratch their faces; she can strike her sister; she can throw temper tantrums; she can hit Hortensio over the head with a lute; she can hit and kick Petruchio; she can give tongue-lashings at will; she can participate in a battle of wits, etc. The objective chosen by the actress must generate action. *What* she does is the action; *why* she does it is the objective; and *how* she does it is the adaptation to the objective.

Thus the character objective is arrived at from perspective or objectivity as well as subjectivity. This means that the director and the actress must seek Kate's objective from the perspective of the spirit or tone of the play. The play is comic and the objective to be played must evoke laughter: Kate's perverse way of achieving her objective—her playing the role of a shrew, a rough, bad-tempered, belligerent, and frustrated young lady. If the actress were to play her objective seriously and subjectively she would create an unlikable, self-centered termagant. Of course, Shakespeare enhances sympathy for Kate by surrounding her with an ineffectual, narrow-minded, and comic father who does not understand his daughter and who does not know how to cope with her; with Hortensio and Gremio, buffoons whose dismay and confusion in dealing with Kate are also laughable; and Petruchio, whose wild clowning, as he holds a wildcat by the tail, excites laughter. The audience understands Kate's perverse behavior and understands her psychology. The arrival of Petruchio on the scene, determined to woo and wed the wildcat (Kate) is a delightful turn of events which whets the audience's appetite for entertainment. Petruchio is one more obstacle in Kate's way. (Her objective is made dramatic because of her obstacles. The possibility of obstacles is one of the important determinants in her choice of an objective to play.) The fact that he takes the audience into his confidence in a soliloquy at the end of 4. 1 and explains his strategy in handling Kate, ending with

> And thus I'll curb her mad and headstrong humour.
> He that knows better how to tame a shrew,
> Now let him speak: 'tis charity to show.

makes the entire proceedings of the play a comical charade and places his actions and Kate's in laughable perspective.

Another determinant of character objective is the outcome of the play—the end of the character's dramatic journey. Whereas Kate discovers her identity and reaches her objective in the journey to Padua, she explains herself and woman's relationship to her husband and love in the last scene of the play. Her realization that

> A woman moved is like a fountain troubled,
> Muddy, ill-seeming, thick, bereft of beauty;
> And while it is so, none so dry or thirsty
> Will deign to sip or touch one drop of it.
>   (5. 2)

is true insight into herself, and her unselfish love for her husband is true love, which Petruchio rewards with "Why, there's a wench! Come on, and kiss me, Kate."

When a character's objective is chosen with such knowledge it becomes an organic part of the play and a through-line of action for the actress or actor.

IMPROVISATION AND REALITY

Plays depicting the life of the past tend to distance the characters from actors and audiences. The clothes, language, customs, and daily routines of such characters, living in a social, political, and economic world different from ours today, are estranging factors. However, they are merely outward shows of thoughts and feelings of people who are essentially like men and women today. The actor and the director must throw off the outer trappings and delve below the surface of past life to find the humanity in Shakespeare's characters. We have already discussed the necessity of establishing psychological bases and character objectives. The modern actor's use of the techniques of improvisation is another bridge to belief in the reality of character.

Shakespearean language is probably the strongest barrier between the past and the actor and audience. The simplest solution is to translate or adapt the language into everyday colloquial conversation. This presents problems and pitfalls, of course. There are the dangers of inaccuracy and distortion—dangers inherent in translations of every kind. However, the guiding principle is to try to invoke the spirit of the original in terms of modern equivalencies.

Using their own words actors can, with repeated attempts to find modern conversational ways of expressing Shakespeare's meanings, gain a greater degree of belief in what they say. (In using such a rehearsal technique the director must act as editor of such textual changes by judging them for logic and truthfulness.) Improvisation of dialogue can lead the actors to improvisation of behavior based on the general psychology of characters and character objective. This kind of improvisation consists of *mirroring* Shakespeare's language, situations, and character behavior in terms of modern images. Othello's encounter with Desdemona at the beginning of 3. 3 easily lends itself to such an improvisation. Desdemona's intercession for Cassio, though expressed in poetry, is readily translated into present-day conversation and character objectives rooted in the sexual psychology of the newly married. In 2. 1, after the arrival of Desdemona, Emilia, Iago, Roderigo, and attendants at Cyprus, considerable dialogue is devoted to bantering witticisms between Iago and Desdemona, underlined with serious insinuations by Iago. The individual words and lines will become clear and believable to the actors if they are paraphrased with simple, direct, modern language and are said to carry out moment-by-moment character intentions. This is true particularly of the colloquy beginning with Desdemona's "Come, how wouldst thou praise me?" and ending with her "How say you, Cassio? Is he not a most profane and liberal counsellor?" To find the spirit of this duel it may be helpful to the actors if they improvise some kind of game which can be physicalized. The words and the actions should be competitive and enjoyable for those playing Cassio and Emilia as well as for the two principal players. This improvisation must parallel Shakespeare's original words and behavior if the intention of the scene is to be carried out.

Another kind of improvisation is useful. It

may be called the *enriching* improvisation in the sense that it helps the actor to fill gaps in building characterization. This involves the improvisation of details which can come from subtextual implications. Such details of dialogue and behavior could be used by the actors to increase their belief in the reality of a particular scene. For example, we can take 1. 3, involving the Duke and the Senators. The situation and characters have their equivalents in any modern government war office or headquarters. The continuing differences between Greece and Turkey over Cyprus as recounted in the newspapers can provide improvisational material to make Shakespeare's scene relevantly realistic and believable. The study of maps, the coming and going of office personnel, the reference to documents, the arrival of dispatchers, etc., can be used to elaborate the life of the scene and character details which the actors playing the Duke and the Senators need.

A third kind of improvisation stems from implied or offstage scenes. An implicit scene is described by Othello when he tells the story of his courtship of Desdemona just before she arrives at the council meeting of the senate. The actors playing Othello, Desdemona, and Brabantio would be helped considerably by improvising this episode in their lives. The improvisation of Othello's and Desdemona's elopement, which has taken place offstage before the second scene of the play, would add to the reality of their relationship and enrich the emotional background for the scene in front of Othello's and Desdemona's honeymoon lodging. This kind of *continuity* improvisation welds together the narrative and assists the actors in achieving a through-line for each character.

The use of improvisation depends upon the actor's and the director's imagination in finding words and actions to mirror, enrich, and fill in events suggested by Shakespeare's text. The demands made upon the imagination by *Othello,* which is for the most part a realistic play, convincing in terms of modern psychological knowledge of character and of our interest in racial problems, are not as great as those made by a less realistic play, *The Tempest.* Yet, like *Othello* and all other plays, *The Tempest* is based on actor and audience willingness to believe certain assumptions. Whereas other plays ask for belief in more easily recognizable characters and situations, *The Tempest* appeals directly to the imagination and the willing suspension of disbelief in

fanciful characters in unrecognizable situations. It must be said, however, that the play begins with a comparatively believable storm and shipwreck. The behavior of the characters is convincing from reports of actual experience of such incidents. Credibility is stretched only when we discover that Prospero caused it all. The immediate acceptance of this fact is induced by Prospero's demonstrated power to summon and control Ariel. Then Shakespeare builds the special world of the play, scene by scene. The director and actors of the play must conceive of and believe in behavior and events in relation to this world. The starting point for the creation of characterization depends upon acceptance of this world. It is an enchanted cosmos where the impossible is possible. It is an

> . . . isle . . . full of noises,
> Sounds, and sweet airs, that give delight and
>   hurt not:
> Sometimes a thousand twangling instruments
> Will hum   (3. 2)

about the ears of all who inhabit or visit this island. Here the ruler is an omnipotent magician who casts spells and forces all—the elements, the human, half-human, and inhuman—to bow to his will. The characters are actors playing roles and they are

>   all spirits, and
> Are melted into air, into thin air,
> And, like the baseless fabric of this vision,
> The cloud-capped towers, the gorgeous palaces,
> The solemn temples, the great globe itself,
> Yea, all which it inherit, shall dissolve,
> And, like this insubstantial pageant faded,
> Leave not a rack behind: we are such stuff
> As dreams are made on; and our little life
> Is rounded with a sleep   (4. 1)

The opening scene of the play can be mirrored in the most realistic improvisation of speech and behavior to serve as groundwork for performances and productional aspects which for actual presentation may become only the abstraction of a storm and a shipwreck, with Ariel darting about in his own beam of light to indicate his control of the elements and the mariners.

Prospero's story of his deputizing his brother to act as Duke of Milan, his absorption "in secret studies" (1. 2) of magic and the supernatural, his brother's usurping of the dukedom, his being thrust aboard a rotten bark together with the child Miranda, their coming ashore on the island, and their life together before the storm and shipwreck can be improvised to enrich their background and make Prospero's narrative to Miranda more believable to the actors. The scenes of Ariel's rescue from the "cloven pine," the discovery of Caliban by Prospero and his bringing up by Prospero and Miranda, Caliban's attempted assault upon Miranda, and other scenes left out or occurring offstage can be rewardingly improvised to make for continuity of playing and belief.

The strange and monstrous shapes, Iris, Ceres, Juno, and the participants in the masque—the most abstract characters in the play—must imagine themselves half human and half spirit and draw creative food from the behavior of birds and animals and even from the appearance of flowers, shrubs, and trees moved by the wind. Their improvisations will depend upon patterns of objectives arising out of the given circumstances of the scenes in which these characters appear.

Improvisations in the rehearsals of *The Tempest,* it must be stressed, should be used by the director and actors to create actor belief and stimulate imagination and not to give the audience an impression of realism. In fact, the more the director of the play can stimulate audience imagination by suggestion, connotation, and imagery, the better. The music, mood, and atmosphere emanating from the language are so pervasive that character detail and excessive visual production will literalize and stifle imagination so necessary for an allegorical dramatic pastoral.

The Tempest is a theatre *game,* and the approach to the use of improvisations in rehearsals should be to capture the spirit of playfulness with joy and childlike naiveté and seek the stimulation of the imaginative resources of the actors. The degree of success of the actors will be reflected in the response of the audience.

CHARACTER INNOVATION

Audience familiarity with some Shakespearean plays is considerable. *Hamlet, Othello, Macbeth, The Merchant of Venice,* and *Twelfth Night* are favorites with the public and are produced frequently. They are also the plays probably most often studied in school. The aspect of these plays which is a matter of general knowledge is the plot. Almost everybody knows what *happens* in these plays. Their unfolding and outcome possess few surprises and little suspense. They have thus suffered a degree of dramatic loss to which new modern plays are not subjected. The director of Shakespeare must compensate for this loss by shifting audience interest to other dramatic potentials.

Shakespeare's characters continue to interest and excite audiences though they know about them in general. They may even have a fairly definite image of certain characters. However, the main characters are so rich and so open to varying interpretations that they have suffered little from familiarity. They remain full of surprises. Acting emphasis and directorial means can dislocate the clichés and create fresh, new, and rewarding views of character. Audience interest and tension can thus be shifted from narrational values to character values. Of course, plot is character in action, and they enhance one another.

In the National Theatre production of *Othello* in 1965 Sir Laurence Olivier's Othello exemplified this in scene after scene. His emphasis upon Othello's race alerted the audience to a subject relevant to modern society and conditioned the response to each scene. His was a *black* Othello, cocky out of a sense of insecurity, gullible in his complacency, and naive not only in sophisticated Venetian society in general but also in human relationships particularly. Audience foregone conclusions as to the unfolding story were forced out of consciousness and almost unbearable suspense and tension were evoked. The predictability of narration was replaced by an unpredictability of person.

Ian Holm's fresh portrait of Hal in the 1966 Royal Shakespeare Company's production of *Henry IV, Part I* colored and gave focus to the play while adding tensile strength and pull to individual scenes.

David Warner's "cool" Hamlet renovated every event in the same company's production of the play. How he reacted became more important than what happened to him. His psychology was in tune with 1966 and informed the overall thrust of the play.

Of course, innovation in character approach to the protagonists of the plays will affect interpretations for all the principal and susidiary characters. The Desdemona of Olivier's Othello was not as girlishly romantic as he imagined her to be but rather was mature and strong in her steadfast love. She loved him for what she saw in his character, not because of his exotic appearance and heroic adventures. She married him realizing full well the prejudices of her aristocratic society and she was prepared to face all opposition. Her defense of him before her father and the Senators, for example, thus brought a new dimension to the scene. Falstaff and Hotspur in *Henry IV* in contrast to Ian Holm's Hal were less laudable in moral fiber than those usually presented. Falstaff was of grotesquely enormous proportions—ridiculous, amoral, and completely irresponsible. Hotspur was presented as platitudinous, romantic, reckless, and thoughtless —given to impulse and self-dramatization. The responsible and committed, though calculating, Hal of Ian Holm appeared estimable by comparison with those who surrounded him. The Claudius opposed to David Warner's "cool" Hamlet was the personification of impeccable statesmanship, and Gertrude seemed to be the victim of circumstances, a natural woman caught by the inexorable machinery of her society.

In shifting the emphasis from narrational to character values the director need not and should not twist and dislocate the character values out of textual validity. The text must support the director's choices of character emphases. In the search for a new view of characters a director may be tempted by what appears to be interpretive inspiration but will ultimately be discovered to be capricious and gimmicky, impossible to substantiate, if the director is honest with himself. The current obsession with modern relevancies in producing the classics sometimes results in heavy-handed distortions and outright superimposition of "bright ideas" by the director. (See Chapter V, "Making Shakespeare Contemporary," for examples.)

Now we turn to a study of the individual characters in *King Lear*. We will analyze each one from a psychological viewpoint to help the actor justify his behavior. However, the actor must remember that the role he is to play is larger than life and takes on the dimensions of an archetypal character. The play is based upon psychologically true characters even though their motivations may often seem to the director and actors to be very slight. An audience watching the play in performance is too absorbed in the events of the play to question plausibility.

CHARACTERS IN "KING LEAR"

Lear

Lear, the center of the play, around whom all other characters revolve, exists and behaves in such absolute authority that he poses a special problem for the actor who looks for his psychological base or bias. The improbability of his conduct from the very beginning of the play has been noted and decried by Goethe, Bradley, and Coleridge, among others. How can it be justified? And justified it must be for the actor in terms of human behavior rather than of criticism. How can an actor *believe* in him? Before the play begins he divides his kingdom, and the Duke of Albany and the Duke of Cornwall are both apparently equally deserving and equally loved by Lear, though Kent and Gloucester thought the King "had more affected the Duke of Albany" (1. 1). When Lear appears he says that he has divided "In three our kingdom" and goes on to express his "darker purpose," which is to find out which of his daughters loves him most in order that he may reward her with his "largest bounty." And thinking to bestow it on Cordelia, he asks her what she can say

> to draw
> A third more opulent than your sisters?

Who ever heard of a father, even though a king, presiding over a public—or a private— "trial of love"? In effect, he seeks to extort from them a loyalty oath. Inasmuch as he has divided the kingdom into three parts, he expects to award the more opulent third to Cordelia because he

> loved her most, and thought to set [his] rest
> On her kind nursery.

And he demanded public avowal of her love —a love weightier than her tongue will permit her to articulate. Goneril and Regan possess the

> glib and oily art
> To speak and purpose not

and are rewarded not only with their own portions of the kingdom but with Cordelia's richer third. Cordelia is cut off without a share and is disowned by her father, who never wants to see her face again and bids her

> be gone
> Without our grace, our love, our benison.

How can this irrational behavior be explained? Lear divides his kingdom

> To shake all cares and business from our age,
> Conferring them on younger strengths, while we
> Unburdened crawl toward death.

He is aware of his age and failing powers. He feels insecure and wants to be assured of his children's love. But he thinks of love as a commodity to be sold and bought—like many modern parents who reward their children with material things in return for "good" behavior and affection. Lear is not only a father but a king, and he wants a public demonstration of love, respect, and his authority. He has taken them for granted. The director will do well to show his authoritarian rule in this first scene. Signs of it are shown in the court's unhesitating kneeling at his appearance and ascent of the throne, his giving the court a signal to rise, his cutting off laughter when Goneril and Regan laugh at his "Nothing will come of nothing" to Cordelia, the prominence of the sword borne in the procession as an emblem of authority, and Lear's threatening Kent with the sword and his calling Cornwall and Albany before him to swear on the sword

> that future strife
> May be prevented now

—a moment of staging which becomes ironical later when we hear of

> division,
> Although as yet the face of it is covered
> With mutual cunning, 'twixt Albany and Cornwall,   (3. 1)

and the portentous presence of attendants and knights—like a dictator's military might, suggesting control and power. Of course, Lear's personal manner and behavior should reflect his absolute authoritarianism.

His view and way of life have become habit, molded into personality. His accustomed authority unfits him to reason with opposition. His immediate and irascible response to Cordelia's and Kent's speeches are sure tokens of parental and regal authority never before questioned. Too, an awareness of his waning physical and, possibly, mental

powers has induced a degree of insecurity which puts him on the defensive. His reactions are thus out of proportion to the stimuli.

Another strong factor affecting his behavior is the primitive and pre-Christian society in which he lives. When Kent tries, on Cordelia's behalf, to intervene and to justify such boldness by his testimony that he has honored Lear as his king, loved him as his father, and followed him as master, Lear immediately thinks in terms of hunting and killing. "The bow is bent and drawn; make from the shaft" (1. 1). He also implicitly equates animals with man as the objects of hunting and killing. His swearing by Hecate, goddess of the infernal world and witchcraft, and his belief in astrological influence are also indications of the conditioning powers of the pagan world he lives in.

Pride and stubbornness blind him to reason. His "Out of my sight!" to Kent elicits profound advice: "See better, Lear . . ." Laying his hand upon his sword, he accuses Kent of trying

> to make us break our vow—
> Which we durst never yet—

a proud admission of intractability. Here is a closed, authoritarian mind—inner-directed.

His hurt is so deep after Cordelia's public embarrassment of him as king and father that he bitterly offers her to Burgundy for

> What in the least
> Will you require in present dower with her,
> Or cease your quest of love?

Burgundy coldly replies that he wants no more than Lear has offered. But Lear even more coldly replies,

> When she was dear to us, we did hold her so;
> But now her price is fall'n.

On such conditions Burgundy will not have her. But France, in spite of Lear's attempts to dissuade him from accepting Cordelia in marriage, nevertheless does, finding "She is herself a dowry,"

> most rich, being poor;
> Most choice, forsaken; and most loved, despised;

Even Goneril realizes

> how full of changes his age is.
> . . . He
> always loved our sister most, and with what
> poor
> judgement he hath now cast her off appears
> too grossly.

And Regan echoes her with "'Tis the infirmity of his age" and adds perceptively,

> yet he hath ever
> but slenderly known himself.

Furthermore, Goneril makes the telling observation that

> The best and soundest of his time hath been
> but rash; then must we look from his age to
> receive, not
> alone the imperfections of long-engraffed condition, but
> therewithal the unruly waywardness that infirm and
> choleric years bring with them.

Unsympathetic and selfish and hard-hearted they may be, but they speak out of experience and insight. The "imperfections of long-engraffed condition" bespeak a way of life that is subject to poor judgment, rashness, and self-delusions. The seeds of madness have already taken root.

The modern actor can find instances in his own life which in their smaller way can explain Lear's psychological bias. Daily self-centeredness has blinded us all to examples of delusions and irrationality. An overwhelming sense of insecurity and helpless rage have attended unexpected and forced shattering of illusions and untruths. The props knocked out from under us, we have cursed and mistreated those who have loved us most. Our little worlds of work or love, or social, political, or economic standing have been threatened or lost. An actor can examine his life for such jolting if not traumatic experiences and thus believe in Lear as a person and psychologically justify him in part or whole. Experience and imagination must be combined to find the basis for a characterization.

A practical obstacle for the actor playing Lear is Lear's unsympathetic introduction to the audience. He is both unreasonable and old. Old age is not often ingratiating. In Shakespeare's other great tragedies, *Romeo and Juliet*, *Hamlet*, *Othello*, and *Macbeth*, the heroes are young or in the prime of life. Fur-

thermore, they are attractive mentally and spiritually. (Macbeth is like Lear in that though he is flawed he becomes pitiable and admirable in the decline of his fortunes.)

However, by finding believable psychological circumstances, either textually or subtextually, the actor has a basis for justification of behavior and can build his character from these circumstances. Lear's simple desire for love—though he seeks to buy it instead of to earn it—can serve to get the actor through the first scene. He can find plenty of evidence for psychological truth in what he says and what others say about him and thus discover a context for his impelling drive and objective. Certainly from the outset, the character is unmistakably and mightily established in detail and in plan by Shakespeare.

As we come to the Duke of Albany's palace, we hear Goneril complaining of her father's striking her servants for chiding the Fool and, in fact, wronging her by day and night and setting all at odds. And he, she says, "upbraids us/ On every trifle" (1. 3). She would bring the matter to a head and urges her steward and her servants to "Put on what weary negligence you please" and even "let his knights have colder looks among you." This is the state of affairs between Lear and Goneril two days after his resignation from the throne and at the very beginning of his first month's visit to her. Our view of Lear and his noisy knights just returned from hunting and his impatiently calling for his dinner can but give us a jolt. Here is Lear divested of his royal robes. Here is our first look at Lear the domestic man, who would still retain the authority of a king. But he still has that in his countenance which the disguised Kent would call "Authority" (1. 4). Lear accepts him in his service.

He then successively raps out orders for dinner, asks for his Fool, and asks where his daughter is. Oswald's impudent failure to answer and immediate exit enrage Lear to demand "the clotpoll" back. And he calls for his court jester again.

> Ho!
> I think the world's asleep.

Wake up, wake up! The king has arrived and nobody greets him or serves him. Desires frustrated are fuel for the actor. The knight returns to say the "mongrel" steward will not come back to answer the King's question about his daughter's whereabouts. The knight apologetically points out that his

> highness is not entertained with that ceremonious affection as you were wont.

Furthermore, he has noticed that not only the servants but also the Duke himself and Goneril show "a great abatement of kindness" toward Lear. This has occurred to Lear, too, but he has thought it only his own excessive suspicion. This is a noticeable admission—so unlike the Lear of the first scene. It is evidence of a kind of introspection which precedes enlightenment about oneself.

Then he calls for his Fool again. Is this indicative of a feeling of loneliness—that everyone who really matters has abandoned him? The knight's reply that the Fool has pined away since the young lady's departure for France gets a sharp and bitter "No more of that; I have noted it well." Oswald's entrance and impudence, after the knight has been dispatched to Goneril to tell her her father would speak to her, and his order to an attendant to call hither his Fool give Lear the looked-for opportunity to vent his spleen. He strikes Oswald with his whip, condones and rewards Kent's tripping him up. But it can be assumed that Oswald will inform his lady of this latest indignity to her household.

Lear is delighted at the appearance of his Fool but he is not ready for his jester's sharp darts with him as target. Not unexpectedly, Lear threatens him with the whip. Yet the Fool continues to hold up the mirror for Lear to see himself as he really is, and Lear, his thoughts turned in on himself, thinks of Cordelia, the third daughter whom he did "a blessing against his will." He listens to the Fool's pertinent quips with paternal indulgence and is only half responsive, so absorbed is he with his own bitter reproaches.

He is the "straight man" feeding the other comic, the Fool. The colloquy between them has been like a vaudeville routine. Lear accepts his role when he asks the Fool, "Dost thou call me fool, boy?" and the reply is "All thy other titles thou hast given away; that thou wast born with." Lear does not deny it, nor does he threaten with the whip. After all, they are just two clowns, one straight and serious and the other devious and funny. Goneril, silent and sullen in her appearance, interrupts the act and is ready for a showdown with her

father, an old fool who is a babe again and who needs restraints as well as soothing words when he is misguided. She lets Lear speak first but when she does speak she launches into a diatribe against the unbridled language and action of the Fool, the quarreling and riotous knights, and her father as well. Lear cannot believe his senses. Can this be his daughter talking to her father, the King? His ironical questions about her identity and his own are responses to the image reflected in the mirror Goneril holds in front of him. This, as pointed out before, has become a hall of mirrors: First the knight, then the Fool, and now his daughter turns a mirror toward him. He sees neglect, loss of respect, influence, and authority; he sees himself as only the shadow of the former Lear—and a fool too. Goneril's demand that he "disquantity" his train is not unreasonable from a practical point of view. Why does an old man need a hundred knights to follow him about in idleness? Their healthy but rough and boisterous entrance into Goneril's great dining hall after riding and hunting can only confirm her allegations that they are men capable of disorderliness, boldness, and debauchery, Lear's assertion that they are irreproachable in their conduct to the contrary. His blindness and unawareness about himself and his daughters lead us to think he is not a dependable judge of his followers.

His irrational response to Goneril's demand—ordering his horses saddled and calling her "Degenerate bastard"—can be justified by the actor who remembers that the hundred knights symbolize for Lear his regal authority. To reduce their number is to make him more insecure. Besides, Goneril and Regan and their husbands had agreed to maintain a hundred knights, as he had stipulated when he invested them jointly with his

> power,
> Pre-eminence, and all the large effects
> That troop with majesty.   (1. 1)

He expects them to live up to their contract; he lives according to the law. His world is inflexibly legalistic and so should theirs be. Too, they agreed that he should

> retain
> The name and all th' addition to a king

—his title and honors. To deny this now is to show ingratitude,

              thou marble-hearted fiend,
More hideous when thou show'st thee in a
    child
Than a sea-monster!   (1. 4)

Cordelia's fault, he exclaims in startling enlightenment, seems small in comparison with those of her sisters, but Cordelia's failure to express her love for her father has disordered his nature and now he strikes at his head that let folly in and judgment out. Can the mind sustain such a revelation? On the verge of madness, he can only resort to cruel, vengeful, primitive curses, the cruelest of all a plea to the goddess Nature to deprive a woman—his daughter—the birth of children. If she must bear a child, he prays, let it be a "child of spleen" (1. 4) to torment her,

                     that she may feel
How sharper than a serpent's tooth it is
To have a thankless child!

He rushes out to join his people only to find that fifty of them will be dismissed at one stroke, "within a fortnight." He is ashamed of his hot tears which shake his manhood in powerless protestation. He can only take refuge in the thought that he has another daughter who, when she hears of this, with her nails will "flay thy wolvish visage." He hysterically threatens to return to his kingly self, which apparently he has cast off forever.

As Lear impatiently awaits his horses, his mind is absorbed with the wrong he has done Cordelia and the wrongs done him by Goneril; he is thinking such conflicting and unresolvable thoughts that he is fearful of losing his sanity. He quivers on the edge of the precipice and piteously pleads not to fall. The announcement that his horses are ready and the thought that Regan will be kind and comforting steady him as he gruffly leaves our sight with a "Come, boy" (1. 5).

After riding all night, first to Regan's, only to find her and Cornwall departed for Gloucester's, then doubling back, Lear, an old man of "Fourscore and upward" (4. 7), arrives at Gloucester's castle, disheveled, hungry, and near exhaustion. Instead of a welcome by his daughter and son-in-law he receives another blow, the sight of his messenger in stocks. And he soon discovers who set him there: his hoped-for benefactors and hosts. Instead ·of accepting this insult and returning to the comfort of his own palace, he majestically and stubbornly seeks out Regan and Cornwall.

Nor will he be satisfied with their excuse that they are ill and have traveled all night.

    The King would speak with Cornwall; the dear
        father
    Would with his daughter speak, commands her
        service.
    Are they informed of this? My breath and
        blood!
    Fiery? the fiery duke? Tell the hot duke that—
                                    (2. 4)

he roars and then stops dead his mounting passion to observe that maybe the Duke is not well and is not himself

    When nature, being oppressed, commands the
        mind
    To suffer with the body.

Of course, he is comparing the Duke's presumed condition with his own. This is another step on the ladder of self-discovery which comes from awareness of others. The actor and the director must mark these steps carefully if the audience is to accompany Lear in his climb from darkness to light. It is to be noted that Lear's thoughts are becoming less and less controlled; they move from Regan and Cornwall to himself, to Kent in the stocks, back to his hosts, and back again to himself and his "rising heart." The Fool tries to calm him with a comic story, but the mute and insolent entrance of Regan and Cornwall steels him for his restrained greeting. There is control yet in the old man—though it be of a desperate kind.

And desperate he is to believe Regan is glad to see him. But too soon he blames Goneril of ingratitude and he is unprepared for Regan's reply in partisanship with her sister. This is another blow to make his old head spin. Job-like, he suffers blow after blow, to be tagged and underscored by the actor. The more Regan sides with Goneril the more fault she finds in her father. And Lear, still unwilling to face the truth of Regan's obvious lack of love and understanding, curses Goneril and desperately holds on to his picture of Regan as "tender-hefted," one who

                        better know'st
    The offices of nature, bond of childhood,
    Effects of courtesy, dues of gratitude:

He refuses to face facts and wildly holds on to his last illusions. When Regan demands that he come to the point, a trumpet is heard within, and Lear is again diverted to the insult to his royal dignity when his messenger was put in the stocks. The appearance of Oswald reminds him again of "the sickly grace" of Goneril. The entrance of Goneril and Regan's taking her by the hand are yet another blow, the visual evidence of his daughters' partnership against him. How can his old heart bear it? The confrontation foreshadowed at the end of the first scene inevitably develops the issue: Lear's need to retain one hundred knights to be sustained by Regan and Goneril. Why does he need one hundred, nay

> five and twenty, ten, or five,
> . . . . .
> What need one?

when there are servants in his daughters' houses to attend upon him? Regan and Goneril are practical; they are right from the point of view of material comfort; they are *reasonable*. But "O reason not the need!" Lear cries in soul-searching protestation. This speech is, as Granville-Barker points out, "a turning point of the play, a salient moment in the development of Lear's character." [5] It is a milestone in his spiritual journey. The inner action of the play begins to rise as the outer action falls. The tempest in Lear's mind will soon burst forth in all its fury. His darting, ubiquitous thoughts, now complete and coherent, now fragmented and chaotic, bring him ever closer to the razor's edge between sanity and madness. His emotions build higher and higher.

The actor playing Lear must husband his emotions and harness them to the plan of the play. He may well wonder how he will be able to top the moments in the play's opening scene. Now, in 2. 4, he goes out into the storm at another peak of emotion, knowing that he must somehow achieve an even higher emotional peak during the third-act storm scene. However, he can rest through the playing of varied emotions in the remainder of the act. His outburst in his mad scene in 4. 6 is his last extended, angry, frenzied moment except for short moments in the very last scene of the play.

Thus far in the play the actions to be

[5] Harley Granville-Barker, *Prefaces to Shakespeare* (Princeton, Princeton University Press, 1946), *1*, 290.

played by the actor of Lear mostly involve the desire for love, respect, authority, security, understanding. The opposition is first in Cordelia, then in Kent, and successively in Oswald, Goneril, Regan, and Cornwall. The Fool is his mental and spiritual adversary who acts as *raisonneur* and conscience, sifting and distilling his experience into revelation. Beginning with his appearance in the third act Lear is on the side of nature and the gods that create the dreadful turmoil overhead in opposition to their enemies—wretches with "undivulgéd crimes/ Unwhipped of justice" (3. 2), the perjured, the counterfeiters of virtue who are incestuous and ought to beg mercy of the gods. If he be one of these, Lear pleads,

> I am a man
> More sinned against than sinning.

His vision opens up to include the world of good and evil. Having suffered the physical hardship of the storm and a partial cleansing of his inner self, he sees beyond himself. His "wits begin to turn" and he becomes aware of others: "How dost, my boy? Art cold?" This show of interest in and sympathy for others is not to be rushed over by the director and actors. It is the prefiguring of a larger and more important moment when in his next scene he prays for the poor naked wretches everywhere. The Fool's reaction to his master's concern for him is most touching. Certainly he throws his arms about Lear's legs and Lear comforts him. His touching little song is sung to cheer up his master while shrewdly commenting upon life.

Led before the hovel, Lear would prefer to suffer the wind and the rain rather than his more painful thoughts. The tempest in his mind

> Doth from my senses take all feeling else
> Save what beats there— (3. 4)

The storm will not give him leave to meditate on things that would hurt him more but he will go inside. He will pray and then he will sleep. Prayer and sleep may help to protect him from the dark turbulence of his mind.

His prayer for the houseless and ragged poor everywhere, suffering in such weather, opens his mind to his neglect. Exposing himself to what they feel, his sympathy for them is the greater and he would "show the heavens more just." Lear has opened himself to the world; he has walked out of the narrow and encrusted confines of himself and is in the open spaces. If he compares Poor Tom to himself when he asks if he gave all to his daughters who have brought him to this pass, Lear progresses to the realization that

> man is no more but such a poor, bare, forked
> animal

And Lear would strip himself of his borrowed royal robes and become man in his primal state. Edgar, who reduced himself to "nothing," reflects the image of the great Lear to show that a king and a beggar are equal.

Lear, momentarily diverted from his mirror by the light of Gloucester's torch and his courtiers' pleas to come out of the storm to the comfort of fire and food, insists on speaking with the madman, who is a learned Greek philosopher. He first asks "What is the cause of thunder?" He surely does not want to know the scientific explanation. His question has metaphysical relevance. He has seen "unaccommodated man" and now wants to know the meaning of existence. (The symbolism of the storm, of which thunder is a part, has universal as well as particular pertinence.) Only the wisdom of a madman is great enough for an answer. We never know if he receives an answer, but we see the old man leaving the hearth to accept Gloucester's hospitality, and he keeps close to his "philosopher."

Left to the comfort of a room near Gloucester's castle while Gloucester leaves to "piece out the comfort with what/ addition" (3. 6) he can, Lear is convinced that a madman is a king, and we are convinced that the king is mad as he turns the room into a courtroom to arraign his wicked daughters. The grotesquerie of the scene may be projected not only by Lear's words and behavior but by those of Poor Tom and the Fool, who wander off into their own thoughts and songs until Kent tries to make Lear lie down, and Lear insists that Edgar, the "robéd man of justice," his "yokefellow of equity" the Fool, and Kent sit in judgment on Goneril and Regan. One mad, another feigning madness, one a Fool, the other dismayed and a powerless victim of his service to Lear, and two joint stools to represent the defendants Goneril and Regan are the *dramatis personae* of a black farce. The imaginary arraignment of the two daughters and Regan's escape from justice make pathetic Lear's pursuit by

the fiends—his daughters and little dogs. The purpose of the trial stems not so much from his desire to revenge himself upon them as from his obsessive quest for the answer to "Is there any cause in nature/ that make these hard hearts?" This question is related to the main theme of the play, which concerns the human condition. And the actor should give the question due focus by pause, meditation, etc., after asking it.

Shakespeare sets off this theme by audience laughter at Lear's remark to naked Poor Tom, "I do not like the fashion of your garments," and by bringing to a close Lear's present journey into fantasy. Now the mentally, emotionally, and physically exhausted old man lies down on his imaginary royal bed and asks that the bed curtains be closed. It is worth noticing that the Fool, ever in tune with his master's mind, should respond to Lear's ambiguous "we'll go to supper i'th'morning" with "And I'll go to bed at noon." It is only natural, then, that the Fool would humor him by also pretending to close the curtains of his bed. The two natural fools of fortune talk in riddles whose keys unlock destinies. Edgar, the Fool, and Kent sit staring into empty space as their master sleeps until Gloucester arrives with a litter to take him away to Dover to escape "a plot of death upon him."

The actor playing this scene of the play must bridge the previous scene mentally and emotionally in order to be in psychological pitch. He must feed upon the circumstance of his being surrounded by outcasts and madmen and a clown—all hostages to the tyranny of the night and hard-hearted fiends. He will do well to continue imaginatively his questions to the "learned Theban" (3. 4) to arrive at a decision to try his daughters. Although a madman, he is a king who can order such a trial before his appointed justices. Pursued by his own friends, he is in tune with his companions, who are equally possessed.[6] The actor then plays from stimulus to stimulus, conditioned by his subtextual score of actions based upon intentions, opposition, adjustments, and emotions.

In the French camp near Dover we hear from Cordelia, who has arrived seeking to rescue her father, that

> he was met even now
> As mad as the vexed sea, singing aloud,

---

[6] See "Free Imagery" for the staging of the entrance of Lear, Edgar, and the Fool in 3. 6.

Crowned with rank fumiter and furrow-weeds,
With hardocks, hemlock, nettles, cuckoo-
      flowers,
Darnel, and all the idle weeds that grow
In our sustaining corn.   (4. 4)

and she sends a sentry to bring him to her. He obviously has escaped the plot of death and is at Dover. Edgar has left Lear, thrown off his disguise as Poor Tom and clothed himself as a poor man, encountered his blinded father, and led him to Dover Cliff, where he saves Gloucester from suicide. Kent, still in disguise, follows up his letter to Cordelia, forwarded by a gentleman he met searching for Lear in the storm, and makes his way to Dover. He has accompanied Lear, who wanders "i'th'town" but "by no means/ Will yield to see his daughter" (4. 3). "A sovereign shame so elbows him" that he "gave her dear rights/ To his dog-hearted daughters" and he is detained from seeing Cordelia.

But evidently Kent abandons Lear, temporarily at least, to find Cordelia. And we next see Lear alone, singing and crowned with wild flowers, in a field near Dover where he meets Gloucester and Edgar.

Lear is in the grip of his wildest fantasy: "I am the king himself" (4. 6), he says as he hands a weed or flower to his subjects and cheese to a mouse, throws down his gauntlet in challenge to an opponent, and goes hunting. When he sees Gloucester he imagines him to be "Goneril, with a white beard." On this rarefied plane of "Reason in madness" he excoriates his daughters; pardons a man whose offense was adultery; expresses his disgust at sexual appetite and woman's body; expatiates metaphorically upon blindness and sight, the image of authority, hypocrisy, appearance, and reality. All of this has pointed relevance to his own life, Gloucester's, and everyman's.

At last, feeling the pinch of his boots, he sits down beside the eyeless Gloucester and commands him to pull off his boots. He knows him:

                    thy name is Gloucester.
Thou must be patient. We came crying hither;
Thou know'st the first time that we smell the
      air
We wawl and cry. I will preach to thee: mark!

                . . . . .

When we are born, we cry that we are come
To this great stage of fools.

This is the most brilliant moment of his enlightenment.

Then his mind reverts to his sons-in-law, upon whom he would steal with a troop of horses shod with felt and "Then kill, kill, kill, kill, kill, kill!" Cordelia's sentry and attendants come upon him at this emotional height to take him back to her, and he flees in childish glee, with them in pursuit.

This scene is the last and longest interlude of unrelieved madness the actor of Lear must cope with. In a sense it is easier to sustain because it does not, like earlier scenes, present Lear weaving in and out of insanity so much. His recognition of Gloucester and his commentary on man's existence are moments of keen lucidity, but the context out of which this behavior and dialogue emanate consists of darting, disconnected thoughts transcending reality. Throughout this scene of the play life is perceived by him in surrealistic terms—symbolically. His imagination and perception are heightened to tower over love.

Now the problem for the actor is considerable. How does he attain and sustain such a level of being? He must, in preparing himself to play this scene, go back to the seeds of the character and review their changes and growth. (In performance he establishes continuity of flowing action, speech, and emotion and he need not consciously make such a review.) In this way he will ultimately arrive at the plane of fantasy required for the characterization. In a sense it means role playing so intensively that the character cannot distinguish between fantasy and reality. Lear does play many parts, but they originate from one personality. He plays parts according to his nature. He does not, like Hamlet, put on an "antic disposition" (*Hamlet,* 1. 5) and take it off at will as Hamlet does. Nor does Lear, like Iago, who is strongly histrionic—he is to a large degree an actor—exult in his role playing. The actor acts Lear's roles in terms of his psychology and logic.

At all times the actor must avoid "acting" madness. Lear's insanest moments must be truthful to the circumstances of his character. Simplicity and economy of business and eccentric behavior, emotion, and action must be the guidelines. The tendency to exaggerate, to be strange or wild, must be avoided. Instead of trying to appear insane he should try not to. This is what he will do if he plays Lear's objectives. Besides, he should let Shakespeare make Lear mad. The actor is most convincing if he simply follows faithfully in the path indicated by the language of the play. Subtextual exploring (looking for motives and justification in the dialogue) is helpful to establish the actor's justifications, belief, and credibility in the character. Too much subtextual study and hypothesizing, however, can complicate and overload a characterization. Furthermore, such an approach can lead to "far-out" and unjustifiable interpretations. The text then becomes a vehicle for exploitation and extremist realism. Details will crowd out and obliterate the clear and simple lines of character.

In the director's and actor's study of the character of Lear the question may arise as to exactly when Lear goes insane. The answer cannot be accurate. Who can pinpoint the moment which is the clear and unmistakable turning point from sanity to insanity? If art imitates nature it will not unequivocally indicate such a point, since rationality and irrationality in life are relative. However, as early as 1. 4 we are aware of the beginning of Lear's loss of mental balance. Under the pressure of Goneril's challenge to his authority and the Fool's oblique commentary, Lear questions his identity and his judgment:

Does any here know me? This is not Lear.
Does Lear walk thus, speak thus? Where are his eyes?
Either his notion weakens, his discernings
Are lethargied—Ha! Waking? 'Tis not so?
Who is it that can tell me who I am?

These questions imply an inner conflict which shakes the foundations of Lear's reason. In 1. 5, while waiting for his horses to be saddled before they carry him and his attendants to Regan's house, he cries out:

O, let me not be mad, not mad, sweet heaven!
Keep me in temper; I would not be mad!

And he shows an awareness of the state of his mind. In 2. 4, when he is in Regan's house and has to face Goneril again, he pleads, "I prithee, daughter, do not make me mad." Before he goes out into the storm his "O Fool, I shall go mad" is an admission of the inevitability of insanity. The tempest in his mind, reflected by the storm without, in 3. 2 is the dramatization of the climactic moment of Lear's mental breakdown. His "My wits begin to turn" signals his recognition of this fact. When Lear sees Poor Tom and asks,

Didst thou give all to thy daughters? And art thou come to this? (3. 4)

he acquires a double image of life which amounts to aberration and he consistently holds it until he awakes in the presence of Cordelia in 4. 7.

Granville-Barker says that "The simple perfection of the scene that restores Lear to Cordelia one can leave unsullied by comment. What need of any?"[7] And he goes on to point out that the First Folio's stage direction "Enter Lear in a chair carried by servants" (4. 7) should be noted and adhered to by the director because when Lear comes to himself, he is royally attired and is seated as if on his throne again. When he rises from it to kneel before his mistreated daughter, the dramatic effect of his action will, the great producer-scholar implies, be subconsciously noticed. Lear must, he thinks too, "pass from the scene with all the ceremony due to royalty; not mothered—please!—by Cordelia."[8]

Seeing Lear asleep in a chair brought in by servants, a modern audience used to realistic drama, it can be argued, might well think a long sleep in a chair would be mighty uncomfortable. (Of course, the doctor could have ordered him transferred from a bed to the chair simply for the purpose of transporting him from one room to another.) Most modern productions show the old man in a sort of bed when he is brought before Cordelia. The sight of an old man asleep and sitting bolt upright in a chair as he is carried in could be strange to the point of comic. (Peter Brook's *Endgame* production of *King Lear* included the business of bringing him onstage in a chair. The effect was in keeping with the director's intention to point up the primitive, crude, and black comic tone of the play.) Perhaps the discussion of this point of staging is contentious and mere quibbling, yet the director must make a decision about it.

The dramatic effect of Lear's tottering from the chair which suggests his throne to kneel before Cordelia may be sensed by the more knowledgeable and perceptive members of the audience. Most members, however, will probably be unaware of such suggestive staging. The more universally telling part of the effect will be the King's kneeling before Cordelia. When she, in turn, kneels to him, the moment is very pathetic. In fact, both actors will tend to dissolve into tears—feeling so strongly the pity of it all and the happiness of

---

[7] Granville-Barker, *1,* 298.
[8] *Ibid.*

the reconciliation deferred so long after so much suffering. Yet it is a questionable interpretation to show Lear weeping. He asks Cordelia not to weep and goes on to say bitterly:

> If you have poison for me, I will drink it;
> I know you do not love me, for your sisters
> Have (as I do remember) done me wrong;
> You have some cause; they have not.   (4. 7)

This is what is left of his rage against his wicked daughters, and he must give vent to it with some anger and force, hardly expressed in tears. Besides, we have seen him fighting against tears in earlier scenes. Tears do not become the image of a granitic Lear which he has established. Granville-Barker would probably agree with this view of the scene.

He is certainly right that Lear should retire from the scene in all majesty—unmothered by Cordelia. Cordelia prepares us for this interpretation when she asks "Will't please your Highness walk?" The "your Highness" is surely said to encourage him to withdraw in royal dignity. It would be appropriate for Cordelia to go out on his arm—just as she might enter with Lear in the opening scene of the play! *Perhaps* some members of the audience would respond to the dramatic effect of *this* parallel action, which is enhanced by more immediately recognizable dramatic action rather than, in the case of the chair's suggesting the throne, being a matter of purely perceptive imagination. Anyway, the actors should follow Granville-Barker's advice and not make their exit with Cordelia embracing her old father or—heaven forbid—depart from the scene embracing one another!

The sight of Lear and Cordelia captured is bitterly ironical in contrast with their reconciliation and last departure from the stage together. In spite of Cordelia's being cast down for Lear's sake, Lear would lift up her spirits by reminding her that even in prison they would be together and could sing, pray, and laugh at the little world of the court; that only heaven could part them, and that only plague and pestilence could devour them. They would create a world of their own and be protected from the malevolent world outside.

Surely, Lear must be absolutely convinced that he is the "natural fool of fortune" (4. 6) when we next see him in absolute silence carrying in his arms the dead Cordelia. His

> Howl, howl, howl! O, you are men of stones!
> Had I your tongues and eyes, I'd use them so
> That heaven's vault should crack!   (5. 3)

is a curse and an exhortation to destroy heaven itself. The gods have brought him down again. His idyllic world with his beloved Cordelia has been destroyed.

> As flies to wanton boys are we to th' gods;
> They kill us for their sport.   (4. 1)

is as appropriate for him to say as for Gloucester. His mind, again unhinged, wavers between illusion and fact: Cordelia seems to breathe ("This feather stirs—she lives!" 5. 3) and yet she is dead ("now she's gone for ever!"); and he recognizes Kent but thinks "He's dead and rotten." Why should a dog, a horse, a rat have life and Cordelia no breath at all? It is a question that breaks his heart and his mind. In his death throes he thinks her lips move and that she breathes. He dies with a smile of joy on his face. But, irony of all ironies, he deludes himself even as she dies. And he dies as he lived—deluded and blind! Man's natural condition. Edgar optimistically believes he has fainted and tries to call him back to life, but Kent intercedes with

> Vex not his ghost: O, let him pass; he hates him
> That would upon the rack of this tough world
> Stretch him out longer.

and the wonder is that he has endured so long, beyond the allotted term of life.

Lear is the archetype for the self-centered, deluded, foolish, proud autocrat (so insecure that the show of authority becomes a necessary prop for self-dignity)—the natural fool whom the gods destroy for sport.

Gloucester

Gloucester is Lear's foolish twin, whose characteristics and life are in outline similar to the King's. Like Lear he is self-centered, deluded, and autocratic. His life, too, is a journey of discovery about himself, others, and the world.

Each successive scene of the play in which Gloucester appears—and he appears in twelve —is a step marking his spiritual progression while revealing some character trait. His speech in reply to Kent's opening dialogue of the play indicates an association with the King close enough to give him knowledge of his former attitude toward his sons-in-law. Now Lear seems to favor both Albany and Cornwall equally, as evidenced by the impartial division of the kingdom. Gloucester's position in court is further suggested by Lear's commanding him in his first words to "Attend the lords of France and Burgundy, Gloucester" (1. 1). Evidently Gloucester is a court functionary for ceremonials like the first scene. Changes in royal policy and the purported abdication of the King signaled by the apportionment of the kingdom must seriously concern an important courtier like Gloucester. The appearance of Edmund, however, sets him to thinking of more pleasurable matters. Such a quick change of mood is indicative of a mercurial temperament and a sensual man. (The birth of Edmund was extramarital.) The subject of adultery is vividly introduced by both Lear and Edgar in later scenes. Gloucester's jocular attitude toward Edmund suggests a certain pride in his sexual exploit and a kind of admiration for his "whoreson," who has been away nine years but who has been acknowledged by him. Gloucester's saying that Edmund will go away again is not explained, but the presence around court of a bastard son, whom he has "so often blushed to acknowledge," though now hardened to it, may still be the source of some embarrassment.

In a remarkably short time and compressed into thirty-three lines Shakespeare has set in motion a two-pronged story while he paints in broad strokes an image of the double protagonists of a single theme.

Gloucester is not present at Kent's banishment but he is at Cordelia's and, unlike Kent, he stays diplomatically aloof from the quarrel between the King and his daughter. However, in his next entrance the banishment of Kent is on his mind together with his disturbed thoughts about France's leaving in anger and the resignation of the King's power and his departure from his court. His apprehensiveness proves fertile ground for Edmund's machinations. Already feeling insecure in terms of official life, he is the more easily persuaded that his older son has turned against him. Too, parental as well as official authority is challenged. The "late eclipses in the sun and moon/ portend no good" (1. 2), as evidenced by the discord in Lear's family, the falling off of friendship between Lear and Kent,

> the bond
> cracked 'twixt son and father. This villain [Edgar]
> comes under the prediction;

When the "king falls from bias of nature" and his son is "unnatural," nature's eruption into eclipses signifies a world out of joint. He has reasons to be credulous of his son's betrayal. He leaves Edmund with the thought:

> And the noble and true-hearted Kent banished; his offence, honesty!

He is a troubled man. Call him gullible if you will.

The actor must believe that his ready acceptance of Edgar's betrayal is justified psychologically. As a type he is the sensual or emotional man but he is also an individual, influenced by his own special set of circumstances. The premise of his character is convincingly motivated for the actor. And the actor must not judge him but believe him if he is to establish a firm basis for his characterization.

Other facets of his character are demonstrated in the following scenes. He wants to make peace between Lear and Cornwall in 2. 4. Yet he is not a true activist, though he protests Cornwall's putting Kent, the King's messenger, in the stocks and he protests Lear's being allowed to go out into the storm but he says and does nothing in the quarrel between Lear and his daughters. His sense of decency does prompt him to act when he makes his decision to side with the King. This decisive action (3. 3) is the turning point of his life. It is a moment of superb bravery to go out into the storm to seek Lear, though Cornwall and Regan have dispossessed him of his own house, closed the doors against him, and threatened pain of death upon him if he aids the King. He tells Lear his

> duty cannot suffer
> T'obey in all your daughters' hard commands.
> (3. 4)

His world has been irretrievably upset and he begins to see the evil in his life.

> Our flesh and blood, my lord, is grown so vile,
> That it doth hate what gets it.

he reflects in his misery, near to madness. He takes the King to his farmhouse adjoining the castle and leaves him to make further arrangements for his comfort.

He returns to bring a litter to transport the sick, deranged Lear to Dover, where he will be able to escape a plot upon his life. Ironically, this action will turn evidence against him in the inquisitional trial Regan and Cornwall will hold.

Captured and brought before his enemies, he speaks ironically in face of the fact that Regan and Cornwall have taken his castle from him and protests that he is their host and deserves to be treated with the respect guests should show. He has values which civilized people hold. Pressed to the admission that he helped the King go to Dover and asked why he did so, he stands up to Regan and Cornwall even while tied to the torture stake:

> Because I would not see thy cruel nails
> Pluck out his poor old eyes,   (3. 7)

His reward is the loss of his own eyes.

Pushed to decisive action, his complacency and conciliatoriness behind him, he shows an innate sense of decency, duty, and justice. The man who earlier appeared self-centered, self-satisfied, reactionary, superstitious, and impulsive achieves spiritual splendor. Like Lear he is not a sympathetic figure at first but gradually wins our understanding and pity.

His protests against the gods, who kill man for sport, against "the time's plague when madmen lead the blind" (4. 1), and against his own "superfluous and lust-dieted" self betoken helpless rage at cruel life and a desire to end it in suicide. His rescue from death by Edgar, his loving and disguised son, only strengthens Gloucester's frustration at powers stronger than man. Yet he is determined to bear affliction till death. The recognition of the demented King at Dover Cliff leads him to observe bitterly:

> O ruined piece of Nature! This great world
> Shall so wear out to naught.   (4. 6)

And his fatalistic frame of mind would permit him to give himself freely to the "friendly" hand of Oswald who would destroy him. Even his second rescue from death prompts him to wish he were mad

> So should my thoughts be severed from my
>   griefs,
> And woes by wrong imaginations lose
> The knowledge of themselves.

Only in our last view of him do we hear him reservedly reconciled to life. After he hears of Lear's and Cordelia's being taken prisoner he refuses to move farther and de-

jectedly says (5. 2), "a man may rot even here." The philosophical Edgar gives him cold comfort with

> Men must endure
> Their going hence, even as their coming hither;
> Ripeness is all. Come on.

Gloucester's reply is an unconvincing "And that's true too." (He is no Hamlet who accepts this philosophy.) Perhaps Shakespeare meant for us to believe that Gloucester is genuinely sincere since, as Edgar says (5. 3), he died

> 'Twixt two extremes of passion, joy and grief,
> Burst smilingly.

No doubt his flawed heart was too weak to support the conflict of life.

Though the redemption of Gloucester may be debatable, the sound basis for his character and its development cannot be gainsaid. The actor can build it piece by piece with belief and conviction. His plight will not allow him to compete with Lear for great pity and sympathy mainly because he never confronts his real adversary, Edmund. We do not see good and evil operating in the presence of one another to demonstrate their qualities. Lear, on the other hand, is shown locked in conflict with his wicked daughters. Too, Lear, being the center of the play, has more opportunities than Gloucester for revealing his inner self, which has greater depth of feeling and understanding than Gloucester's. Our intellect rather than our emotions responds to Gloucester. Yet he is a memorable character.

Kent and Edgar

Kent and Edgar appear to be personifications rather than convincing human beings. This impression is intensified by their unrealistic disguises maintained without apparent purpose. Why do their disguises succeed even in the presence of those who know them intimately, like Lear and Gloucester? Credibility is stretched when even the Fool and Albany see them. And why does Edgar persist in his disguise when Gloucester is blind and knows that Edmund has betrayed him? Why doesn't Kent reveal himself to Gloucester when they meet on the heath? The choric nature of much of this dialogue also adds to the allegoric qualities of the two characters. The fact of the matter is, of course, that they function as dramatic devices to suit the purposes of their creator. The actors who impersonate

Kent and Edgar face difficult practical problems of acting.

Kent establishes in the second scene of the first act his honesty and candor. He sees Lear's stubbornness and unreasonableness and has the temerity to so label them. He sees through Goneril's and Regan's hypocrisy and understands Cordelia's reserve and refusal to act falsely. He perceives the difference between flattery and love, appearance and reality. His devotion to Lear as king and father, master, and patron is manifest. Duty does not dread to speak "When power to flattery bows" (1. 1), and his life is held "but as a pawn" to wager against his king's enemies, nor does he fear to lose it when Lear's safety is the motive. His admonition to Goneril and Regan to prove the truth of their "large speeches" is more of a prophecy than a challenge.

His devotion to Lear is like a dog's to its master; it is completely selfless and unchangeable. His offer of his service to Lear points up the Lear of majesty and authority and defines a true and honest subject who would serve his king. His loyalty and his forthright bluntness of speech and action are first demonstrated in his dealings with the pretentious and impudent Oswald. He suffers the punishment in Cornwall's and Regan's stocks with patience and devoted equanimity until fortune smiles once more and turns its wheels. He is an unidealistic man reconciled to the good and evil of life.

The first scene of Act 3 shows him separated from Lear by the storm and acting as a functionary of the playwright to inform the audience of the division between Albany and Cornwall and the coming of the French army to Britain. He then sends a courtier to Cordelia to tell her of her father's tragic plight. He next leads Lear to the shelter of a hovel to wait while he offers to return to Gloucester's castle to demand courtesy and hospitality of Regan and Goneril. He remains by the side of his master, tries to protect him from the storm, watches him go mad, and follows him to Dover. In 4. 7 he functions as the agent to explain plot complexities and progress. Seeing Lear and Cordelia together again and reconciled, he retains his disguise in conformity with his unexplained plan yet to be carried out and disappears until the encounter between the forces of France and Britain has been concluded. His

> My point and period will be thoroughly
> wrought,
> Or well or ill, as this day's battle's fought.

once again implies his purely dramatic function and suggests his allegorical nature.

> Told the most piteous tale of Lear and him
> That ever ear received, which in recounting
> His grief grew puissant and the strings of life
> Began to crack: (5. 3)

Suspecting the approach of death, Kent comes to the British camp near Dover to tell his king and master goodnight forever. Later, when Lear puts down the dead Cordelia and asks "Are you not Kent?" Kent answers, "The same:/ Your servant Kent." There is no further need to disguise himself. His disguise has enabled him to serve his master; that was its purpose. He has reached his goal. And when Lear dies Kent declines Albany's offer that Edgar and he should rule in the realm "and the gored state sustain" by saying,

> I have a journey, sir, shortly to go:
> My master calls me; I must not say no.

Kent's life work being over, he will follow and serve Lear even in death. Kent is the personification of service—selfless, honest, forthright, and openly dedicated. The audience sees him at first as a simple, honest, outspoken, unpretentious, and fearless man. And then, following some grand design, he disguises himself, is accepted in Lear's service, is released from the stocks for baiting Oswald, becomes Lear's personal caretaker, and plans his rescue and reconciliation with Cordelia. Once this is accomplished he sheds some of his more human traits and behaves more and more like a morality figure. At the end of the play, speaking in metaphor and rhyme characteristic of his symbolic role, he announces the fulfillment of his dramatic function.

The actor's own personality is needed to flesh out this character—if more roundness is desired. To add dimension to the character the director must select an actor for Kent who possesses interesting qualities of personality and whose presence and behavior appear real and truthful at all times. Otherwise, Kent will seem flat—as he is written. It can be argued that his function in the play does not require dimensionality. He establishes himself vividly in the first part of the play, and the average actor can make the most of his simple and obvious traits as the basis for a convincing characterization. Interest in him drops off as the play unfolds and interest in other characters grows. He is a likable character from start to finish and the actor has that consolation anyway. The character also has a clear objective: to serve. All of his actions are based upon it, and there is no inconsistency within Shakespeare's simple and uncomplex design. The actor needs only to come to terms with this design and allow the character to live within it.

The design for Edgar is complex. He starts off with hardly enough dialogue and action to make a clear impression. All we know about him before his appearance in the play is that he is the legitimate son of Gloucester and older than Edmund. He and the Fool are, as indicated in the stage directions, the only principal characters who do not attend the meeting of the court. (In my vision of the production the Fool hides behind the King's chair during the court scene.) "Pat! he comes, like the catastrophe of the old comedy" (1. 2) —right on cue for Edmund's villainous purpose. The actor playing Edgar must assume he is something of a recluse—serious and introspective if one is to believe him capable of as much philosophical insight as he demonstrates later on in the play. He seems naive in the extreme to believe Edmund. But it can be reasoned that an introvert with imagination —for his creation of the role of Tom o'Bedlam and the playing of it must be imaginative —might believe Edmund's story of his father's rage. And Gloucester was indeed in a rage. Though Edmund does not describe Edgar's alleged offense, his father immediately (and truly) jumps to the conclusion that some villain has done him wrong. Too, Edgar probably knows that his father's temperament is mercurial. And why should he doubt Edmund? He knows his brother only superficially; Edmund has been away from home nine years and is a comparative stranger. Why should Edgar suspect his brother, who is apparently an outgoing, charming, and handsome fellow? In fact, Edgar may find this stranger-brother fascinating. Besides, if we can believe Edmund, his brother is

> noble
> Whose nature is so far from doing harms
> That he suspects none;   (1. 2)

And Edmund is so convincing in his words and behavior about the matter, so suddenly introduced, that Edgar must believe him. Edmund's advice to "go armed" if he should stir abroad is indicative of the seriousness of his father's anger. The actor with a convincing image of Edgar based on the assumptions above need only believe moment to moment and respond as Shakespeare demands.

It is conceivable that the director and actor can take a cue from Regan's

> Was he not companion with the riotous knights
> That tended upon my father?   (2. 1)

and present Edgar intoxicated in his first scene with Edmund and thus susceptible to Edmund's story. Yet this interpretation of Edgar hardly fits in with the deeper nature of the character demonstrated in the rest of the play.

Once entered upon the fiction of the character, the actor, imagining himself hiding from the wrath of a choleric and volatile father, can only come out of hiding, hear that the Duke of Cornwall and Regan, Gloucester's patrons, are coming to Gloucester's castle and that the Duke of Albany has been aroused—probably at his father's instigation—and must respond to Edmund's every suggestion, including the sham duel at swords. Edgar's running away, on his brother's advice, can seem only wise. The situation seems indeed desperate. And he acts and reacts impulsively; it is no time to think.

Unlike the circumstances and actions constituting the realistic premise of Kent's character, Edgar's demand a greater suspension of disbelief on the part of the actor and the audience. The actor can find subtextual as well as textual justification for believing the basis for his character. The audience, however, ultimately accepts the premise of Edgar's character not because of its plausibility but because it is provocative and intriguing. Edmund's unabashed and blunt admission of his villainy over "A credulous father! and a brother noble" (1. 2) is so disarming that audiences find it attractive and furthermore accept his behavior out of sheer delight at his outwitting two such gullible people. Too, this "let's-pretend" basis of the mode of the play makes a strong appeal; it is an established rule of the game of theatre, and Shakespeare exploits it.

Pursued and hunted everywhere like any criminal, Edgar naturally decides to disguise himself. It is interesting that to "preserve" himself he thinks of taking

> the basest and most poorest shape
> That ever penury in contempt of man
> Brought near to beast.   (2. 3)

This thought—an ever recurring theme in the play—coming from the naive Edgar of the previous scenes is surprising. Yet it is appropriate for a morality play character to utter and it prepares the audience for more philosophical commentary by Edgar. Of course it is brilliant foreshadowing for Lear's new vision of himself when he realizes the parallel between himself and Poor Tom and man and beast. Reducing himself to nothingness as a Bedlam beggar ("Edgar I nothing am.") repeats the process to be exemplified by Lear and Gloucester in their progression from man's highest but darkest to his lowest and most enlightened state. This stripping of illusions and ignorance is found in the clothes imagery as well as that of blindness and sight. Thus Edgar functions in relation to one of the main themes of the play and is motivated on the symbolical level as well as the realistic.

He, in 3. 4, hides behind his role as Tom o'Bedlam when face to face with his father and his other court acquaintances, the disguised Earl of Kent, and the court jester the Fool. His wild, disjointed talk and behavior become a necessity to shield him against recognition when his father appears on the stormy heath. And the actor must play this intention throughout the scene. A word of warning about his role of Poor Tom. He must avoid making him too animalistic—too much like Caliban. He is a sane person assuming an "antic disposition," and too much exaggeration physically or vocally can make him repulsive and give the impression of amateurish playacting. Economy of movement and realistic detail must guide the actor. The foul fiend that continually bites his back not only suggests the madness of a beggar but the madness growing in Lear. In the fantastic arraignment of Goneril and Regan, Edgar breaks out of his role and speaks as himself when in pity for Lear he says (3. 6), "Bless thy five wits!" His first aside,

My tears begin to take his part so much
They mar my counterfeiting.

and "Poor Tom, thy horn is dry" find him wrestling with himself and coming to the end of his strength to play out his role. When Lear is taken away in a litter and he is left alone, he demonstrates his function as a dramaturgic device by commenting upon his and Lear's plight. His "Tom, away" indicates his intention to throw off the character of Poor Tom,

but he meets his blinded father and must continue to play his part; however, his choric commentary becomes more frequent. Thus he alternates between pretending to be a beggar-man, expressing his own personal reaction, and making thematically pertinent remarks. He is character, actor, and chorus.

When he arrives at Dover (4. 6) with his blind father he has dropped the language of Poor Tom and has changed his clothes into some probably furnished by the old tenant at Gloucester's request. After his father remarks that he thinks his voice is altered and he speaks "In better phrase and matter," Edgar resorts to some of the most beautiful poetry in the play when he imagines the shore below the supposed cliff at Dover. Gloucester's attempt at suicide and Edgar's saving him are purely symbolic. However, Shakespeare grounds the scene in realism in forcing Edgar to pretend to be still another character to further fool the suicidal Gloucester. The purpose of treating the scene in this manner is to underline the metaphysical aspects. Gloucester is taught a lesson about the absurdity of man's victimization and his need to bear affliction till he cries out "enough" and dies. Edgar's part is to humor Lear in his madness by giving the password "Sweet marjoram" and to guide the audience as to the scene's meaning:

O, matter and impertinency mixed!
Reason in madness!

When Lear runs away, followed by Cordelia's sentries, Edgar pushes the plot forward by asking the Gentleman about the coming battle between the French and the British. His saving the life of his father and killing Oswald ties him to the main plot when he finds Goneril's letter to Edmund. His motivations stem almost exclusively from his dramatic function. His reappearance in the play is to help organize the denouement by giving Albany the letter and setting up his role as "champion" to challenge and fight Edmund and bring evil to account.

He returns to his part as leader of his blind father, leaving him in a field between the two warring camps in the shadow of a tree, and prays "that the right may thrive" (5. 2). He darts around like the puppet he has become, more a part of the play's machinery than its life. His purpose again is to advance the theme as he reenters to announce that "King Lear hath lost, he and his daughter ta'en"—small comfort, but he gives Gloucester a chance to appear reconciled to the bitter role of a man who must endure his "going hence, even as their coming hither." And "pat," he comes again, "like the catastrophe of the old comedy" (1. 2), at the sound of the trumpet to act out his part in the doomsday ritual Shakespeare has carefully planned (5. 3). His language is formal, heraldic, and moralistic. (Even Edmund becomes formalistic in speech.) Edgar's "brief tale" about his life as a madman in beggar's rags, his meeting his blind father, his failure to reveal himself until "some half-hour past," his father's death, the appearance of Kent in lamentation over Gloucester's death, and Lear's sad story is told in morality play language—stilted and undramatic. The actor can only jog along with the rhythm of the verse and accent the allegorical nature of the scene. Only at the entrance of the Gentleman with Goneril's bloody knife does Edgar speak conversationally. His last speech, however, is in verse and serves as an epilogue to the play.

The character of Edgar consists primarily of role playing and more often takes on the aspect of art than of life. In many ways it is the most difficult part in the play for an actor, especially one trained in the realistic theatre dependent upon psychological motivation and response. Charm of the actor's personality can enhance the character and give the appearance of humanity. A sound psychological basis and moment-to-moment belief are necessary to give life to the symbolic nature of the character. Quick change of attitude and emotional adjustment are demanded. Absolute subservience to the author's every dramatic color is obligatory.

The Fool

In no other of Shakespeare's tragedies does the court jester or fool play a speaking part. (A clown appears briefly in *Othello* but his presence is dispensable and is usually cut in modern productions.) The Fool in *Lear* is organic to the play. His objective as a character makes a vivid contribution to the theme: to show everyone, especially Lear, how foolish he is. His mirroring function has already been alluded to in the discussion of Lear's character. He is thus primarily an agent of the author. His existence as a person must usually be discovered by implication rather than overt explanation or action. His humanity, however, is his most endearing quality to the audi-

ence. The director and actor must be alert to all possible evidence of it.

His "double talk" must be recognized as such: It has an inner meaning as well as an outer. His first words in the play make this clear and an audience understands it. But before we follow the sequence of his speeches let us look at the references to him before he makes his appearance in the text.

The first are made by Lear in 1. 4. He calls for his "knave," who is a boy. Whether this means in age or in looks we don't know. However, it connotes affection on Lear's part. Lear calls for him three times and says he has not seen him in two days. Lear has missed him. The Knight's answer is

Since my young lady's going into France, sir, the fool hath much pined away.

This attests to his love for Cordelia. And Lear, in self-reproach, angrily barks at the Knight: "No more of that; I have noted it well." He wants his boy to entertain him and cheer him up from his dejected thoughts centered on Cordelia.

When the Fool arrives making a saucy offer of his fool's cap to Kent, Lear brightens up and affectionately asks how is his "pretty knave." The Fool at once offers his cap to Lear, who is better suited to wear it. His double talk continues and mirrors Lear's ironical predicament. His "Truth's a dog must to kennel" is pointed at Lear's unwillingness to face truth. Lear's "Dost thou call me fool, boy?" and the Fool's answer,

All thy other titles thou hast given away; that thou wast born with.

reveals the heart of the matter for Lear and all human beings. The audience laughs delightedly and is at the same time brought up short by the depth of the Fool's observation. His

they'll [his daughters] have me whipped for speaking true, thou'lt have
me whipped for lying; and sometimes I am whipped for
holding my peace. I had rather be any kind o' thing
than a fool:

describes the ironical position he holds as court jester and as human being. Audience laughter is mixed with pity—the combination of emotions typically evoked by the Fool.

now thou art an O
without a figure. I am better than thou art now;
I am a fool, thou art nothing.

cuts deeply. Nor does the Fool let up in his caustic and profound remarks trying to make Lear see what has happened to him and what he has become. The Fool plays his bitter role with uninhibited effervescence and calculated direction. He continues his pointed conundrums even as Lear departs from Goneril's house and builds his attack to "Thou should'st not have been old till thou/ hadst been wise" (1. 5), which he says more in sorrow than in jocularity. Yet he keeps alive the exacerbating thoughts which Lear responds to with a pitiful plea to heaven to help him maintain his sanity. This last scene of the first act shows the Fool keeping up his role as entertainer with only halfheartedness. He is so much wiser than his master, yet he must flagellate him with the truth. He would make the blind see.

Forever remarking upon the ways of the world, the Fool pokes fun at Kent's "cruel gestures" to raise a laugh and comments upon man's treatment in comparison with animals'. The man-as-animal imagery is picked up again—started by Lear's reference to Goneril as a "Detested kite" with a "wolvish visage" (1. 4).

The Fool sends Kent "to school to an ant" (2. 4) to teach him not to follow Lear's example of trusting to summer days and finding himself unprovided for when winter comes. He remains silent and apart from the action of the rest of the scene and simply watches the terrible quarrel between his master and his daughters. However, Lear's "O Fool, I shall go mad!" finds him sorrowfully clinging to the old man as he goes out into the storm.

He is just a pitiful boy, "a piece of court tinsel so drenched and buffeted"[9] by the storm when next he is seen (3. 2). Lear's comforting words,

I have one part in my heart
That's sorry yet for thee

said before they start out with Kent for shelter, delight the Fool and set him to childlike dancing about and singing his charming "He that has and-a little tiny wit" to cheer up his master. His contrastingly pathetic and comic words and behavior add to the grotesquerie and mockery of Lear's. The image of a white-

haired, half-crazed old man defiantly and exultantly shouting at the elements, with his court jester—the last vestige of royalty—clinging to his tattered and wet garments, is branded upon the mind. The drama of contrasts and the juxtapositions of emotions project Lear's and man's ironical posture.

At the beginning of the next scene with Lear and Kent, just outside the hovel (3. 4), the Fool can only shiver in the wind and rain until he, ever mindful of his master, rushes to him to ward off further thoughts of filial ingratitude which lead to madness. The Fool is at Lear's side when he, "houseless poverty," is urged to go into the hovel. His cry in terror as he rushes out,

Come not in here, nuncle, here's a spirit.
Help me, help me!

is childishly pitiful. (His human characteristics seem to come to the surface more often since his master has shown concern for him.) Here he wishes to protect the King and asks for help for himself. He, finding the "spirit" harmless, is able to make a little joke about him but he is not unmindful of Lear's progress in madness forwarded by the appearance of Poor Tom:

This cold night will turn us all to fools
and madmen.

He is at the same time functioning as the playwright's mouthpiece speaking on the main theme of the play. The announcement of the arrival of Gloucester is heralded by his curiously timely allusion to "an old lecher's heart." Lear's increased interest in the mad beggar as a learned philosopher and the source of knowledge of the nature of things, it will be noted, leaves the Fool silent and neglected. Does he sense his replacement by another court jester? Anyway, he is no longer in the center of the action and tags after the others as they are led away by Gloucester.

In the opening of the last scene in which Shakespeare shows him (3. 6), he seems to be bidding for Lear's attention. He is probably buoyed up by his master's calling him "sapient sir" and joins in the mad trial of Goneril and Regan. He may even take Poor Tom's hand as they dance and sing antiphonally,

Come o'er the burn, Bessy, to me.
  Her boat hath a leak,
  And she must not speak
Why she dares not come over to thee.

---

[9] Granville-Barker, *1*, 291.

This mad fooling comes to an end with Lear's lying down upon an imaginary bed in exhaustion, asking that the bed curtains be drawn, and saying "we'll go to supper i'th'morning." The Fool's enigmatic rejoinder "And I'll go to bed at noon" are his last words, conceivably prophetic of his death.

The Fool as court jester must have meant something to an Elizabethan audience which was quite different from what he means to a modern one. He was immediately accepted as a convention and a symbol. He was the personification of wit and wisdom, and audience confidant. For today's audience he is still the source of comedy and is recognized as commentator. But he is not the uninhibited clown he once was. In fact, the modern actor often makes him too coy and self-consciously funny. The Elizabethan actor who portrayed him was the supreme entertainer, funny man, singer, and acrobat. Today it is best to play him dryly and not to force his comedy. His singing is more acceptable if it is ballad singing, and his tumbling about must be restrained. The "cap and bells" Elizabethan clown has become a cliché. It is advisable, in my view, not to have him wear the traditional cap but something subtly suggesting it. He can be seen as a kind of Stan Laurel comic—an understater of laugh lines who gives them the "dry mock." Ease and effortless behavior should mark his characterization. A naturally comic appearance and voice will enhance the role. His goal should be thoughtful laughter and not guffaws.

He is the only principal character in the play without a name. He is generic and operates on two levels simultaneously. However, the actor need only play his guiding objective, to which he must string his smaller units of intention to find and project the character's humanity, realism, and symbolism. Next to Lear himself, the Fool is beloved and moves the hearts and minds of the audience.

Cordelia

The nature of Cordelia's character in the symbolic context of the play was alluded to in the introductory remarks in this chapter. She, like the other characters, must be seen by the director and others on both the symbolic and realistic levels. It must be granted that she is "less real than symbolic" because her behavior in the first scene may seem implausible mainly because she loves and yet remains silent. She does indeed seem to be the embodiment of the idea that muteness is important to Shake-speare's intention "to dramatize the proposition that plainness is more than eloquence, that beauty is to be purchased by the weight, that meager lead, which rather threatens than promises aught, buys more than silver and gold." [10] These are intellectual and critical reference points.

Theatrically, Cordelia establishes her humanity in her very first words in an aside to the audience (1. 1): "What shall Cordelia speak? Love, and be silent." In contrast to the fantastic love trial to which Lear is subjecting his daughters and Goneril's and Regan's obvious hypocrisy in expressing affection for him, Cordelia's behavior is admirable and understandable. Her sincerity is heartwarming. What, indeed, can she say in the face of such overblown flattery? She is neither so eloquent nor so emotionally free as her sisters. Unhappy as she is at their obvious untruthfulness and at her father's apparent belief in them, she cannot heave her heart into her mouth and express her profound love for him. Since Lear makes the entire occasion legalistic, Cordelia tries to communicate with him in legalistic terms and says she loves His Majesty according to her "bond, no more nor less." This sounds hard if taken at face value, but if the actress says these words with effort to show her inner struggle, they will be softened, and the audience will sympathize with her. And who can argue against the rationality of her assertion that her sisters cannot love her father "all" if they have husbands who are entitled to half their love? Certainly the audience must find her reasonable even if Lear does not.

Lear does not understand that Cordelia's heart can go with her words, that truth can have its own value. And her "So young, my lord, and true" is an urgent but unsuccessful effort to communicate with him. Lear's demonical outburst in reply can but silence her. How can she make him understand?

Lear is not reasonable. His excessive anger borders on madness. It is out of proportion to the circumstances. Kent's efforts to make him "See better" fail. What can poor Cordelia do but love and remain silent when Kent's intercession for her resulted in banishment? She does make a final effort to vindicate herself after the King of France speaks of how strange it is that the one Lear loved most should so quickly lose his favor. Her admission that she has not

---

[10] Fraser, p. xxx.

that glib and oily art
To speak and purpose not, since what I well
  intend,
I'll do 't before I speak—

only evokes the hard, authoritarian, and self-centered reply that it would have been better had she not been born than to have displeased him. His subsequent rejection of her with

Thou hast her, France; let her be thine, for we
Have no such daughter, nor shall ever see
That face of hers again. Therefore be gone
Without our grace, our love, our benison.

can only leave her in tears. Yet she is strong enough to control herself, to tell her sisters she knows what they are, and to prophesy that time will uncover their evil cunning.

Cordelia is the victim of the conflict between feeling and reason. Too, perhaps defensive pride reveals itself in her words and deeds. This public trial of her love for her father must be embarrassing for one so emotionally reserved. In fact, it is humiliating to be treated so in front of her sisters and the court. Is it any wonder that she fights back? She is no Ophelia but a strong, proud young woman who is sincere and honest, though being so costs her disinheritance and banishment from her home and native country.

Her reserve has been called fatal. Shakespeare does not tell us why she is reserved, but we can imagine that she has had little opportunity to be affectionate with a father so lacking in understanding, so dictatorial and selfish. Evidently the Fool and Kent know and understand her better than her father, as evidenced by their love for her. Even the King of France, in a limited acquaintance with her, treasures her enough to accept her to be "queen of us, of ours, and our fair France." Nor can "all the dukes of wat'rish Burgundy . . . buy this unprized precious maid" of him.

Her return to Britain with the French forces ready to make war against Lear's enemies is primarily in the interest of her father:

O dear father,
It is thy business that I go about!
. . . . .
No blown ambition doth our arms incite,
But love, dear love, and our aged father's right.
(4. 4)

She is a selfless love personified, a servant to the King, her father. Her mission in life is recognized in her symbolic role. She even possesses prescience that her "life will be too short,/ And every measure" (4. 7) will fail her when she asks Kent how she will love and work to match his goodness. When she and Lear are made Edmund's prisoners she thinks only of her father (5. 3):

For thee, oppressèd King, I am cast down;
Myself could else out-frown false Fortune's
  frown.

She knows her destiny:

We are not the first
Who with best meaning have incurred the
  worst.

Contrary to Kent's wish, "The gods to their dear shelter take thee, maid" (1. 1), she is abandoned by them and hanged by her father's enemies. The gods do not defend her! She, like Lear, is a "natural fool of fortune" (4. 6), a puppet who plays out her destiny at the end of strings manipulated by her creator. Yet she is all too human, with strength and weakness, and the actress must find the creative stimuli which will make her truthful and recognizable. The audience is ready to love and believe in her.

She will find her second scene, in 4. 4, the most difficult to act. First of all, the audience sees her after the Doctor evidently has told her something about Lear and she identifies him with "Alack, 'tis he!" and then describes how he was seen. (The stage directions indicate that they enter, and obviously they have been talking.) This means that the actress must be thinking of the Doctor's remarks before she speaks. Perhaps the Doctor has seen an old man wandering about and has asked Cordelia if he could be Lear. These imaginary remarks must be verbalized in her mind in order to continue the conversation convincingly. In addition to this difficulty, the actress must reestablish her character after a long physical absence from the stage, though her spiritual presence has been felt in many scenes. It can be reestablished only if she fills in her life imaginatively between the time of her departure for France and that of her return to Britain. In the present scene she also has the problem of speaking to someone and thinking aloud, and her dialogue is not easy to articulate and communicate. However, the actress must play each moment for its full emotional value. The audience will apprehend in a general way, though it may not comprehend each detail of thought and feeling. As a scene, it is transitional in the general pattern of plot progression, rather than critical. It is a part of the urgency, excitement, and movement of the play and should be played in relation to the rapid, suspenseful rhythm of the cumulative power of the organizing forces contributing to the denouement of the play. The focus of audience attention is no longer on Lear himself but on those surrounding him, for and against him. The emphasis is on outward action rather than on the inner drama of the protagonist. This scene pushes the plot forward and develops character only in Cordelia's last speech, already referred to. Yet the scene is dominated by Cordelia and reflects her character at each moment. The actress must seek for the widest possible emotional and mental color range to give the scene intrinsic interest. By no means should the director allow her and the other characters to rush through the scene for pure plot expositional values. Too, the Doctor is a new character and should be of interest to the audience, though Shakespeare has given the actor little to say or do. The actor playing the part can be cast specifically to evoke interest by his presence and personality, which will add a dimension not in the writing of this scene. However, his character is more firmly projected in the next scene in which he appears, and the actor may study that scene to find more varied character facets which form the basis of the character.

The urgency of finding Lear and bringing him to Cordelia and the appearance of the Messenger announcing that the British are on the march quicken the tempo of the scene. Audience interest, however, is on Cordelia and her actions in behalf of Lear.

The seventh scene of Act 4, marking the reconciliation between father and daughter, almost plays itself. It is highly gratifying for the audience, so long has it been wished for and anticipated. It is inherently so full of emotion that, as has been pointed out in the discussion of Lear's character, the two principal actors need only to restrain their personal emotions and remember that Lear and Cordelia are not sentimentalists but are characters of dignity and strength.

Albany

In the first words of the play Kent says that he thought the King loved Albany more

than Cornwall, and Gloucester held a similar view. But now that the kingdom has been divided and each has been given an equal share, it is not apparent whom Lear loved more. When the court assembles, the King indicates his impartiality and declares his desire to proclaim his daughters' inheritances in order to prevent future strife. Evidently he knows of the rivalry between the two families. However, it can be assumed by the director and actor that Albany probably had found favor with his father-in-law, and there is ample evidence to indicate Albany's affection for the King.

In the first scene of the play Albany speaks once and then only in unison with Cornwall in trying to dissuade Lear from striking Kent. His next appearance and words come in the fourth scene. Here he arrives in the middle of the quarrel between Goneril and her father and is ignorant of the cause. He is conciliatory toward Lear and when he sees the old man in a rage, weeping hot tears, he protests against Goneril's behavior though he admits his great love for her. He is obviously torn by his devotion to them both. Although he cautions Goneril not to make matters worse between her and Lear, he takes no definite stand and trusts to the future. Goneril speaks of his "milky gentleness" but she does not condemn him.

Obviously Albany is a gentle man who is in love with his wife and dominated by her in this scene. (It is possible that he is passionately in love with Goneril, who may be sexually attractive and physically satisfying to him. She would take advantage of this fact, and her behavior toward him in the fourth scene could indicate it.) The fact that, when the audience next sees him, he turns against Goneril in outrage and anger and from then on shows his strength, proves that he is not a weak man. It is important, therefore, to cast an actor in this part who is tall, physically magnetic, with a likable personality and a pleasant voice. It should gradually occur to the audience that there was reason for Lear to like him and that he respects and reveres the King.

Albany not only is mild mannered but he is also religious. In trying to find out the reason for Lear's curse against Goneril he asks (1. 4): "Now, gods that we adore, whereof comes this?" When he castigates Goneril for mistreating Lear, "A father, and a gracious agéd man" (4. 2), he calls upon the heavens to "Send quickly down to tame these vile offences." And above all is his imprecation that the heavenly powers "defend" Cordelia in the last scene of the play.

In the fourth act Albany, responding to his sense of justice and human decency, is a changed man—and Oswald prepares the audience for his new appearance while informing his mistress Goneril of Albany's reaction to news of previous events at Gloucester's castle. The actor of Albany should not, however, lean heavily upon this dialogue to mark the transition in his character. In the previous scene with Goneril after Lear's departure for Regan's house, he can show Albany torn between his love for Goneril and his feeling for Lear. In this scene the audience should recognize signs of rebellion against Goneril. He takes Goneril's side only momentarily. In other words, the director and actor should point up his ambivalence and thus foreshadow the complete change which comes over him between the first and fourth acts. And incidentally, Goneril, like other characters in the play, is proved blind. She does not see the true identity of one close to her:

> It is the cowish terror of his spirit,
> That dares not undertake; he'll not feel wrongs
> Which tie him to an answer.   (4. 2)

Indeed, Albany not only turns against Goneril but also swears revenge on those responsible for blinding him.

On Albany's entrance in Act 5 at the head of his troops, it is obvious that he is a man of action and cognizant that France invades the land together with others who find Lear's cause just. However, he is persuaded to combine his forces with Edmund's and Regan's against the common enemy, forgetting personal grievances temporarily. The letter delivered to him by the disguised Edgar will change his course of action. In fact, insofar as his relationship to the play's main sequence of events is concerned, his course of action is dictated to him by an omnipotent force, that of his creator Shakespeare. Though his reply to Edmund (5. 1), "We will greet the time," may be construed to mean that he will be ready for the French army, it also may imply his readiness for all eventualities, military, personal, and dramatic. Albany is a different man after his disillusionment with his wife and his assumption of command of his soldiers. He is no longer hesitant and ambivalent. He seems propelled by an invisible force and aware of

his destiny to play out the role created for him. He is the reigning power in Britain, now that the Duke of Cornwall is dead, and he realizes his royal obligations too. He is a man of some political stature now, and his bearing reflects it.

His arrival on the battlefield, after Lear and Cordelia have been made prisoners by Edmund, is of such impressive dignity and his language is so formal that his words and deeds have a ritualistic coloring. It is obvious that a confrontation between good and evil is imminent and that the Duke of Albany is the figure who will judge Edmund, Goneril, and Regan. Except for the domestic bickering between Goneril and Regan over Edmund, the first part of this scene is heraldic and proper for a joust between knights. Goneril and Albany humanize it by their emotional outbursts against one another and Goneril's coldly wrathful departure from the scene. Afterward, Albany resumes his office as master of ceremonies and presiding judge and questions Edgar to bring out his, Gloucester's, and Kent's stories. He continues to function in this role until he resigns his royal rights to Kent and Edgar.

Albany is a rewarding character for the actor. His objective is definite and his progression is clear. His humanity is obvious and affective, and his symbolic value is easily sensed. His function is organic to the play and he operates logically out of his context. The actor creates the character from a sound and convincing psychological basis and builds from ambivalence to effect a firm, strong, and favorable impression upon the audience.

Edmund

Edmund is one of "Hell's Angels"—in the mythological and in the modern sense: He is Mephistopheles in a black leather jacket decorated with shiny, raised metal buttons, sitting astride a red motorcycle. He is, as he announces in his first soliloquy (1. 2), a child of nature.

> Thou, Nature, art my goddess; to thy law
> My services are bound.

He is untouched by civilizing moral or ethical values. He is a hoodlum. He is untouched by custom, conventions, or other restraints. He was conceived as a result of his father's and mother's natural desire—uninhibited by marriage or moral conviction. He is a logical result of their union, biologically and spiritually. Born out of his parents' self-gratification, he pursues life for his own pleasure. He is a rebel with a cause—his victimization by bastardy. He seeks status and

> Edmund the base
> Shall top th' legitimate . . .
> Now, gods, stand up for bastards!

Edmund is attractive physically and mentally. An iconoclast and a rebel are ingratiating because they dare to do what the conforming majority do not. As such he is unpredictable, surprising, and therefore comic. His frank and open wickedness, like that of Mephistopheles, is charming and amusing. All in all, Edmund is colored by modernity: His prototype in contemporary society is to be seen everywhere—not so much in action as in attitude. The expression of this attitude in frequent soliloquy achieves an intimacy with the audience and enhances his appeal.

His soliloquies are also prologues and epilogues to his actions, informing the audience what to expect and inviting it to see his actions on a double level. He is himself when alone in soliloquy and the actor of a role when with others. Like Iago, he is a most convincing actor—and must be one in order to succeed in his relationship to other characters. The greatest demands made upon his histrionic powers occur in the scenes with Gloucester and Edgar. His artful leading and persuading of his father in 1. 2 is reminiscent of Iago's seduction scene with Othello. His dissembling serves him well in 2. 1, when he not only persuades Gloucester of Edgar's physical attack upon him but of Edgar's threat against his father's life. Gloucester rewards him by making him his heir. His "virtue and obedience" to his father win the patronage of the Duke of Cornwall. He also manages to call himself to the attention of Regan when he agrees with her contention that Edgar was a "companion with the riotous knights" who served her father. The "base" thus tops the legitimate!

As Edmund climbs the ladder of power he continues to be the actor with infinite flexibility and versatility. He plays many moods and emotions and is quick to respond, to adjust mentally, physically, and emotionally to changing circumstances. Chameleonlike, he changes emotional colors to fit the moment and to enhance his position. In the scene (3. 3) in which Gloucester reaches his de- cision to side with the King, Edmund gives the impression that he sympathizes with his father and condemns the actions of the Duke of Cornwall and Regan. Shakespeare gives him only a short line of dialogue to verbalize this: "Most savage and unnatural!" But words could not be more dramatic. They not only comment with truth upon the Duke and the Duchess but, later, when Edmund is alone and expresses his intention to betray his father, they underline Edmund's own actions with shocking irony.

It is interesting to note the theme of generational cannibalism expressed in the rhyming two lines that end Edmund's soliloquy and close the scene. His "The younger rises when the old doth fall" is the ultimate rationalization of a young man who falsely accused his brother Edgar of writing a letter expressing youth's rebelliousness against age and alleged parental tyranny. The letter reveals Edmund rather than Edgar. When Edmund tells his father,

> But I have heard him oft
> maintain it to be fit that, sons at perfect age, and fathers
> declined, the father should be as ward to the son, and
> the son manage his revenue.   (1. 2)

he imputes a way of thinking to Edgar that is true only of himself. Of course this theme of generational rivalry and struggle for power is further dramatized by Lear's conflict with his daughters and proclaimed in Goneril's and Regan's speeches at the end of the early scenes of the play and most forcibly before Lear rushes out into the storm.

Edmund's expectation of reward for the betrayal of his father is fulfilled handsomely when Cornwall makes him Earl of Gloucester (3. 5); the son becomes the father in title and in material goods. Again Edmund in this scene ironically portrays his devotion to loyalty, a loyalty to his patron stronger than that to his father, "Though the conflict be/ sore between that and my blood," he says. His quick agreement not to be present when Cornwall vows to have his revenge on old Gloucester proves how weak is his feeling of loyalty to his father. Edmund, newly elevated to the title of Earl of Gloucester, his mind and heart charged with a desire for more power, barely considers what will happen to his father. Besides, he has been designated escort to the

King's daughter, the Duchess of Albany. On top of this honor he is entrusted with the organizing of armed forces to help defend the country against the army of France, now landed on British soil. Both assignments have fascinating possibilities for Edmund.

We see what they are so far as Goneril is concerned. (Regan later says in 4. 5,

> She gave strange oeillades and most speaking looks
> To noble Edmund.

when she last saw them at Gloucester's castle.) And when Goneril and Edmund arrive before the Duke of Albany's palace, Goneril orders Edmund back to Cornwall to make his troops ready and lead them. She gives him a remembrance, kisses him passionately, and encourages his love for her and his ambition for political power.

Returning to Gloucester's castle, he learns of Cornwall's death and assumes command of his troops. The audience next sees him at the head of Cornwall's army and accompanied by Regan (5. 1). It is obvious that he is in a position of power, militarily and personally. Regan is his for the asking. The entrance of Albany and Goneril and their forces finds him heady with power, and he even speaks sarcastically to Albany when the latter speaks so fairly of the "just and heavy causes" of those who are partisan toward the King. He urges Albany to draw up his forces for battle. Then, in a soliloquy to the audience, he evaluates his position with both Goneril and Regan and wonders which one he shall take: He has sworn his love to both and shall he take "Both? One? Or neither?" (5. 1) Besides, Albany is in the way and it is up to Regan to "devise/ His speedy taking off." He plans to imprison Lear and Cordelia without pardon when the battle is won. And he means to rule over all.

When the battle is over and he has his royal prisoners, he orders the execution of both. When Albany arrives with Goneril and Regan (5. 3) and commands that the prisoners be handed over to him, Edmund answers like a seasoned modern politician and diplomat. The King and his daughter are under protective custody until they can be brought to trial. Throughout the quarrel over his status and prerogatives and up to the fateful encounter with Edgar and trial by sword he tries to brazen it out in desperate delusions of grandeur. Though a knight and entitled to decline to duel with one of lesser rank, he agrees to fight his unknown adversary. Even after he has been vanquished he is still thinking of the privileges of blood and office to forgive the victor "If thou'rt noble." Then when Edgar reveals himself he agrees that the gods are just and their father's sins have cost him his eyes. The wheel has come full circle, and Edmund is at the bottom of its turn—where he started.

In death, Edmund realizes, he will become one with both Goneril and Regan, who have met their death too. "Yet Edmund was beloved," he says. He has achieved that status anyway and in spite of his nature tries to do some good and confesses his and Regan's order that Cordelia be hanged in prison. Up until the end of the play Edmund is psychologically consistent and convincing, but he, like the other characters, becomes a figure in a morality play when he realizes that death is imminent. His contrition and change are indeed arbitrary but they conform to well-established theatrical convention, and the audience recognizes and accepts that convention. The quick tempo of events helps to suspend disbelief. Besides, there is audience gratification at his ultimate transformation. The unmoral has become moral. Shakespeare wrote in the popular tradition. The actor need have no qualms about Edmund's last scene nor ask any questions about psychology; he need only trust Shakespeare, who has proved over and over that he knows his business.

Goneril and Regan

With Edmund at the apex these two characters form a triangle of lust and evil. In their overblown speeches proclaiming their love for Lear, they are suspect of hypocrisy. The simplicity and restraint of Cordelia's asides provide the contrast in sincerity. Her words of farewell to her sisters leave no doubt of her attitude toward them. Nor are we in doubt as to Goneril's and Regan's opinion of her. The masks of these two fall completely when they are left alone and we see them in their cunning and in their considerable strength. It is clear too that they have estimated Lear's physical, mental, and psychological condition with accuracy and truth. Regan's

> 'Tis the infirmity of his age; yet he hath ever but slenderly known himself.   (1. 1)

in particular makes a deep impression on an audience knowledgeable in psychology.

In spite of their obvious jealousy and hatred of Cordelia, whose victimization has won our sympathy, they are realistic and reasonable. The trouble is, of course, that they are coldly reasonable. This evaluation of their father is clinical rather than human. Moreover, they realize the inherent danger to themselves in

> the unruly waywardness that infirm and choleric years bring with them.

The lines are unmistakably drawn, and war is inevitable between them and Lear.

In this colloquy at the end of 1. 1, Goneril and Regan establish their similarity of character in certain respects, but differences also emerge. Goneril is the dominating figure, with Regan in subservient agreement, but Regan's more economical language is not only more rational but also more memorable. Goneril is the more impulsive and emotional of the two; and she is the stronger as well as the older. She is also the more active of the two: At the end of the scene Regan says, "We shall further think of it" but Goneril insists "We must *do* something, and i' th' heat" (1. 1; italics mine).

It is important for the director and actresses to communicate the contrast between these two to the audience. First of all, the contrast can be projected by the physical appearance and emotional tone of the actresses. Regan might be small and delicate of stature and feature and soft of voice, and Goneril Amazonian in size and deep-throated. Opposite casting might be the fresher approach if the tragic grandeur of the play is not diminished. Both, however, are monsters, animalistic, and prototypes of evil, and this must not be scanted. The magnitude of their presence must be apparent to counterbalance Lear's own monstrous behavior. In spite of his unsympathetic qualities it must be clear that those of Goneril and Regan are even more unsympathetic.

Some actors find it difficult to play unsympathetically, so avid are they for audience approval and so strongly do they tend to judge their roles from a point of view of morality, fairness, and justice. Too, actors tend to think in terms of what *they* would do and say rather than what the *characters* would do and say. They investigate a role in the context of their own psychology, thoughts, and feeling. The modern psychological Stanislavski approach to Shakespeare, especially, must be controlled and modified to conform to the allegoric or symbolic nature of his characters. Justification and belief must be founded upon theatrical circumstances, not personal, everyday, prosaic ones. The actresses playing Regan and Goneril need to think of Lear's autocratic and repressive hold over his court and his children. Rebellion against unreasonable parental authority is justifiable against their father. Years of suppression and self-centeredness, once broken by the wealth and power with which he invests them in the division of the kingdom and his abdication from the throne, can only result in their excessive reactions. They revolt in a spirit of revenge against real and imagined parental wrongs. They become drunk with new and unaccustomed power. Certainly the two actresses will have no difficulty in finding sufficient examples in the behavior of children today. And like such children they are not entirely unjustified in their behavior.

Lear's choleric and arrogant dealing with Goneril's servants and the unbridled behavior of a hundred knights quartered in her house inevitably cause continual disturbances. Goneril is justifiably upset. Lear is a troublesome and unreasonable guest. His outbursts of anger and his incredibly barbaric curse against her must arouse at least a degree of sympathy for her even though she urges Oswald to incite her servants to impudence and disrespect in order to bring to issue the conflict between her and her father.

His angry flight to Regan can bring him little comfort. The two sisters have already prepared themselves for his irrational behavior and they have leagued themselves against him. Cornwall and Regan confront him with cold arrogance. Regan's argument that he is old and should be ruled by discretion is unfeeling and unsympathetic, and her assertion that she is away from home and without provision needed for his entertainment is evasive. What does he need of even fifty followers, since their upkeep and number are cause enough to dispense with them?

> Should many people, under two commands, Hold amity? 'Tis hard, almost impossible.
> (2. 4)

Why does he need so many attendants when there are twice as many servants in her home to serve him? She and Goneril are reasonable and practical. They are impervious to his spiritual needs, the needs of a man who was once king.

They try to justify themselves in practical terms:

> This house is little: the old man and's people
> Cannot be well bestowed.

says Regan. Goneril rationalizes that

> 'Tis his own blame; hath put himself from rest,
> And must needs taste his folly.

Regan counsels Gloucester to shut up his doors:

> He is attended with a desperate train,
> And what they may incense him to, being apt
> To have his ear abused, wisdom bids fear.

They try to justify their unfilial behavior in thrusting him out into the storm.

Threatened by the arrival of the army of France to side with Lear and fearful of losing their power, they rapidly degenerate to hate and primitive cruelty. They lust for blood and they have a ready victim: Gloucester. Goneril's lust takes a second direction, with Edmund as its object. Regan, not without jealousy of her sister's opportunity to be with Edmund on their journey to the Duke of Albany, gratifies her own blood lust in the torture of the "Ingrateful fox" and "filthy traitor" Gloucester (3. 7). Not satisfied with Cornwall's putting out one of his eyes, she screams that "One side will mock another. Th'other too!" Drunk with blood, she takes up a sword against the servant who wounds Cornwall, "runs at him behind," and kills him (in accordance with the stage directions). In a frenzy of cruelty she informs Edmund's father of his betrayal and commands:

> Go thrust him out at gates, and let him smell
> His way to Dover.

Would it be incredible for her to spurn the mortally wounded Cornwall when he says,

> Regan, I bleed apace.
> Untimely comes this hurt. Give me your arm.

I think not. She might go toward him, appearing to intend to help him, and then contemptuously walk away from him and allow him to stumble offstage in the agony of death. Her lust has, like Goneril's, taken another direction.

Edmund is now the center of their world and their only goal. Possession of him and possession by him motivate their every thought and action.

Goneril has momentary advantage over Regan in accompanying Edmund to her palace. She makes the most of it and offers Edmund her love and her person as future reward. But in sending him back to Cornwall to help draw up his forces, she does not know that the Duke is dead and that his widow awaits Edmund with open arms. In her confrontation with Albany she breaks off with him and completely destroys her marriage. These actions constitute irrevocable errors and hasten her eventual downfall. Her letter to Edmund, which later falls into Albany's hands, seals her fate completely. On her return to Regan's house with Albany, she finds her sister and Edmund together and in an aside proclaims her willingness to lose the battle between Britain and France rather than allow Regan to sever the bond between her and Edmund. She agrees to go to Regan's tent and there, as the audience learns later, she poisons her sister.

The denouement of their story comes when they face one another after Lear's and Cordelia's imprisonment and they struggle for Edmund. Mortally ill, Regan is assisted offstage, and Albany confronts Goneril with her letter to Edmund after Edmund's duel with Edgar. Realizing that Edmund has received his death wound, she tries to destroy the incriminating letter and, failing that, she refuses to admit knowledge of the letter and, like Iago, seals her lips in her last defiant words (5. 3): "Ask me not what I know." With this she leaves the scene to commit suicide.

Oswald and Cornwall

These two minor figures of evil are vivid. Though the audience sees Cornwall first and hears about the rivalry between him and Albany, he does not speak and establish himself until the second act. Oswald is introduced in the third scene of the play. In making him privy to her outspoken thoughts about the King, her father, Goneril makes it clear that Oswald is more than an ordinary steward. His oily compliance with her orders in haughtily failing to answer Lear's question about the whereabouts of his daughter and his impudent withdrawal from the presence of the King mark him as a man to be reckoned with. His return to the King in a token show of subservience—possibly to give direction to other servants who are lackadaisically starting to prepare Lear's dinner—results in rudeness to Lear, and he is struck by the King. His surly and defiant "I'll not be strucken, my lord" (1. 4), said as he starts stalking out, so outrages Kent that he trips up Oswald. This humiliating treatment is not suffered gladly and will be remembered by Oswald.

The opportunity for revenge on Kent presents itself when at Gloucester's castle he tells Cornwall of the King's striking him and Kent's tripping him from behind. Kent is forthwith put into the stocks, and Oswald delightedly exits with Cornwall and Regan. (Kent's angry but comical description of Oswald, prior to the arrival of the Duke and the others, as a servant aspiring to gentility—conceited, fastidious, sycophantic, effeminate, and foppishly dressed—paints a complete portrait.)

Oswald's action in the play illustrates these traits. The overruling one is his ambition—his desire to elevate himself above his class. His actions at the beginning of the scene in which he meets Kent and asks where he may stable his horse may, for example, be interpreted to show condescension to Kent which would reflect pretensions to a high social level. His asking if Kent is a servant of the house might be part of this attitude. Of course, the darkness of early morning might explain his protesting that he doesn't recognize Kent. But it is consistent with his character to pretend he doesn't know a person as poorly dressed as Kent. Another approach to the scene by the actor playing Oswald is to recognize Kent as the man whom he fears because of his tripping him and threatening him at Goneril's palace and then to pretend not to know him.

Not unlike Edmund, he is completely devoid of principles, would like to be socially and professionally "legitimate," and uses his wits to climb to power. Confidant of Goneril, he finds himself in a bargaining position with Regan and, on the promise of a reward to kill the blinded Gloucester, actually attempts to kill the old man. But Edgar saves his father and slays Oswald. Oswald's last words are a request for a decent burial and an anguished cry that death is untimely: He dies without achieving his ambition. Shakespeare, in effect, allows Oswald to write his own epitaph—and gives the actor a sound and clear basis for characterization.

Cornwall, though almost unnoticed by the audience in scene 1 of the play, makes a definite impression in 2. 1 when he and Regan arrive at Gloucester's house. His alliance with Edmund in the words

> you shall be ours.
> Natures of such deep trust we shall much need;
> You we first seize on.

shows authority and suggests a man to whom the use of force is a natural habit. His reaction to Kent's complaints about Oswald and his subsequent stocking of Kent demonstrate his arrogant, hard, and cruel nature. His reply to Gloucester's protesting such treatment of the King's messenger with "I'll answer that" (2. 2) implies the possession of power to support his words. Gloucester's warning Lear of

> the fiery quality of the duke,
> How unremovable and fixed he is
> In his own course.   (2. 4)

makes clear his choleric and stubborn character. He will not brook opposition. Like any petty tyrant drunk with new-won power, he takes every opportunity to show it. He showed it to Kent and, after Regan and Goneril defy Lear, he boldly admits to Lear that it was he who stocked the King's man and, demonstrating a cold disregard for the welfare of others, suggests that all withdraw into the house out of the impending storm. He insists that Gloucester let Lear go his way into the storm since he "leads himself" and he orders that the doors be shut against the old man.

Revenge is a natural motivation for such a man. When he learns from Edmund that Gloucester has aided Lear and has allegedly betrayed him by siding with the French, it is not surprising that the revenge he will exact will be horrible. He gets Edmund out of the way on the pretext that the revenge he is bound to take will not be fit for Edmund to behold. This is not a demonstration of his consideration for Edmund's feelings but a practical precaution not to have the son present at his father's inquisition and torture. His speech to Regan before Gloucester is brought before him reveals him in all his savage, animalistic anger. Though he says he may not pass judgment upon Gloucester's life without a formal trial, yet his power shall indulge his wrath, "which men/ May blame, but not control" (3. 7). And only blood will assuage his anger. The gouging out of Gloucester's eyes is a characteristically primitive act for Cornwall. When his servant protests his action, Cornwall is consumed with passionate rage. Under ordinary circumstances a nobleman trained in swordsmanship should be able to defend himself in a duel with an unpracticed servant but, screaming with anger at the effrontery of a serf, he completely loses control and is mortally wounded.

This despicable man of brute force, devoid of human feeling, is nevertheless a weakling. Dominated by a strong and autocratic father-in-law who is King, he finds power suddenly in his grasp. Unused to it, he uses it prodigally for fear of losing it. The consort of a princess, he is ever mindful of her rank, and newly won power is compensation for his feeling of inferiority. On his arrival at Gloucester's castle he defers to Regan except when he uses his new authority to ally Edmund with him. When Lear arrives he permits Regan and Goneril, the royal princesses, to do the talking. Once he interrupts the quarrel to assert his authority in stocking Kent. He seems to be trying to assert himself and live up to his new status. His "Leave him to my displeasure" (3. 7) in response to Regan's and Goneril's "Hang him instantly" and "Pluck out his eyes" seems another effort to assume authority. And though Regan takes the lead in calling for death by hanging, Cornwall takes his cue for bloody torture from Goneril but complies with Regan's advice to put out the other eye. In some ways the inquisition of Gloucester and his torture appear to be a contest between Regan and Cornwall to outdo each other in savage revenge. Usually Regan takes the lead and Cornwall follows. Actually he is dependent upon her; this is a consequence of the difference in rank between the two and a difference in personal, social, and political degree of security. His dependence upon her is most vivid and ironical when, at the end of the scene in which Gloucester is blinded, he moans,

I have received a hurt. Follow me, lady.

. . . . .

            Regan, I bleed apace.
Untimely comes this hurt. Give me your arm.

Her rejecting him, as I have suggested in the staging of the scene, will point up his dependence upon her and his inherent weakness. Gloucester's word picture of the man is in-

complete. The actor can find the rest in his actions and psychology in order to give reality to the embodiment of evil.

PROBLEMS

1. Compare *A Midsummer Night's Dream's* "level of being" with that of *The Merry Wives of Windsor.*

2. Make a similar comparison between *Much Ado About Nothing* and *Cymbeline.*

3. Determine the psychological basis for the following characters: Oberon and Titania in *A Midsummer Night's Dream;* Benedick and Beatrice in *Much Ado About Nothing;* Imogen and Posthumus Leonatus, and Guiderius and Arviragus in *Cymbeline;* Bushy, Bagot, Green, Henry Percy, and Sir Stephen Scroop in *King Richard II.*

4. Find an objective for each of the characters in problem 3. Select a scene made up of units of the objective for a character and rehearse the scene for presentation to the class. The class should not be told what the overruling objective for a character is but should try to determine it on the basis of the scene presented. The director should check his intentions with the reactions of the class.

5. Select a scene and plan the outline of a "mirroring" improvisation and work out the improvisation in class. At a later date present to the class the scene from the play which served as the basis for the improvisation.

6. Find subtextual material for an "enriching" improvisation. Work out the improvisation for the class and later present the scene from the text.

7. Present a "continuing" improvisation to the class and then present the scene from the text which is dependent upon the implied scene.

8. As an exercise in "character innovation" base the characterization for Duke Orsino from *Twelfth Night* on an intense hippie type. Do the same for Olivia and Viola. Present scenes to the class for criticism.

9. Visualize Macbeth as a young man married to a matronly Gertrude in the scenes prior to Duncan's murder. Emphasize a domineering mother–poetic-son relationship.

10. Find innovative psycho-political approaches to Caesar, Brutus, and Cassius in *Julius Caesar.*

11. Find untraditional characterizations for Malvolio, Aguecheek, Maria, and Sir Toby Belch in *Twelfth Night.*

12. Base the following characters on ani-

mals, birds, or flowers: Troilus, Cressida, Helen, Hector, Paris, and Agamemnon in *Troilus and Cressida*.

13. Do the same for five characters from *Richard III*.

14. Present scenes illustrating problems 9–13.

Chapter IV

SHAKESPEARE'S THEATRICALISM AND DIRECTORIAL PROBLEMS

In my discussion of the Shakespearean "mode" (Chapter II) it is apparent that his works are an amalgam of dramatic conventions and realistic techniques. Shakespeare, like all dramatists, drew upon dramatic tradition, though he was the product of his age and though he introduced certain innovations. The medieval morality play, interludes, the commedia dell'arte, the wandering Elizabethan minstrels and storytellers, and the village comics are reflected in his works and mix the past with the contemporary. His innovations consist mainly of his poetic treatment of language and his enrichment of character by his psychological insight. He shifts the emphasis from narration to character and theme. Nevertheless, it has been noted that characterization remains tied to the past. His great character studies represent prototypes and some must be seen in terms of allegory if the meaning of the plays is to be communicable.

In structure, the plays, except for the tightly structured *Macbeth* and *Othello,* are loosely organized and all are multiscened with frequent changes of locale. Shakespeare utilizes the conventions of the soliloquy, the aside, the choric figure, the prologue and epilogue. His most important convention is the use of verse —both blank and rhymed—for most of the principal characters. Edmund in *King Lear* and Iago in *Othello* are exceptions; they speak in prose. However, even their language is poetic by virtue of its imagery. Shakespeare was a poet-dramatist who relied heavily upon convention.

His frequent reminders to the audience that they are watching a play—through soliloquies and asides as well as the play-within-the-play —emphasize convention. His direct and indirect appeal to audience imagination illustrates the ambivalence between convention and realism. This ambivalence is a clear invitation to the audience to recognize the different levels of illusion and to respond to his plays with multiconsciousness. Clearly his theatricalism is characteristic of his mode of expression.

Today's director should be sensitive to theatricalism and should try to discover it in each of the plays. It makes special demands upon him, special and different from those made by the modern naturalistic-realistic theatre. To try to meet these demands it is helpful to the director to summarize the outstanding characteristics of the distinct modes of expression used by Shakespeare and by the dramatist of naturalism-realism. (The playwright today is seeking new forms and is inclined to experimentation but he writes primarily for a theatre which is basically naturalistic or realistic. These two terms are often used interchangeably, but historically and aesthetically they are words intended to represent actuality, though they differ in their means to achieve this end. The dramatic movement called realism was a revolt against naturalism. The realists wished to represent life by selected details, ordered by artistic principles. The naturalists wished to do the same thing by photographic, unselected, and unarranged details. The difference between realism and naturalism is one of degree, not of kind. Taste, selection, order, and control are used by the realist to achieve intensification or suggestion of actuality rather than duplication. There is, therefore, a range of difference between the two but they are alike on some points. With this understanding we can proceed to compound the two terms into naturalistic-realistic for the sake of convenience.)

The characteristics of Shakespeare's mode may be summarized as follows:

1. Loose structure
2. Use of conventional devices
3. Reminders to audience that theatre is not life
4. Appeal to multiconsciousness of audience
5. Appeal to audience imagination

6. Physical theatre and stage emphasizing conventional
7. Nonlocalization of scenes
8. Frequent shift of locale
9. Emphasis upon spectacle
10. Dramatic use of time
11. Archetypal characters

The characteristics of the naturalistic-realistic mode are, in summary:

1. Loose to relatively tight structure
2. Elimination of conventional devices and stress upon motive and causality of character and plot
3. Attempts to persuade audience it is watching life
4. Appeal to one level of consciousness
5. Appeal to sense of verisimilitude
6. Fourth-wall stage attempting reproduction of lifelike environment
7. Controlled shift of locale (some exceptions)
8. Absence of spectacle and concentration upon few characters except in social or political plays in which group or mob is important
9. Use of actual time

As the director works with Shakespeare in terms of theatricalism he is gradually led away from naturalism-realism, interpretively and directorially. The factor perhaps most significant in forcing the separation is Shakespeare's approach to characterization without regard to environment, which is thought by naturalist-realists to strongly influence the shaping of character.

Environment therefore is usually presented on the stage with a high degree of fidelity to actuality—often photographic. In Shakespeare the psychology of character is not so much explicit as implicit and elastic for the purposes of the playwright. Environment is not a shaping force and therefore is suggested and general. The place of action is furnished for dramatic reasons, not realistic ones. Working through the power of suggestion, Shakespeare substitutes a world of the imagination for specific localization. His stage is empty space to be filled and transformed to suit his imagination: The king's throne room becomes a battlefield; a bedroom becomes a tomb; a tavern becomes a council chamber; the door to a castle becomes the door to a house or an opening to a cave; his characters take their environment with them.

However, it must be pointed out that modern audiences, though used to realism on the stage (and on the screen and television), will respond cooperatively to appeals to their imaginative powers. When Rosalind says "Well, this is the forest of Arden" (*As You Like It,* 2. 4), even though there isn't a single tree onstage, they are willing to make believe that Rosalind has indeed arrived at the forest because they have already accepted the romantic premise of the story, have been caught up in the mood of the play, have given their allegiance to Rosalind and Orlando in their struggle against their enemies. They have yielded to the beauty of the language and the charm of the world of the play. These persuasive elements are so strong that they evoke a reality more convincing than papier-mâché trees designed and painted to look exactly like oaks and birches. In fact, stage trees will actually appear artificial in contrast to the word picture painted by the poet-dramatist. Therefore, the announcement by one of Shakespeare's characters of where he or she is constitutes a dramatic device effective on a modern stage as well as on an Elizabethan one.

Locale is also established by the presence of a character associated with it. For example, the Provost and Abhorson the executioner in *Measure for Measure* serve to create the environment of a prison. Stage properties also denote place: The executioner's ax denotes the prison; the throne chair, the king's palace; the bed, the bridal chamber; tankards, the tavern; tables and eating equipment, a banqueting room; flags and sounds, the battlefield. These devices assist the imagination to create an image of place for audiences. The director thus finds Shakespeare an active collaborator. However, the actual staging of one of his plays requires perceptive analysis and interpretation and imaginative use of the physical space of the stage.

BASIC STAGING OF KEY SCENES

We have already seen how the director may determine the placement of scenes on a reconstructed Elizabethan stage or on a modern stage setting designed to suggest the basic form of the Elizabethan stage with areas approximating the upper stage, the inner stage below, and the forestage platform. Now we can approach the problems of staging behind a proscenium arch.

Inasmuch as a play of Shakespeare's suggests many locales for its action, such locales may be expressed to some extent by parts of the set or by the set as a whole while nevertheless allowing for free play of the audience's imagination. More important than the localizing qualities of a setting are the demands of the scenes, especially the key scenes according to the structure of the play, in terms of spatial dimensions needed to contain the action—levels, places for the characters to sit, the visual relationship of acting areas, provisions for entrances and exits, and the need of furniture properties. Of course, the director's image or concept of each scene should be an overriding guide and organic to his vision of the play as a whole. However, each scene as written acquires basic illustrative physical action. If we select *Othello,* for example, we can choose the key scenes and determine their physical demands and their placement. (Two scenes have already been considered in connection with an Elizabethan stage in the section "His Stage and Ours.")

The key scenes expressing the narration and theme of the play are: 1. 1 (Iago and Roderigo awakening Brabantio); 1. 3 (Othello at the Senate); 2. 1 (Othello's arrival at Cyprus); 2. 3 (Cassio's drunken fight with Roderigo and Montano and his demotion); 3. 3 (the persuasion of Othello by Iago); 4. 2 (the "brothel" scene); 5. 1 (the attack on Cassio and death of Roderigo); 5. 2 (the murder of Desdemona, the arrest of Iago, and the suicide of Othello).

Act 1, scene 1, shows Iago and Roderigo roistering drunkenly in the middle of the night and, plotting to be revenged upon Othello, waking Desdemona's father Brabantio. His house is indicated by Roderigo's "Here is her father's house; I'll call aloud." They shout below his window and charge Othello with elopement with his daughter. In the first part of the scene it is essential that Iago and Roderigo be below the window and unseen by Brabantio. In the Elizabethan theatre, as I have pointed out before, Brabantio probably made his entrance on the upper stage and Iago and Roderigo shouted up to him from the forestage or main platform. The intention of the scene is to make them terrorizing unlawful hoodlums breaking the silence and peace of the night. They threaten the order of Brabantio's world. They are raucous, rough, obscene, disorderly—faceless evil lurking in the darkness. Iago is of course the devilish manipulator of the dupe Roderigo. He is protected by the cloak of darkness, and his voice, unlike that of Roderigo, is unknown to Brabantio, the law-abiding and respected Senator

whose sleep and happiness are forevermore disrupted.

The director is assisted by a level and an opening at least suggesting a balcony or window. However, it is possible to communicate the dramatic values of the scene without Brabantio's appearing above his assailants. It is possible to stage the scene by keeping Iago and Roderigo in the dark or in shafts of light, in order for the audience to see their faces and byplay only when they speak, and thus create the illusion of their being hidden in the darkness out of view of Brabantio. The spatial demands of the scene are small since the characters are few in number and huddled together, Brabantio and his attendants as well as Iago and Roderigo. It is helpful to play this confrontation between the two forces downstage to make the greatest emotional impact upon the audience. This is the initial scene of violence that will increase in intensity as the play progresses, and the audience should be assaulted by sight and sound emanating from an area of the stage in close proximity to them.

The third scene of Act 1, taking place in the Senate, consists for the most part of a formal trial of Othello, accused of seducing and marrying the daughter of a noble Senator. The latter part of the scene is a sort of tag which revives the second level of the narrative devoted to the schemes and plots of Iago and Roderigo. The assembly of the rulers of Venice is an emergency session to make defensive preparations for war against the Turks. It is a solemn and tense occasion worsened by the conflict between one of the noble Senators and the country's military chief. This is the core of the scene, and when the conflict is resolved Othello is appointed officer in charge of prosecuting the war and prepares to depart for Cyprus. This segment of the scene can be imagined by the director and, indeed, demands of him a certain amount of pageantry, with brilliantly gowned Senators surrounded by several attendants in dress fitting for the occasion. Fanfares announce arrivals and departures. The characters are generally static and formally grouped. A sense of ritual pervades the proceedings. The size of the scene insofar as numbers of characters are concerned should not be so large as to diminish the importance of the main characters, who are Othello, Desdemona, and Brabantio, and they should be positioned onstage to constitute the focal point of the stage picture. The Duke and the Senators represent the power of the country but are secondary in dramatic importance. They generally react as a group and depend upon the principal characters for their dramatic existence. Only three Senators and the Duke are actually needed to represent the Senate. Gratiano, Cassio, and Iago must be present for the proceedings. Officers, scribes, and attendants are background figures only and are environmental decoration. In all, the characters should number as many as ten and not more than twenty. Therefore, space should be provided accordingly. If the Senators sit down on stools provided for them, the overall space must be increased accordingly. In addition, their being seated could force Othello, Desdemona, and Brabantio into disadvantageous positions onstage unless the Duke and Senators are placed downstage or on a line with them. The acting area needed for this third scene of the play could include a stepped level right or left center stage for the Senators and the Duke, to give them an appearance of

regal power, and a center area on floor level for the principals. When the Senators, the Duke, and the principal characters depart, and Iago is about to leave, Roderigo appears out of the shadows, and the two are left alone in a small area of the stage to pursue their function in the narrative.

The first Cyprus scene of the play (2. 1) is divided into four sections: Montano and his attendants establish the quay of Cyprus, describe the storm, and welcome Cassio; Cassio welcomes Desdemona, Iago, and Emilia, and all banter uneasily as they await Othello; Iago fences with Desdemona and Cassio and eventually reveals his ulterior motive to ensnare Cassio in a web of circumstances to strip him of his lieutenancy; Othello arrives and is welcomed in triumph; and Iago instructs Roderigo to taunt Cassio into a fight and bring about Cassio's demotion. It is a growing scene in the sense that the number of characters is progressively increased and, as Iago spins his

"Othello's Arrival at Cyprus" in the proscenium-stage production of Othello *at Yale, directed by Frank McMullan, 1966. Set: John Stevens; costumes: James Harris. Photo: A. Burton Street.*

cunning and intricate web, the tension is increased. It is interesting to note, too, that the play and its characters move from the civilizing influence of Venice to the primitive and secluded island of Cyprus where both Othello and Desdemona are cut off from all outside help and become prisoners of a diabolical power—Iago. On this hell's island nature's storms subside but man's storm of suspicion and passion grows. The scene is one of great physical activity, engendered at the outset by the storm, then diminished as the characters wait for Othello's arrival, and then exploding into the frenzied movements of the Cypriot people who enter from diverse places and take their positions of subservience to their conqueror. The appearance of the soldiers who march into position to form an avenue of flags adds to the moving image, which is frozen when the lone majestic figure of Othello strides in triumph to the arms of his "fair warrior!" With the departure of Othello and Desdemona all the figures in the picture spring to life again and movement takes place over all the stage until only two figures remain in view, huddling once again in secret conversation. One leaves hurriedly, and the other remains behind as he languidly rationalizes his outpouring of hate. The stage space is put to use cumulatively in synchronization with the dramatic progression of the scene until the full stage is utilized.

The third scene of Act 2 opens with a celebration of Othello's victory over the Turks. Native girls dance with Othello's men; food and drink are in plentiful evidence. Othello and Desdemona appear to bid all good night and retire after Othello appoints Cassio officer of the night's watch.

Cassio then urges Iago to accompany him to the watch but Iago persuades him to join the revelers in a stoup of wine. Cassio assents to a drink even though he confesses his weakness to the effects of alcohol; he wants to show his friendship for the men and wishes to drink to the health of Othello. In a few moments he is drunk but pulls himself together and marches out unsteadily with the officers of the watch. Roderigo is pushed out after them to provoke a fight with Cassio.

Iago persuades Montano that Cassio is a habitual drunkard and unfit to be Othello's lieutenant. Then Cassio enters driving Roderigo before him and striking him with his sword. Montano tries to stop him and Cassio turns on him. Roderigo escapes while Cassio and Montano fight. Iago pretends to separate them while Roderigo, at Iago's command, rings the alarm bell. The fight and the ringing of the bell bring revelers, officers, men, and Cypriot people to the scene. Just after Montano is wounded and Cassio would strike him again in his anger and drunkenness, Othello enters, draws his sword, and stops the fight. The testimony of Montano and Iago's description of what happened convince Othello of Cassio's guilt, and he strips him of his lieutenancy. Desdemona enters to ask what is the matter but is told by Othello "All's well, dear sweeting; come away to bed," and is led away. Montano is helped away.

The scene that follows shows Iago hypocritically comforting Cassio and insisting on his friendship for him. He eventually convinces him that Desdemona can help him to regain his place. And Cassio exits to complete his watch.

Roderigo then rushes onstage angrily complaining that he has been cudgeled by Cassio, has spent all his money, and still has not been rewarded by winning Desdemona away from Othello. Iago urges patience and rids himself of Roderigo. Alone onstage, he tells the audience of his next step in his plot to arouse Othello's suspicion of Cassio's relationship to Desdemona.

This is obviously a scene involving many people and a great deal of movement, much of which is intense and violent. It is another full-stage scene. The setting should provide different levels to permit entrances above and below, the grouping of people above and below, and space for background and foreground action. The entrance to Othello's quarters and the area in front of it should be juxtaposed to the reveling and fighting area. The place where the watch is to be held should be above these two areas and the entrance to it opposite Othello's area.

The famous temptation and seduction scene (3. 3) is long but simple in its spatial demands. The core of the scene depicts the developing relationship between Othello and Iago. Cassio, Desdemona, and Emilia have short accessory appearances and action which seem to vary the mood and intensify the thrust of the main line of progression.

The beginning of the scene requires a small playing area on one side of the stage for Cassio, Desdemona, and Emilia. When Othello and Iago arrive onstage and see Cassio steal away guiltily, they should be preferably on an upper level and on the opposite side of the stage. This positioning of the two parties will assist the audience to believe that they are not immediately seen and heard by one another.

When Desdemona and Othello come together for her plea on behalf of Cassio, Iago remains on the upper level and at a distance from them. They could play their scene in the same area where Cassio stood. And Emilia remains to one side until she and Desdemona depart.

Iago rejoins Othello approximately center stage and both move downstage center for most of the dialogue. Then Iago exits up right and Othello follows him part way for

> This fellow's of exceeding honesty,
> And knows all qualities, with a learnéd spirit,
> Of human dealings.

turns back to center stage for the rest of his soliloquy, and is met there by Desdemona as Emilia observes from one side. The handkerchief is dropped there and is returned by Emilia.

As Emilia moves right center she is stopped by Iago, who reenters from where he left the stage. They play out their scene in this area, and when Iago commands her to leave him he comes down center stage for

> I will in Cassio's lodging lose this napkin,
> And let him find it. . . . .
> . . . . .
> The Moor already changes with my poison:
> . . . . .
> Look where he comes!

to the end of the soliloquy.

The rest of the scene between Othello and Iago should utilize less and less space as it develops to its climax—and the climax of the play. It can be imagined as a complex web of movements with Othello, the fly, kept in the center as Iago, the spider, spins his insinuations and lies. Their movements are longer and looser at first and gradually get shorter and tighter. The element of the chase, with hunter and hunted, is the key to the choreography. Iago enters, and Othello escapes but only to be progressively more strongly enticed until he is finally trapped. Iago moves behind him, in front of him, away from him, and to him. Othello moves away from Iago, to him, away from him, and finally stops moving, giving up the struggle; and kneeling down to swear revenge on Desdemona, he is joined by

his captor. Together they sway in demonic ecstasy as they pledge themselves to one another and to the death of wife and friend.

The first scene of Act 5, showing the attack on Cassio and the death of Roderigo, takes place on a street near Bianca's lodging. The audience knows that Bianca has invited Cassio to supper, and he has told Iago he intends to accept. The plot agreed upon between Iago and Roderigo at the end of 4. 2 is further evidence of the locale of the action. The action requires, first of all, a place for Iago and Roderigo to hide. Iago's "Here, stand behind this bulk; straight will he come" suggests that they hide behind one of the pillars holding up the roof of the Elizabethan stage while Cassio passes in front of them on the forestage. Othello could enter at one side of the stage or, more probably, on the upper stage to overhear Cassio's cry, "I am maimed for ever. Help, ho! murder! murder!" Hearing this as he enters, Othello recognizes Cassio's voice but he mistakes Roderigo's "O, villain that I am!" for Cassio inasmuch as he comments "It is even so." Othello departs and is followed onstage by Lodovico and Gratiano, who are attracted to the scene. They appear, like Othello, either to one side of the stage or on the upper stage. When Iago appears onstage with a light they recognize him, and Iago addresses them. Later they come from one side of the stage or from the upper stage and join Iago and discover Cassio. The subsequent entrances of Bianca and two attendants with a chair for bearing Cassio off brings the total number of characters onstage to eight. (Emilia later enters to find out what has happened and to join Iago in condemning Bianca.)

Though the scene takes place on a street which has little depth in actuality, considerable stage space is needed in depth and width. A deep forestage and an upper level are desirable if the action is to be clear and effective and if the constantly shifting focus is to be sharp. Like any act of violence in a street or other public place, it is a magnet which attracts people from every possible direction. Therefore, several places of entrance should be possible from stage right and left, and upstage. It should be pointed out here that the need for Desdemona's bed in the next scene should be considered. If an Elizabethan type of stage is to be used, the bed would naturally be placed in the inner stage behind the drawn curtain during the action of the scene we have been discussing. However, if a "space" stage behind the proscenium is being used, the bed must be brought into place in darkness at the end of this scene, and the noise of the movement of the bed should be covered by strong, loud, strident music which should end suddenly. A long pause should follow—the stage in darkness except for a point of light from a candle held by Othello, who walks a long distance from upstage slowly and in silence toward Desdemona's bed.

This short scene, preceding the last scene of the play, is one of a brief period of restrained movement and hushed but agitated voices followed by screams, shouts, and increased and hurried movements. The tempo and intensity accelerate to the point in the scene when Cassio is borne offstage when they decelerate slightly through the condemnation of Bianca and the exit of all the characters. The music at the end of the scene is a striking contrast to the violence. Such a scene of so much movement and emotional pressure requires clear choreography of movement, change of focus, and careful timing. The director must achieve order while communicating to the audience a sense of chaos. Obviously, a perceptive analysis of the physical needs of the scene in terms of space is essential.

The last scene of the play focuses upon the deaths of Desdemona and Othello, which take place on the bed. The bed, of which the audience becomes aware as Othello approaches it with his candle, not only indicates Desdemona's and Othello's bedroom as the place of action but is weighted with symbolic values. It is a property around which the action of the entire play revolves. It is conceivable that the director and the scene designer might very well visualize the rest of the play in reference to this scene in which the bed appears. (I think it theatrically wrong to use the bed in any other scene. It must be reserved for the climax and denouement of the play.)

The bed must be placed on the stage to give it the significance it deserves. In an Elizabethan theatre the inner stage, where the scene would be located, had certain built-in disadvantages, mainly, restricted space around the bed and limited lines of sight, and therefore had shortcomings for the actors and the audience. However, the bed in the inner stage had visual centrality enhancing its dramatic importance. In a modern setting the director and designer must insure its importance and at the same time provide for space for the presence and action of the characters, especially after Emilia discovers the dead Desdemona and cries for help, bringing in Montano, Gratiano, Iago, Cassio, Lodovico, and attendants.

The placement of the bed upstage center, a choice location visually, does force all the actors except the player of Othello to play below the bed and thus turn upstage. Placing the bed center stage causes it to stand between the audience and actors above it and divides the action upstage and downstage of it. All things considered, the most practical position for the bed is right or left of the center of the stage. This will permit a free acting space on the side of the stage opposite the bed. This space will permit uncluttered grouping of the actors, an adequate area for Othello's attempt to murder Iago, Iago's successful murder of Emilia, and his escape.

If the bed is right or left stage, another problem concerning its position is the question of whether it should be parallel to the proscenium opening, at right angles to it, or diagonal to it. The least advantageous position is at right angles to the proscenium opening. A position parallel to it permits action below and above joined with action on the other side of the stage. This is workable. A position diagonal to the proscenium opening has advantages for the scene between Othello and Desdemona and allows Othello to fake the smothering and choking of Desdemona while covering the action with his body and shielding such action from the view of the audience. The diagonal position of the bed permits the actors to share the scene with Othello as each one comes into focus. Othello can stay behind the bed or come down to the onstage side to speak. At the moment of his suicide he can be upstage and at the head of the bed and separated from the others by it. Thus he will fall on the bed just above Desdemona's body, and his head and arms will fall on Desdemona's breast—uniting them again though in death.

When Lodovico says (5. 2)

> The object poisons sight;
> Let it be hid.

the curtains to this inner stage of the Elizabethan theatre could be closed. On our modern stage some other device must be used. A curtain could descend to hide the bed, curtains around the bed could fall, or the lights could blot it out. A more theatrical solution, I think, is to allow attendants with long pikes to surround the bed and to dim the lights on the rest of the stage, having the light on the bed grow smaller and smaller until it goes out and plunges all into darkness. This ending of the play is in a mode of theatricalism and may serve to frame the entire play. At the beginning of the play the stage curtain is up and the setting is discovered by the audience when it enters the theatre, lighted to emphasize shadows and highlights—a place of performance rather than a specific environment—and then when the performance begins, appropriate sounds of a bell striking midnight are heard and the lights dim down to complete darkness. Out of this darkness, areas of the setting emerge to suggest a poorly lighted alleyway. As the bell tolls the audience hears strident voices quarreling in the distance. The action thus begins in darkness and materializes in constricted areas of light. As the play progresses the areas of light are enlarged, and then after the turning point in the action, Iago's temptation and persuasion of Othello in 3. 3, the darkness gradually returns, and finally the stage is enveloped in darkness again for the end of the play.

CONTINUITY

Shakespeare's plays are not plays *of* scenes but plays *with* scenes. Yet this fact does not seem to be clear to many directors. It has already been pointed out ("The Text and the Director's Working Script") that the plays were divided into scenes not by Shakespeare but by editors, beginning with Heminges and Condell, the editors of the First Folio in 1623, who, though quite inconsistent in marking act and scene divisions, made some attempt to conform to Elizabethan scholars' understanding of classical principles of playwriting. Though the published versions of the plays down to the present show act and scene divisions, the director must remember that in actual performance on Shakespeare's stage there were no breaks in continuity of action to indicate separate scenes. Continuous flow of performance in today's theatre is essential whether the performance takes place behind a proscenium, in-the-round, or on a thrust stage. Entrances and exits of characters and change of scenery, properties, costumes, and lighting should not be allowed to disrupt continuity of performance. One or two intermissions, probably not granted Elizabethan audiences, must be determined for modern audiences.

To approach the problem of establishing and maintaining performance continuity, the director must consider entrances and exits. In general, they should overlap. This overlapping was quite easily done on the Elizabethan stage, where action could shift to the forestage, upper stage, or inner stage. For example, a scene taking place in the inner stage can be brought to an end and blotted out by drawing the curtains as entering characters appear on the upper stage or the forestage. In *King Lear* the exit of Lear, Gloucester, Kent, the Fool, and Edgar at the end of 3. 4 into the inner stage, which becomes the "hovel" on the heath, and the entrance of Cornwall and Edmund on the platform or forestage in 3. 5 can serve to illustrate this overlapping of exit with entrance. (Some editors place the Cornwall-Edmund scene in "A Room in Gloucester's House" and thus indicate the use of the inner stage, but such scene localization need not bother the modern director, who must see any stage for Shakespeare's plays in terms of fluidity and nonlocalization of scenes, especially when, as in this scene, the locale is Gloucester's house in general and may be inside or outside. Some editors probably place the scene inside because of the reference to Gloucester's house and the secretiveness implied in the conversation between Cornwall and Edmund. If so, such editors are thinking of the realistic play and not Shakespeare's.)

The overlapping of entrances and exits is accomplished by timing. If the overlapping is between an inner-stage scene and a forestage scene, as in the example from *King Lear,* the curtain to the inner stage starts closing immediately after Edgar's last line, "I smell the blood of a British man" (3. 4), and Cornwall says as the curtain is closing "I will have my revenge ere I depart his house" (3. 5). Not only are the action and dialogue made continuous but the tempo also is accelerated by the emotional intensity of Cornwall's speech and the quickness of his movements. In addition, audience attention is shifted from one place of action to another. This shift brings visual change and variety and tends to add to the general vibrancy and excitement of the performance. These technical aspects of staging are involved in insuring the flow of all scenes of a play, wherever the scenes may be located onstage, whether inner stage and forestage, upper stage and inner stage, upper stage and forestage, or whatever.

A special problem of overlapping of scenes

occurs with the entrances and exits of groups of characters, especially in battle scenes. If the action occurs in one general area—though scenes may move to different camps and parts of the field as in Act 5 of *Henry IV, Part I*—they may be placed on the forestage or platform, even though camp tents may be set up and dismantled by both opposing forces. The action flows back and forth across the stage with intermittent single combat between the adversaries mixed with general combat until the climactic moment of conflict between the antagonist and protagonist—in this instance, Hotspur and Prince Hal. In addition to selecting places of entrance and patterning the action of these scenes, the director must insure the flow of scenes by blending sight and sound. To avoid the lapse in dramatic continuity which may occur when one group must leave the stage before a rival group enters, the director must shift the focus from one group and one area to another group and area immediately. He must not hold up the pulse of the scene by forcing the audience to wait until the last man of a group disappears from view before the dialogue and action can continue. In 5. 2 of *Henry IV, Part I*, Worcester, Vernon, Hotspur, Douglas, officers, soldiers, and messengers are onstage and must exit before 5. 3, when the two forces come together in general and then individual combat. To blend the scenes, the minor characters may rush off after Hotspur's "Now, Esperance! Percy! and set on." This leaves the stage to only four characters: Worcester, Vernon, Douglas, and Hotspur. Hotspur can finish his speech calling for trumpets to sound and urging all to embrace, and then as martial music is heard the four embrace and exit immediately to one side of the stage as the officers and soldiers of both sides enter, fighting, from the opposite side of the stage. Such staging will avoid the pile-up of characters at the exit, which breaks the flow of the action. Of course, when lights are used to pick out areas of action, they may fade down on one group of characters and cross-fade to another stage area and group. Lights thus change audience focus of attention and avoid a disruption of action continuity occasioned by the necessity of clearing the stage of a large group. However, the cross-fading of lights forces the group to exit in the dark, a dangerous and possibly noisy procedure. The technique of leaving the speaker of the scene's last line of dialogue onstage while most or all of the other characters exit before him is ad-

visable as general procedure for overlapping entering and departing large numbers of characters.

The techniques for achieving continuity of action discussed above, though illustrated on an imaginary Elizabethan stage, may be equally effective on the proscenium, thrust, or arena stage. The form and space of each stage will dictate the placement and timing of entrances and exits. (Entrances and exits through the aisles of any kind of theatre usually lengthen the time they require and raise the possibility of overemphasizing them and/or delaying the continuance of the dramatic pulse bridging two scenes.) Transitions need to be carefully timed and controlled. An overly long entrance or exit may be shortened by dimming the lights and bringing them up on another acting area. In general, entrances and exits on a proscenium stage are shorter than those on other kinds of stage. In order to judge and prescribe the timing for scene transitions, it must by now be obvious that the director must be aware of the rhythm of the moment emanating from the structure and curve of intensity of the play.

The overall rhythm dictates the variation of this rhythm demanded by each scene and the transitions between scenes. Rhythmic variations result to a significant extent from a change of mood from one scene to the next. Let us return to the last two scenes in *Henry IV, Part I* for an example. After the battle scenes and Hotspur's death there is an abrupt change of mood, from suspense and general excitement and pity to black comedy. This comic vein is opened with Falstaff's uneven fight with the brave and noble Douglas, when Falstaff falls down as if he were dead while Hal and Hotspur meet in the play's climactic conflict. It is forgotten by the audience during this fight and Hotspur's death. But it is revived when Hal sees the recumbent Falstaff and, not without a sense of irony, ruefully eulogizes his friend. Falstaff's rising from the ground in fright at the prospect of being disemboweled, his seeing the still form of Hotspur beside him and fearing he too has been counterfeiting death, his stabbing the corpse with the purpose of telling the King that he, Falstaff, had slain the noble Hotspur, his starting to lug the body away, his confronting Hal and Prince John with the preposterous story of his death, and his ultimately admitting his boasting and lies bring the scene to a seriocomic ending with news of a victory for the King. This sequence of events from the beginning of Hotspur's and Hal's confrontation and combat to the last scene of the play constitutes a thematic continuum. It emphasizes the theme of idealism and honor juxtaposed with practicality and discretion in the horrible and senseless context of a war for political power. To give the moment its powerful emotional and intellectual impact, a pause is needed to allow the audience to absorb its full shock and thematic thrust before the last scene of the play begins. The moment ends when the trumpets sound for an empty victory, and King Henry, Prince Hal, Prince John of Lancaster, Westmoreland, and officers and soldiers of the King take their formal positions for the final judgment of the uneasy victors over the vanquished Worcester and Vernon, the King's division of his powers, and his decision to continue the conflict. Granted this interpretation—and interpretation is the guide to the director's use of rhythmic tempo and accent—the two last scenes of the play are joined for continuity and dramatic effect.

As pointed out before, two agents useful to the director in bridging scenes are light and sound, which must be integrated with actors' movement and speech. First let us consider light. Stage light changes are a part of the rhythmic flow of scene into scene. To avoid the impression of stopping the action of the play by blacking out the lights, the director must cross-fade them. Thus the scenes can blend into one another much as they do in a motion picture. Shakespeare, as I have said, wrote cinematically. Images dissolve into succeeding ones; sometimes they collide in sharp contrast. The opening scene of *Hamlet*—misty and penumbral—is shockingly joined with the court scene with its riot of color and joyous gaiety of celebration. Hamlet, shrouded in black, is the connecting link between the two visual images created by the two scenes. A slow fading to darkness or a quick blackout serves to break the continuity of performance, gives a sense of finality, or forces the emotional impact of a scene to resonate in the minds of the audience.

As a transitional aid, light, by its intensity and color, builds mood and atmosphere and helps to achieve modal variety. When the last two scenes of *Henry IV, Part I* merge in silence and without action, the lights may suggest the end of a bloody day, slowly turning from a cloudy blue to the pink of dusk at the entrance of the King's party and, as the scene progresses, gradually intensifying to create a bold, bloody world of contention and war.

Special sound effects and music (church bells and trumpets, for instance) are effective scene connectives in Shakespeare because they may function in the place of dialogue or action and support the dramatic qualities of the moment and even add an emotional or intellectual element. They can be used to "cover" the entrance of a royal procession, marching soldiers, soldiers in group conflict, a gathering mob, a single character, and so on: the procession and assembly of the court to watch the play-within-the-play in *Hamlet;* soldiers who in *Coriolanus* line up before Corioli when the Senators appear on the walls; fighting soldiers who come onstage after Hotspur and his supporters embrace and plunge into battle in *Henry IV, Part I;* the gathering mob in *Julius Caesar* or *Coriolanus;* the entrance of Edgar to challenge Edmund in *King Lear;* or the appearance of Richard after he has been crowned king in *Richard III.* (This scene can be staged so that Buckingham and others await Richard near the throne as he enters alone to the blare of trumpets.) Sound effects and music not only join scenes but change the mood and stimulate interest in the oncoming scene. For instance, the tolling of church bells may serve to bridge the first two scenes of *Richard III.* It not only heralds the entrance of Lady Anne with the corpse of Henry VI and sets the emotional climate for such an event but the mournful sound of church bells also contrasts ironically with the cynical thoughts, speech, and behavior of Richard. And, of course, thoughts of death and religion connoted by the bells are jarringly juxtaposed against Richard's outrageous wooing of Lady Anne. Contrast of mood is effected in the reconciliation scene between Lear and Cordelia by supplanting the sweet music ordered for Lear by the stinging, harsh beat of the drum heard as Lear and Cordelia, the physician, and attendants depart and Edmund and Regan and their forces arrive.

The use of all kinds of sound in the modern productions of Shakespeare has become almost conventional. Special scores, including electronic music and other popular sounds, are composed for many purposes. Sometimes the music is used as a background for scenes, as a comment on scenes, or as a prelude to scenes. Directors and composers thus impose sound on the plays where it is not indicated in the text. The reasons for this imposition of sound are usually interpretational but sometimes theatrical—in the belief that Shakespeare can be made more exciting by music and special effects. The introduction of contemporary musical and other sounds is presumed to add an extra dimension to a Shakespearean production—relevancy. Dependent upon the director's interpretation, these sounds can be enormously effective and enhance the dramatic event if other elements of the production support them. Often, however, they call attention to themselves and seem to be extraneous. Returning to the use of sound as a connective between scenes, it must be conceded to be a potent tool in the hands of the director. It must be carefully selected for interpretational and technical purposes and not for diversionary or exhibitionistic reasons.

Sometimes sound may be used incidentally to cover scene and property changes. It maintains and furthers the dramatic pulse of the play while assisting the modern director who does not have an Elizabethan stage facility with an inner stage and curtain to hide such changes or an Elizabethan audience who will accept the sudden appearance of persons bringing onstage a stool, table, or bed in the middle of dialogue.

The problem of scene and property changes for Shakespeare on the modern proscenium stage has been one of the most difficult to solve. For many years scene and property changes have been allowed to break the flow of action so essential to Shakespearean production. Opulent productions in the name of spectacle and realism in the nineteenth century and too frequently in the twentieth century have required a great deal of time to set up the scenery and furnishings before proceeding to a new scene. Musical interludes were introduced to cover these changes. They sometimes lasted as long as forty-five minutes. This was Shakespeare with light opera—or vaudeville! The cumulative impact of his plays was considerably diminished. The enlightened director of today must be sensitive to the curve of intensity, the form, and the style of the plays and the overall emotional effect intended by the playwright—or even to carry out his own interpretational intentions. He can employ a number of methods to prevent scene changes from disrupting continuity of performance.

He and the designer can utilize the form of the Elizabethan stage and provide an area for interior scenes that can be cut off at will by a curtain, screen, or lighting for the placement of furniture and other properties. A revolving stage provides a facility for concealing one part of the stage where scene changes can be made while the performance can continue on another. Scene changes *à vista* have become popular at the Stratfords in England, the United States, and Canada. This device calls for quick raising, lowering, and "tracking" of scenery and properties integrated with entrances, exits, light, and sound. This means that in some transitions dialogue and action can be continued while scenic changes are made in the background without distracting the audience. One of the simplest devices—and similar to Elizabethan stage practice—involves the use of costumed attendants or characters in the play to remove and set up features of the setting and properties in stage areas not lighted or used by the actors or to make such changes upstage of the performers, who continue their dialogue or action. If the director uses costumed attendants to make scene changes as a convention and part of his scheme of production, he sometimes calls attention to the device. However, the continuous use of this convention—actually stopping the flow of the play to point up a directorial conceit—becomes monotonous and soon wears thin for the audience. It is more desirable to use the convention unobtrusively. Let the audience accept it as a necessary and useful device which is an integral part of the theatricalism and naiveté of Shakespearean stage conditions. It becomes a part of the acceptance of the play as play and performance. Quite frequently servants and attendants can set the stage as part of the story line. In *King Lear*, 1. 3, Goneril orders Oswald, her steward, to prepare dinner; he can supervise his servants in the setting up of tables for Lear and his knights in the background and in dim lighting while Kent appears downstage in bright light for his soliloquy. When the lights come up on the whole stage after Lear's hunting horns are heard, the servants can continue preparing dinner and be present when Lear calls for his dinner. In *Richard III*, 5. 3, Richard orders: "Up with my tent!" His soldiers set up the tent on one side of the stage. On the other side Richmond's soldiers set up his tent.

In his overall approach to this problem of scene changes and continuity the director may profitably remember the basic appeal of Shakespeare's plays: their appeal to audience imagination and willingness to make believe. The setting of properties and even scenic elements by attendants in the background or to one side of the stage while the performance continues becomes peripheral action for the eye, and the audience will willingly pretend it is not taking place. As others have pointed out, attendants involved in these actions are similar to the black-clothed property man in the Japanese theatre who is supposed to be invisible to the characters onstage and the audience in the theatre. The convention is accepted. It works on the audience's imagination. The director's techniques of joining scenes by overlapping entrances and exits, by lighting, by sound, and by strongly established conventions will not only guarantee the ebb and flow of performance but will also enhance dramatic impact.

Finally, a pattern of continuity should evolve for the director through his concept and scheme of production and through the process of rehearsals. Each scene change has its own dramatic function and should be approached by the director from this point of view before he decides on the techniques to be used. Variety, contrast, and theatricality are a part of a well-conceived, imaginative score for the director to follow. He marks his score with signals for directorial implementation.

COMBAT

Shakespeare's scenes of combat, by individuals or groups, are usually the least convincing aspects of a production. The main reason for this is the director's attempt to make them completely realistic (and thus try to copy cinema and television techniques). Everyone has seen a Shakespearean production in which actors fiercely hack away at one another's swords (usually of tin), missing the sword and hitting a tin- or wooden-sounding shield, all accompanied with unconvincing grunts and groans, many grotesque grimaces, and much straining of muscle. In an attempt to make it all realistic several of the combatants will sometime during the melee suddenly appear with a red bloodlike liquid on their hands, faces, and even clothes. Instead of achieving greater reality with "blood," they invite the audience to ask how the business was done. Under the influence of the Theatre of Cruelty and other avant-garde movements, directors and actors nowadays work out elaborate patterns of acrobatic movement and brutal behavior to stress man's cruelty—all for its

shock effect. To increase the sensationalism of a fight the actors are sometimes given more than one weapon each—broadsword and dagger, pike and spiked ball on a chain, and the like—together with spiked gloves or knuckles or even spiked leggings. Of course the actors elect to perpetrate a whole catalogue of acts of mayhem, with as much "blood" as possible, before delivering the *coup de grace* to a victim. Medieval engines of war, cannons, smoke, pikes, bows and arrows, pistols, instruments of torture, battering rams, wagons—all are used to add conviction to the scenes. But do they really? Do they not call attention to themselves and become objects of curiosity and wonder? Stagecraft takes precedence over stage life.

The skill of the actors in handling swords and other weapons may help to achieve a degree of reality in scenes of conflict (Elizabethan actors were accomplished swordsmen). Yet every audience subconsciously is aware that the people it is watching are actors who are pretending to hurt or kill one another. It knows that actors must give other performances; they can't kill off one another. The most realistic scenes of physical violence onstage can have only a momentary impact before the audience assures itself it is all make-believe. Such scenes may have greater thematic force than emotional, and some of today's directors try to justify them accordingly. Regardless of the actor's or director's skill at duplicating life at its ugliest and most horrible, the illusion created is only superficially convincing, depending as it does upon the audience's willingness to believe. Possibly one of the greatest of the historical plays based on themes of violence and brutality in war is *Henry V*. And it has been pointed out many times that Shakespeare's use of the Chorus fully proves that his kind of theatre depended upon the audience's suspension of disbelief and use of its imagination.

The Chorus joins 2. 4 with 3. 1 in *Henry V* with a narrational segment that begins with

Thus with imagined wing our swift scene flies,
In motion of no less celerity
Than that of thought.   (3. Prol.)

and brings the audience with Henry and his expedition to France to

see a siege:
Behold the ordinance on their carriages,
With fatal mouths gaping on girded Harfleur.

As he finishes his appeal to our imagination,

> the nimble gunner
> With linstock now the devilish cannon touches,
> And down goes all before them. Still, be kind,
> And eche out our performance with your mind.

The exit of the Chorus flows into the entrance of King Henry and his soldiers with scaling ladders as the explosion of cannon blends with trumpets sounding "alarums." Thus Henry and his forces may come onstage with great energy and in some numbers. Obviously, Henry and the soldiers stop fighting momentarily, and before making another charge, they

> Stand like greyhounds in the slips,
> Straining upon the start.

As they rush off to attack the enemy the trumpets sound again and cannon go off. Shakespeare provides the salient features of war, actually and imaginatively. The behavior of the actors and the resourcefulness of the director can complete the image of war. And the image is more important than the prosaic details. The audience hears the characteristic signs of war—the sound of artillery and martial music—and sees with its mind's eye the full military details. The director need select only the significant actual equipment to be used to symbolize battle scenes. Such a selection depends, of course, on the intention he finds in each scene.

The first scene of Act 3 shows the English expeditionary force in the full sweep of a campaign, moving from victory to victory. The King has grown to his full powers as a leader of men, exhorting them to expend every ounce of energy and prove their love of England. Henry and his soldiers symbolize the romantic and patriotic view of war. They are led by large, colorful banners flapping in the breeze stirred by moving standard bearers and they are surrounded by pikes and swords brandished in aggressive gestures. The deafening noise of ordnance and the sharp, thrilling sound of trumpets stir their blood mightily.

Following this band of England's noble best is the rag-tag common soldier represented in contrast by Nym, Bardolph, Pistol, and the Boy, who find no glory in war. The Boy sums up their feelings:

> Would I were in an alehouse in London! I would
> give all my fame for a pot of ale, and safety.
> (3. 2)

This view of one of the components of the army is a fitting prelude to the King's thoughts which he expresses at Agincourt when he reveals his disgust with war and his kinship with the common man.

Nym, Bardolph, Pistol, and the Boy represent not only the common man but, specifically, the little man of London, practical, cynical, tough, and with a strong sense of comic irony. He has no illusions based on romantic ideals. In contrast with the Londoners, who represent the true Englishman, are the middle-class Welsh Fluellen and Gower; the Scotsman Captain Jamy; and the Irish Captain Macmorris. They are opinionated, quarrelsome, and nationalistic—fragmenting prototypes of Britain. All these elements in our first view of Britain at war function organically in relation to the play's metaphor for nations, patriotism, jingoism, and man at war.

This reading of the scene expresses one director's view of its dramatic intention. The staging of it to communicate an image of one aspect of war would certainly include, in the first section, banners and flags of England (distinctive from those of France, which will identify the adversaries later on), pikes, swords, drums, and trumpets for use by King Henry, members of his court, his officers, and soldiers. Nym, Bardolph, Pistol, and the Boy, the second group, might follow, pulling and pushing a supply wagon. The third group of warriors, consisting of Gower, Fluellen, Jamy, and Macmorris, would have their swords, knives, water bottles, knapsacks, and personal belongings to busy themselves with as they halt for rest and conversation. For the director, the choice of these stage properties characterizes the event and emphasizes the contrast between military echelons, class groups, and national factions temporarily joined by war. (To point up the Welsh, Scottish, and Irish representatives, attendants might carry small banners of different colors and heraldic signs denoting each of the three nationalities.) The presence of these physical objects will feed the actors' imaginations and stimulate convincing selective behavior as they come onstage and as they play out the scene. The choice of visual and aural stimuli evoked by certain significant military implements and the actions of the actors will support the Chorus as he appeals to the audience to be kind and piece out the performance with their minds.

Shakespeare is selective and impressionistic

in his structure of the play. He gives us only a few possible scenes of actual physical combat. Most of the scenes revolve around parleys between Henry and the French representative, camp life involving subsidiary comic characters, views of the French in their tents and in the field talking about the conflict, and views of Henry with his soldiers about to begin an attack, just after an attack, or awaiting an attack. His main interest is in the development of Henry as a character and he therefore selects events and dialogue which will best demonstrate Henry's views and reactions. War is only the context or pretext for the focus on character. (The director in today's theatre, concerned about a playwright's relevancy politically and socially, can of course shift the emphasis to the subject of war itself. Michael Kahn, the director of the play in the Stratford, Connecticut, Shakespeare Festival in the summer of 1969, saw the play in terms of "war games." This metaphor served to point up an ironic theme involving war and children's games turned into adult games of politics and power struggles.)

When alarums and excursions implying group fighting are indicated in the stage directions coming down to us, they are of brief duration and usually precede a scene of combat between only two characters, as in *Henry V*, 4. 4, in which Pistol overcomes a French soldier. The scene proceeds, it will be noted, through the human but humorous complications of an Englishman's trying to understand French. The spectacle of a young boy acting as interpreter to the boasting, arrogant bully, the tall "Auncient Pistol," and the gallant, unfortunate, and very polite Frenchman is great comic relief from an otherwise serious and pathetic event.

The next scene (4. 5), giving us a quick view of the French, involves alarums but no excursions, if the director is influenced by stage directions. If not, he may add excursions to bridge the scene with the previous one and continue the fighting to make the French scene flow into the King Henry–Exeter scene (4. 6) and, incidentally, show the audience a moment of battle between the two forces. There is a possibility of creating warlike activity to connect with the next scene. The King's command that "every soldier kill his prisoners" might be demonstrated in the interval between the scenes if prisoners should accompany Henry, his forces, and Exeter at the beginning of the scene. Yet these bridging moments of physical combat are fragments, bits and pieces, to give the impression of war. The play as a whole is a mosaic of scenes about war and of war to form a poetic image—symbolical and real.

The staging techniques of hand-to-hand combat must be utilized with directorial imagination and fidelity to the event. The alarums and excursions between and in scenes must be handled for variety and conviction, appealing both to audience imagination and a sense of actuality. Group and single combat must avoid uniformity of physical behavior. Too often the audience sees all actors doing the same thing, whereas each encounter is between two or more combatants, each one fighting according to his character, skill, and cunning. A group of fighting men breaks up into two soldiers fighting one another, two against one, or one surrounded by a group. Each encounter should be carefully choreographed, showing each soldier meeting his adversary or adversaries in constantly changing physical postures and behavior. He fights with his sword, his hands, legs, head, and body. When swords are down, individual grappling, wrestling, tripping, and even biting and using sticks or other objects take place. Some fight standing, some kneeling, some rolling on the ground, each seeking to achieve supremacy over the other. Each encounter is a life-or-death matter. The duration and tempo of all group fights are short and quick, kaleidoscoped into fleeting images, the total picture impressionistic but adding up to an imaginatively convincing moment.

It must be remembered, by the way, that the comments above on scenes of combat are meant as general interpretive and technical points of reference, guidelines, or signals to the director in trying to solve staging problems and, at the same time, adhere to a point of view toward the play as a whole. In rehearsal the director should work with the actors to be creative within the framework of interpretation and technique. First of all, actors cast in the smaller speaking and nonspeaking parts of servants, messengers, attendants, and such, who become part of the fighting forces of a play, can find satisfaction in their roles if, with the help of the director, they can create characters for themselves. In some instances, the actor in the role of an attendant might naturally become a soldier in his master's army. He therefore would play the same character at court and at war. Even the actor who appears without speaking and only in the battle scenes should discover a definite character for himself and behave in battle as that character. The director should encourage two or more combatants to improvise in private rehearsals their pattern of movement and behavior in each encounter in the various battle scenes of a play. He and the actors can then integrate the various separate fights by adapting and editing what the actors have created on their own. Nothing should be frozen into a definite pattern until improvisations can be set as definitive. Let the actors create with properties of their choice, reflecting their characters and the special circumstances of a fight. The director should act as a stimulant, moderator, and editor. His main responsibility will involve control of duration of each encounter, clarity and definition of movements, and focus of a scene for the communication of the narrational and thematic aspects. By all means he should work for order in moments which give the audience the impression of chaos.

The scene between the Romans and the Volscians in Brecht's adaptation of *Coriolanus* was staged ritualistically, strongly influenced by the Kabuki theatre. The two sides lined up against one another up and downstage. With rasping, dissonant martial music filling the theatre and accompanying the action, the Volscians chanted "Au-fid-i-us" and the Romans "Mar-ci-us" as they prepared to hurl themselves on one another. Finally, the two sides came together with a terrible and horrendous clash of swords and swords to shields; eventually each combatant grappled with his opposite in hand-to-hand conflict. Every movement of each soldier was superbly choreographed. In the foreground Marcius and Aufidius wielded their heavy weapons with deadly aim, and when their swords were knocked out of their hands they became locked in a titanic struggle of strength until Marcius eventually gained supremacy and Aufidius was rescued from death by his colleagues. The whole picture was a mixture of reality and symbolism. At times the group appeared to be moving in slow motion. The costumes of both sides, incidentally, added to the effect of supermen of Roman and Volscian myth embroiled in a death struggle. They wore large, primitive-looking helmets, long tunics, and high boots, all made of black leather. They often sug-

Battle scene from the Berliner Ensemble's Venice performance of Coriolanus, *directed by Manfred Wekwerth/Joachim Tenschert, 1966. Photo: Percy Paukschta.*

gested individuals and groups working like a huge war machine. Here was actuality mixed with imaginative metaphor. It was the most terrifying and beautiful stage battle I have ever seen. It was art of the highest order. Moreover, it was exemplary for any stage director of Shakespeare.

Shakespeare's scenes of combat demand adherence to his overall theatricalism, which is a synthesis of selected, significant, and connotative words, actions, physical objects, and sounds. The level of illusion is imaginative rather than realistic. Most important, it is truthful and therefore universal *and* relevant.

CEREMONY

A prominent part of Shakespeare's theatricalism is ceremony, connected, of course, with royal and noble personages and events, and most identifiable with the tragedies and histories. However, even some of the comedies and seriocomic plays have scenes pervaded with an atmosphere of ceremony created by such personages as Theseus and Hippolyta in *A Midsummer Night's Dream,* the King of France in *All's Well That Ends Well,* Leontes and Polixanes in *The Winter's Tale,* Antiochus, Simonides, and Pericles in *Pericles, the Prince of Tyre,* the dukes in *The Comedy of Errors, As You Like It, Twelfth Night,* and *Measure for Measure.*

Ceremony arises from events involving the crowning of a king, processions, recessions, council meetings, the knighting of subjects, trials by a royal judge, trials by arms, proclamations, and so forth. Often they are characterized by the theatrical element of spectacle, which consists of large numbers of characters in colorful attire, fanfares and other musical signs of pomp, heraldic banners and sovereign flags, halberds, and formal grouping expressing not only the dramatic content of scenes but also protocol and the hierarchical levels of court life. Ceremony is a dramatic value lifting the play to a poetic level higher than that of prosaic everyday life.

What are some of the directorial problems in scenes of ceremony? In the royal procession at the opening of *King Lear,* which I have mentioned briefly in the discussion of the director's "double vision," it serves to establish the primitive and authoritarian court of Lear, a monarch who has ruled not only the court but his daughters by power. His entrance may be heralded by the wild sounds of a horn, which prompt Gloucester to say "The king is

coming" (1. 1). In the interval before he actually appears Goneril and Cornwall and Regan and Albany hurry onstage, coming from entrances right and left of the throne chair set in the center of a thrust stage and as near as possible to the back wall of the stage, opposite to the corner aisle down which Lear and his entourage enter. The elder daughters and their husbands join Gloucester, Kent, and Edmund. All are near the throne. They kneel as the procession moves to the center of the stage and proceeds between the two groups to the throne level. At the head of the procession are two banner bearers, followed by an attendant who holds a broadsword in front of him as a symbol of Lear's might. He is followed by two knights in chain armor who carry long pikes. Behind them are two attendants carrying a map and the cushion on which rests Cordelia's coronet. Then come Lear and Cordelia with two more knights with their pikes protecting their monarch from the rear. One banner bearer stations himself on one side of the throne and the second on the other. The sword carrier stands to the left. The first knights move to the extreme right and left of the throne chair. The attendants bearing the map and coronet station themselves to the left and right, to be near Lear when he calls for these objects. Lear seats Cordelia on a bench to the right of the throne and then ascends the throne. The two knights in the rear of the procession plant themselves in the two aisles which serve as entrances. Lear seats himself and signals the court to be seated. Grouping themselves around the bench to the left of the throne, Regan sits on the bench and the others stand, Goneril and Cornwall nearest the throne and Albany beside the bench. Gloucester positions himself near the throne on the right; Kent stands next to him to be able to play his scene with Lear; Edmund stands on the right near the aisle used for the procession.

It will be noted that editions of the text of *King Lear* simply say: "Enter King Lear, Cornwall, Albany, Goneril, Regan, Cordelia, and attendants." Nothing is said about a royal procession. The director may wish to play down the courtly aspects of the scene and make it more of a council meeting, emphasizing the familial. Lear, it may be thought, has called his family together to read them his will and has asked Gloucester and Kent to be witnesses. He will call in France and Burgundy after he has made his settlement upon his daughters. This is a valid view of the scene. Other dramatic values are emphasized in the other staging. Most notable come from the separate and furtive entrance of the elder daughters and their husbands, the entrance of Lear and Cordelia, and the pomp and ceremony of the procession. The milieu of the play is established as a context for the characters' root actions which hurl the play into black tragedy.

A word about the constituents and sequence of the procession. First of all, a horn blower or trumpeters could have been used to head the procession and announce the coming of the King. Those who follow do so in a sequence which expresses something about the occasion and the participants. The flag bearers make the event formal and official and they belong near the head of the procession. The knights protect the royal party and those bearing the map and the coronet. Lear and Cor-

delia, coming at the end of the procession, are emphasized. (In some instances the royal personage might enter near the head of the procession, preceded only by musicians, standard bearers, and attendants, and followed by the principals of the scene who are the focal point of the conflict. The king, prince, or duke is, in effect, the judge of the quarrel.) The sequence of characters in a procession will depend upon the concept and purpose of the procession.

Lear's departure from the stage with Burgundy constitutes the recession, which is led by the two knights positioned at the two aisles. Lear and Burgundy are followed by Gloucester, Edmund, Cornwall, Albany, the attendant with the sword, the bearers of the map and coronet, the banner bearers, and finally the two knights who stood on either side of the throne. The recession is covered by the sound of the horn or trumpets. The

The opening scene of King Lear *as staged by Frank McMullan for the Champlain Shakespeare Festival, Burlington, Vermont, 1967. Set: William Schenk; costumes: Fran Brassard. Photo: Horace B. Eldred.*

tempo is quick, and all exit accordingly and in marked contrast to the deliberate and slow pace with which they entered in the procession. Goneril, Regan, the King of France, and Cordelia are left onstage for their scene.

The words "sennet" ("A signal call on a trumpet or cornet for entrance or exit on the stage"[1]), "trumpets," "cornets," and "hautboys" usually, though not always, indicate a formal procession bringing the characters onstage and taking them off. However, the director, in studying the text and coming to an entrance or exit by a group of characters, should determine the dramatic effect desired at this moment. He then decides upon the degree of ceremony he wishes to create by the staging. In considering the entrance of Duncan to Macbeth's castle, for example, the First Folio carries the stage direction: "Hautboys and torches. Enter King, Malcolm, Donalbain, Banquo, Lennox, Macduff, Ross, Angus, and attendants" (1. 6). This is not a state event, but ceremony does surround the King and his followers even at the arrival at the home of a friend for an overnight visit. Some directors have chosen to make this a royal procession of attendants with hautboys or trumpets preceding soldiers or bodyguards, attendants bearing trunks, the other lords, and finally Duncan. Emphasis on pomp and circumstance does point up the kingly presence and makes his murder the more reprehensible in terms of the divinity of kings and Macbeth's relationship to his monarch. The enormity of the crime is increased. On the other hand, a simple entrance for the King and his party would underscore the friendliness, trust, and human relationship between Duncan and Macbeth and thus intensify the shock of the murder. Indeed, Macbeth, prior to the murder, argues against it with the thought that

> He's here in double trust:
> First, as I am his kinsman and his subject,
> Strong both against the deed; then, as his host,
> (1. 7)

and I would argue against a procession for these dramatic reasons: because this is not a state event demanding formality and, if the stage direction "Hautboys" can be used as a clue, the occasion is soft and tender in friendship, since hautboys are oboes which

---

[1] *Webster's New Collegiate Dictionary* (Springfield, Mass., G. & C. Merriam Co., 1949), p. 770.

announce Duncan's arrival with music appropriate for such an occasion. Furthermore, Duncan's

> This castle hath a pleasant seat; the air
> Nimbly and sweetly recommends itself
> Unto our gentle senses.   (1. 6)

is in key with the tone of the scene created by his arrival—and stands in ironic contrast to Lady Macbeth's welcome and the subsequent horrible events. Thus I see a center-stage entrance of the King, his sons, his noble friends, and attendants, preceded by the sound of oboes from offstage, down a ramp or some steps if on a proscenium stage, or their entrance through an aisle or other entryway opposite a thrust stage, and a door or arch through which Lady Macbeth would come to greet Duncan. The group would appear by twos and threes, brushing their clothes and comporting themselves as men do after riding horses some distance, and approach Macbeth's castle, a place they see for the first time. The royal guard would doubtless head the party and station themselves at the castle entryway, followed by Lennox, Ross, and Angus, the King and Banquo, Malcolm, Donalbain and Macduff, and, finally, attendants with luggage. There is obviously both informality and an atmosphere of ceremony attendant upon this interpretation of this entrance. There are, of course, many other views of this scene and ways to stage it. Each stage direction indicating an entrance must be analyzed for its dramatic import relative to the play as a whole.

Henry VIII is a play in which pageantry and ceremony play a significant part. The play is weak but its ceremonial and pictorial aspects are strong. It contains six formal scenes, events of state, in which protocol and symbolism are emphasized. The three most elaborate and impressive are the trial of Queen Katharine in the Hall in Blackfriars (2. 4), Anne Bullen's coronation procession (4. 1), and the christening of Elizabeth at the Palace (5. 4). All of these mark the entrances and processions with the sound of trumpets and/or cornets. The order of precedence is indicated in many modern texts, and the director is well advised to follow the stage directions unless he can devise a more effective plan to accord with his personal interpretation of the events.

Though the ceremonial and pictorial elements in these scenes in *Henry VIII* are the outstanding dramatic values, the characters must not be neglected—not even the small characters who can add texture as well as color. It must be noted that once the characters are placed in their sequential order and then moved to their stage positions, a small number of principal characters takes stage, and audience attention is focused on them. In the trial of Queen Katharine, she and Cardinal Wolsey are central, and after her departure Henry, Wolsey, and Bishop Lincoln have a colloquy. The remaining characters, however, can give depth to the scene by their behavior during pauses and during critical and climactic moments. They must not be allowed to be merely decorative—wax figures in colorful costumes posed carefully by the director. On the other hand, they must not steal the audience's attention when it belongs on the principals. They are, after all, restrained functionaries who are prevented by a sense of decorum from overacting or over-reacting. Nevertheless, they are human beings with feelings and convictions. It is suggested that, after the director has established the silhouette of a character for each participant, the actors be encouraged to respond freely and naturally to the sequence of situations. The director can eventually edit their behavior to contribute to his controlling directorial design of the scene.

Looking at these ceremonial scenes from the point of view that the theme of the play concerns itself with capricious monarchical power, the background functionary characters can be treated as part of the cold machinery of autocracy. They would become automata, functioning and behaving impassively, unaware of human predicaments, and without the feeling and thought of three-dimensional characters. Queen Katharine then would be seen as an object maneuvered by court intrigue, powerless to guide her own destiny, a hostage to a mechanized world. Such a treatment of this scene and subsequent ones would bring into sharp focus the hollowness and emptiness of ceremony.

Anne Bullen's coronation procession, organized according to the explicit stage directions of the editors, as a further contribution to this theme would be as impersonal as a military parade down Fifth Avenue. The gossipy comments of the three Gentlemen watching the procession would serve the spectators in the same way as those of television and radio commentators at public events of national importance, though the Gentlemen in *Henry VIII,* obviously satirized by their creator, would give the occasion a biting edge.

The christening of the infant Elizabeth is dramatic as a piece of royal pageantry, a colorful incident out of a history book. As part of the denouement of the play, it is a mechanical manipulation by a playwright determined to instruct his audience in the facts of their English heritage. The scene requires the precise management of actors and speech suggested by the pat structure organized by Shakespeare.

The King's council chamber is the setting for two ceremonial meetings with smaller processions, but they have a formality and dignity which are very impressive. Hierarchical protocol and ritual are dramatic only secondarily to the trials of the Duke of Buckingham and Cranmer, the Archbishop of Canterbury. The formal reception given by Cardinal Wolsey, at which King Henry meets Anne Bullen, has an atmosphere of ceremony. Hautboys provide the music for the assembly of the guests, the entrance of Henry, and the dance for the matchmaking sponsored by Cardinal Wolsey. Drums and trumpets and the discharge of cannon make it a royal fete portending a change in the court and in national life. Even these minor ceremonial scenes, to feed the ironic theme concerned with self-indulgent and capricious authoritarianism, must be directorially organized to gleam with polish and to function with smooth precision. An air of impersonality and pre-ordination lends the scenes their historicity. They seem to have already taken place. They are removed from the present. The audience is in for no surprises; they watch with more knowledge than the characters have; they know their history, and *Henry VIII* is only a review lesson.

The play contains many humanizing touches, especially in character delineation. The politicians seem less real than the other characters. Henry, Katharine, Anne, the Old Lady, the three Gentlemen, and the common people are remarkably alive, with their flaws and human quirks. A director can bring freshness and modern psychological and political relevancy to a production of the play by emphasizing the richness of these characters while stressing the grace and beauty of the ceremonial scenes peopled with flesh-and-blood characters rather than mere functionaries. The actors' corporeal differences and personalities can add dimensions to characters drawn only in outline. Interpretation can be creative as well as reproductive, and staging techniques are supportive. Though Shakespeare indicates a need for ceremonial design, the director selects and organizes directorial detail to reflect his personal view of the event.

The ritual necessary to a scene of combat consists of the ceremony and rules governing knighthood. The seconds, the Marshal and the Herald, as well as the adversaries and the spectators, recognize the event in terms of politeness and gentility which have crystallized into customary ceremony and pageantry. The deadliest trial at arms is sanctioned by honor, custom, and legality, and horrible physical violence achieves the status of nobility and heroism.

In *King Lear*, 5. 3, Edgar appears as a disguised and unknown challenger to Edmund after Albany, acting as challenger, judge, and moderator, calls the Herald to appear to order the sounding of the trumpet and to read the challenge. "A trumpet sounds" and the Herald reads:

> If any man of quality or degree
> within the lists of the army will maintain upon
>   Edmund,
> supposed Earl of Gloucester, that he is a mani-
>   fold
> traitor, let him appear by the third sound of
>   the trumpet.
> He is bold in his defence. *First trumpet*
> Again! *Second trumpet*
> Again! *Third trumpet*
>   *An answering trumpet heard. Enter Edgar,*
>   *in armour*
>   *Albany*. Ask him his purposes—why he ap-
>   pears
> Upon this call o'th'trumpet.
>   *Herald*.   What are you?
> Your name, your quality, and why you answer
> This present summons?
>   *Edgar*.   Know my name is lost;
> By treason's tooth bare-gnawn and canker-bit:
> Yet am I noble as the adversary
> I come to cope.
>   *Albany*.   Which is that adversary?
>   *Edgar*. What's he that speaks for Edmund,
>   Earl of Gloucester?
>   *Edmund*. Himself: what say'st thou to him?
>   *Edgar*.   Draw thy sword,
> That, if my speech offend a noble heart,
> Thy arm may do thee justice; here is mine:

Edgar then accuses Edmund of being a traitor to the gods, his father, his brother, and

Albany and threatens to prove it with his sword. Edmund says he should ask his name

> But since thy outside looks so fair and warlike,
> And that thy tongue some say of breeding
>   breathes,
> What safe and nicely I might well delay
> By rule of knighthood, I disdain and spurn.

and after a few more lines Edmund asks for the trumpets to speak; they fight and Edmund falls mortally wounded.

These passages from the play demonstrate the formality and convention of speech and action. The director who seeks to make these speeches naturalistic and prosaic fails or refuses to recognize the theatrical value of stylization which derives from the ceremonial. The manners and grace of the characters and the formal composition of the stage picture express this stylization which is part of the mode of the play.

Another ceremonial scene emanating from knighthood's code of behavior is the challenge to combat by arms ordered by Richard, who at the end of *Richard II*, 1. 1, decrees that

> At Coventry upon Saint Lambert's day.
> There shall your swords and lances arbitrate
> The swelling difference of your settled hate.
> Since we can not atone you, we shall see
> Justice design the victor's chivalry.
> Lord marshal, command our officers at arms
> Be ready to direct these home alarms.

In 1. 3 the lists are set out, Heralds, the Lord Marshal, and others attending. The Lord Marshal learns from Aumerle that Henry Bolingbroke, Duke of Hereford, and the Duke of Norfolk are ready and awaiting the trumpet's call to battle. King Richard and noblemen enter at the flourish of trumpets; Richard takes his seat on the throne, and John of Gaunt and the others take their places. A trumpet is sounded and is answered by another within. Then Norfolk in armor enters, preceded by a Herald. Richard asks the Lord Marshal to demand of him the cause of his arrival and who he is, and the Marshal asks Norfolk to

> Speak truly, on thy knighthood, and thy oath,
> And so defend thee heaven and thy valour!

Norfolk does so. The trumpets sound and Bolingbroke enters in armor, preceded by a Herald. Richard requests the Marshal to demand of Bolingbroke his identity and his cause, and the Marshal asks

> What is thy name? and wherefore com'st thou hither,
> Before King Richard in his royal lists?
> Against whom comest thou? and what's thy quarrel?
> Speak like a true knight, so defend thee heaven!

After Bolingbroke does so, the Marshal cautions all not to touch the lists or barriers of the jousting field. Bolingbroke asks to kiss his sovereign's hand and, this done, takes his leave of him, his cousin Aumerle, and his father John of Gaunt. Both appellants in the conflict appeal for victory. Lances are then received by Bolingbroke and Norfolk. The Heralds representing both repeat their names and challenge, and the Marshal orders the trumpets to sound and the combatants to step forward. At this juncture the King throws down his "warder" and stops the fight.

The similarity between the two scenes from *King Lear* and *Richard II* is obvious. Both have the same pattern of speech and action leading up to the point of actual conflict. Questions and answers governed by the code of knighthood take on a ritualistic appearance. Indeed, the atmosphere of such scenes is quasi-religious. These scenes differ from the ceremonial ones involving processions, trials, council meetings, and other affairs more related to the state. They are formal physically but contain no set pattern in speech. Both kinds of scene do consist of the pageantry of flags, colorful costumes, large numbers of people, and music. All of these scenes require formal pictorial composition.

The pictorial has long been recognized as a theatrical value in Shakespeare's plays. The audience appeal of color, large numbers of characters, and music is great. And ceremonial scenes have a fascination for the eye and imagination. Their visual design in terms of composition—the deployment of characters and the placement of furniture properties—should be carefully worked out by the director in collaboration with the scene, costume, and lighting designers. Very often ceremonial scenes are key scenes in the structure of the play and are meant to be emphasized in production. Their formalization helps to accent them. Othello's appearance before the Duke and Senators of Venice (*Othello*, 1. 3), the

first scene of *King Lear,* and Queen Katharine's trial in the Hall of Blackfriars in *Henry VIII* (2. 4), as ceremonial key scenes, illustrate this. They represent crises and turning points in the lives of principal characters, and the dramatic and formal nature of the occasions underlines their significance. Their pictorial dramatizations should support the nature of the occasions.

A pictorial dramatization depicts character relationships and storytelling values, as well as the spirit of a moment, and involves the director's use of design elements such as focus, balance, line, level, mass, variety, and unity. The use of these elements varies in accordance with the kind of stage available. The proscenium stage allows the audience to view the performance from only one side, and pictorial elements of staging are organized for that one view. The director is working with a framed picture and analyzes his compositions as though he were a painter. The thrust stage and the in-the-round stage force him to work as a sculptor. In both kinds of work he must be aware of and control the audience's focus of attention. He wrestles with these problems, however, only after he has analyzed a scene to determine what character or characters are most often the focal points of interest. This has a bearing on his choice of placement of characters and furniture properties. And audience lines of sight are always a consideration. Large groups on the stage, as they are in many ceremonial scenes, present acute problems of focus on any kind of stage. Different members of the audience in a theatre with a thrust or in-the-round stage never see the stage from the same vantage point; the audience is on two sides and in front or sitting on four sides. In addition, the performers individually and as a group are in constant movement, and their movement is generally circular. The experience for the audience is like watching a top spinning at a moderately slow speed.

Balance or visual weight on a nonproscenium three-dimensional stage must be considered axially, except when the pictorial dramatization is composed parallel to the back wall of a thrust stage. On a proscenium stage it is a matter of visual weight placed on either side of the stage. Axial balance requires constant checking by the director if he is interested in achieving continually changing and aesthetically satisfying visual images for the audience. On the three-dimensional stage the center becomes the focal point of action— and the actor is drawn to it. Other actors radiate around this central figure. The spatial interval and the number of actors creating a radius affect the balance. Inasmuch as the stage picture revolves, the balance (and other design elements) is continually changing.

Line, level, mass, variety, and unity are points of consideration for the director when organizing and composing his actors on all kinds of stages. Their use on a proscenium stage is similar to that for a canvas to be framed. The thrust stage, though open on three sides to the audience and with its back wall on the fourth side, like a proscenium stage, really orients the actors toward the audience sitting on the front side, opposite to the back wall. The designer and director work out a suggested environment for the play by changing certain architectural elements of this back wall—as they do for the Shakespeare festival at Stratford, Ontario. The most important pictorial dramatizations are placed in front of this back-wall setting, and the central part of them runs parallel to the setting and, like a crescent, curves right and left to follow the sides of the stage. Compositional elements are used here by the director as painter cum sculptor. There is a feeling of plasticity. The in-the-round stage encourages the director to work for complete plasticity in his groupings. Line on this stage tends to be circular in large outline, though segments may vary. Level helps connote psychological, social, and political status. Actors relating to one another in massive groupings must be relegated to the corners of the in-the-round stage in order to protect audience lines of sight. Large, tightly knit groups must be avoided even at corners. Variety of level, physical posture, line, and mass is just as important on in-the-round stages as on others. Unity of composition is achieved by spatial tying-in and harmony of use of the other elements.

The focus in the Senate scene in *Othello* is mainly on Othello and the Duke and the Senators, massed together with the Duke on a dais. Of course, the focus in any scene shifts, and in this one it moves to Brabantio, Desdemona, and individual Senators. The audience's attention moves from one side, the Duke's and Senators', to the opposite side, Othello's. Even though the Duke and Senators comprise the judge and jury at a trial of Othello and are of superior legal and social position, they should not be placed on a proscenium stage

upstage of Othello but on one side of the stage to allow Othello to play on the same plane with them. The opposing forces divide the scene between them, though Othello is responsible for most of the dialogue. This kind of analysis of a scene is necessary to determine character placement and furniture props. The Duke may sit in state under a canopy and raised above the Senators, who sit on either side of him, while Othello, Brabantio, and Desdemona stand opposite them. The main focus in the first scene of *King Lear* is on Lear, though the focus shifts to Goneril, Regan, Cornwall, Albany, Cordelia, Burgundy, the King of France, and Kent. Since Lear dominates the scene, his throne chair might be up center. The positioning of characters and furniture props associated with them depends upon their dramatic significance and not on their social or political stations. Kings, queens, and princes do not necessarily belong upstage, as some directors and designers evidently think.

Symmetrical balance in pictorial dramatization emphasizes the formality and stylization of a scene—it appears consciously composed and unnatural. Asymmetrical balance is equally pleasing to the eye and actually creates more interest visually. It helps to make an occasion less formal, more spontaneous. Formality does not depend entirely upon compositional balance, it must be remembered. An atmosphere of formality may exist when the language or action or behavior of the characters is ceremonial, dignified, and lacking in spontaneity. The use of line created by the spatial relationships between characters—straight, curved, indirect, and so on— affects the mood and meaning of a pictorial dramatization. Level onstage may connote social, political, or psychological relationships and helps achieve visual variety. Visual mass and weight influence compositional balance and affect the mood of a scene. The large group of characters in the Queen Katharine scene in *Henry VIII* is made up of clusters of officials and functionaries and creates weighty masses constituting a larger mass. It is a heavy scene visually. Visual variety is achieved by levels, body postures, line, and placement onstage. The more variety, the less the formality of a composition. The positioning of the Senators seated in a row below the Duke in the *Othello* scene creates a strong impression of a formal mass or block of dignitaries opposed to Othello. A sense of visual unity in a stage picture enhances the dramatic impact of a key ceremonial scene.

COMEDY

Shakespeare wrote less than a half dozen plays out of a total of thirty-seven attributed mainly to him that possess an all-pervading comic spirit. "Problem comedies" like *Measure for Measure, The Winter's Tale, All's Well That Ends Well,* and others, usually considered to be comedies because of their happy endings, have a serious thread woven throughout them. At least, this is the modern reaction to a reading of the plays. The director in dealing with the serious aspects can, of course, lighten them or even make fun of them and thus create a unifyingly predominant light tone. This is by way of making concessions to today's audience conditioned by the comedy of popular writers of comedy for Broadway, films, and television. On the other hand, the director influenced by the avant-gardists can use the serious elements of the comedies as a key to their performance. He can turn them into black comedies, Absurdist plays presented in Brechtian, Artaudian, or Grotowskian performances. A director's choice of interpretation is wide in today's theatre. In our study of Shakespeare's theatricalism, however, we should look at the comedies in the context of that theatricalism.

As a creative writer of comedy in his era, he was heir to certain theatre conventions which were accepted as a part of the popular tradition. His use of character, plot, language, and theme followed this tradition in the main but always with certain innovations that gave his work individuality and contemporaneity. We find characters borrowed from medieval drama, Plautine comedy, the commedia dell' arte, and Jonsonian plays of humor mixed in with characters from contemporary drama and everyday life. All these characters were identifiable and accepted by the Elizabethan audience on a heightened level of illusion. They were the focal point of audience interest. And so they are for audiences today.

The director of Shakespeare in today's theatre will do well to make them his focal point of interest too since they are the chief source of comedy. Shakespeare's emphasis on word play, especially punning, to arouse laughter often makes his dialogue a liability. What was laughable to the Elizabethan is not necessarily so to a modern audience. The puns seem simple-minded to us when we understand them. And much of his "comic" dialogue is made up of obsolete words and unidentifiable references. (It is remarkable, however, how amusing a great deal of the language is in a good modern production of *Love's Labour's Lost,* a play long thought unplayable.) In modern comedies the dominant element is the witty, offbeat, or wisecracking conversation of the characters. "A laugh a line" has saved many otherwise deficient plays. Shakespeare's comedies arouse laughter for different reasons. Sometimes his plotting is obvious and naive, but usually the basic situation is amusing and believable because it is the result of human fallibility, misunderstanding, or complicated but dramatically intriguing circumstances.

A vain, self-indulgent, fat old man, who believes the ladies find him irresistible, makes credible the plot premise of *The Merry Wives of Windsor.* Compensatory vanity in Malvolio in *Twelfth Night,* lack of attention and love in Katharina in *The Taming of the Shrew,* self-dramatization in Orsino in *Twelfth Night,* and mistaken identity of the Dromios in *The Comedy of Errors* create basic situations that make these plays universally acceptable as well as amusing. Even though many of these characters are a part of the popular tradition and are thus prototypes, they are nevertheless human.

They are human though cut out of life on the bias. They are, as Henri Bergson puts it in his highly esteemed work on *Laughter,* "in the grips of an attitude."[2] Falstaff in *The Merry Wives* sees life only from his particular self-deluding angle of vision. (In the *Henrys* he has some perspective on himself and is more three-dimensional as a character. He admits that he is not only witty but the source of wit for others.) However, at the end of *The Merry Wives* he realizes what an old fool he has been. The smaller characters are like automata, completely controlled and motivated by their attitudes. Shallow is a belligerent, choleric, little old man, the victim of his memory of his youthful strength and bravado and his idea of his status as a gentleman with a coat of arms. His legalistic language, even in less than legal circumstances, pervades his conversation: His mind is attuned to the business of his office as justice of the peace. His cousin Slender is caught in the mold of timidity and gentility. Simple, servingman to

---

[2] *Laughter,* tr. C. Brereton and F. Rothwell (New York, Macmillan, 1917), pp. 132–200.

Slender, lives up to his name as frankly as a character from a morality play. Pistol sees himself and the world through the eyes and highfalutin language of a character from an old melodrama. Corporal Nym is obsessed with "the humour of it" and Bardolph, "gotten in drink," moves in an alcoholic haze. Ford becomes "horn mad" and green-eyed with jealousy.

Sir Hugh Evans is trapped by the Welsh language in violent conflict with English and by his pretensions as a scholar. Dr. Caius is similarly victimized by his Frenchman's fractured English and Gallic temper. Mistress Quickly is obsessed with her view of herself as a matchmaker. All are wound up and set in motion by their *idées fixes*.

Malvolio in *Twelfth Night* is the complete automaton with his delusions of grandeur. Katharina, the shrew, is a mechanical toy manufactured by her anger at the world. Trinculo and Stephano in *The Tempest* are soaked in alcohol, obedient to its caprices. Even Caliban is fixed by his animalistic view of the world.

Though the little peripheral, and a few of the principal characters of comedy remain in the grips of an attitude throughout the play, some like Falstaff in *The Merry Wives* and Katharina in *The Taming of the Shrew* gain perspective on themselves. They, of course, are the most human characters, who learn through the crucible of experience. (Malvolio, though a principal character, still clings to his vision of himself to the end of *Twelfth Night* and threatens all who see him for what he is with "I'll be revenged on the whole pack of you," 5. 1.) Another important feature of Shakespeare's structuring of his comedies is his dramatic sense, which tells him to show his rigid characters in juxtaposition with resilient and normal characters. Mistress Page, Mistress Ford, and Page in *The Merry Wives of Windsor* are shown in their normality in contrast to the whole gallery of characters shown on the bias. Malvolio, Orsino, and Olivia stand out from Viola, Maria, Sir Toby, Sebastian, and the Captain in *Twelfth Night;* Katharina from Petruchio, Baptista, Bianca, and most of the rest in *The Taming of the Shrew;* Caliban, Stephano, and Trinculo from Gonzalos, Prospero, Miranda, and Ferdinand in *The Tempest*. Without this contrast the self-deluded characters would not be comic but would be psychologically eccentric and possibly pitiful.

These comically flawed characters, too inflexible to adjust to the world as it is, try to force the world to adjust to them. The resultant conflict and tension are laughable because we see the difference between their conception of themselves and the way they really are. The crises and decisions springing from these characters create the events that make up the plot premise and the complexities of the narrative line. Not totally unlike some of the serious plays, the comedies are complicated by numerous peripheral events adding variety and humor. Falstaff in *The Merry Wives* is responsible for the main situation, but Shallow, Slender, Sir Hugh, Dr. Caius, and Mistress Quickly stir up comic incidents resulting from their rigidity of thinking and the competition and scheming for winning the hand of the lovely Anne Page. Ultimately, of course, Shakespeare weaves them into the main pattern of which Falstaff is the center. The audience is willing to involve itself in these foolish lives because they are so appealingly human and because the audience can sit in its Olympian superiority and avoid actual anxiety or even inconvenience suffered by the characters. Its objectivity, however, is only relative. It is concerned enough to participate vicariously in the predicaments which so recognizably mirror everyday life.

An especially dramatic aspect of these laughable events and characters is the use of parallel and contrasting situations and themes. The campaign for Anne Page mirrors, in contrast, Falstaff's strategy for Mistress Ford and Mistress Page. Of course, the greatest contrasts are among characters. They are contrasted not only psychologically but physically. The tall, skinny Slender stands beside the small, wiry or plump Justice Shallow. Both are outlined against the tall but solidly built and overly dignified Sir Hugh Evans. Falstaff stands in relief from his page, the tiny Robin; the elongated and angular Pistol; the dried-up crabapple of a Nym; and the stocky, lumbering Bardolph. Dr. Caius is slender, graceful, and precise in manner and movement. The buxom or possibly stringy and down-to-earth Mistress Quickly is compared with the delicate and genteel Mistress Ford and the forthright and amply endowed Mistress Page. (The physical and psychological contrast between these two makes for greater audience interest.)

They raise our laughter because of the contrast or incongruity between what they think they are and see themselves as and the predicaments into which they are forced. Falstaff, in all his vanity and dignity, is ridiculous having to make his escape in a basket of dirty clothes which, with him in it, is eventually dumped into the Thames; and he is equally amusing running out of Ford's house dressed as a woman. The green-eyed jealousy of Ford drives him into some melodramatics incongruous with the true facts of the relationship between his wife and Falstaff. The middle-aged Sir Hugh and Dr. Caius are unevenly matched duelists prompted into conflict by misunderstandings about the courting of Anne Page. The last scene of the play presents Falstaff in the epitome of incongruity when he goes to Herne's Oak for his supposed assignation with Mistress Ford and Mistress Page and is humiliatingly pinched and taunted by the fairies. (There is humor too in his repeated and foolish agreement to the three abortive attempts to effect a rendezvous with the ladies. In his delusions of his prowess as a lover he moves like a robot to comic predicaments, each successively more ridiculous than the one before. The comic principle of repetition as a source of laughter is illustrated also by the four narrative threads of romantic courting: Falstaff and the wives; Slender and Anne; Dr. Caius and Anne; Fenton and Anne.

Mistaken identity and surprise play their comic part in the fairy scene. Slender and Caius, each thinking he is eloping with Anne, steal away a fairy who turns out to be a boy; and Falstaff learns that Mister Brook was Ford in disguise—he has been cozened at every turn—and the audience, aware of the truth all along, has a good laugh at all concerned. Shakespeare well understood the comic relationship necessary between audience and characters.

The director who is alert to these sources of comedy will take care to reflect them in the process of staging the plays. He and the actors will find the particular psychological bias of each character and build characterizations accordingly. Each character acts and reacts from incident to incident in terms of his particular bias, believing in it and finding, imaginatively and creatively, circumstances on which to build realistic detail to give rich texture to each moment of his fictive life in the play. The modern actor must discover in the life of a past era contemporary equivalents of behavior that bring conviction and reality to his character's underlying and dominating desire on which is based his through-line of action.

Comedy is serious for the actor and laughable for the audience. His character sees life from his particular angle of vision, and the actor believes in it utterly; and though in rehearsal and performance he is subconsciously aware of his comic inflexibility, he never allows the audience to be aware of it. He is convincingly serious and naive about all he thinks and does. By all means he must avoid trying to be funny or giving the appearance of it. He must play lightly and with ever changing tempi of thinking, speaking, and acting. The director must tie together each moment rhythmically to continue the pulse beat of the various parts making up the whole. The performances of all the actors must cohere even while they work in contrasts. Elaborate character detail and pauses can make for turgidity. An impression of spontaneity—a feeling of the first time—is necessary even though great care has been taken in the planning and organization of performances. A comic character acts emotionally and on impulse; if he took the time to think, he would solve his problems and extricate himself from his predicaments. If he should, during the course of his career, appear to think, his mind can operate only in the groove created by his psychological intractability; his thinking results in comic rationalities.

Shakespearean characters, especially comic ones, have become stereotyped in performances over the years. They are the victims of tradition. And the mechanization of their minds and behavior has made them fit conveniently and easily into molds. Their freshness after repeated display in our Shakespearean festivals has gone stale. They must be approached in a new light. For example, Falstaff in *The Merry Wives of Windsor* can be conceived by the actor as a person who believes profoundly in his sincerity. In fact, he can believe that he alone is sincere and all around him false. This kind of self-delusion creates its own brand of vanity. His pretensions to nobility and the privileges of knighthood can serve as a basis for the claims which he considers only justifiable and right. In his dialogue and behavior after the moments of comic humiliation, he feels himself more sinned against than sinning. Even his decision to seduce the merry wives to gain access to their husbands' money is motivated by the conviction that the world owes him a living, and foul means to gain it, in accordance with his rationalization, are fair. Besides, he is responding only to the "leer of invitation." In fact, by social hierarchical right and privilege Sir John is doing the Windsor burghers a favor—he thinks. This kind of reasoning on his part takes on a modernity which the play does not traditionally have inasmuch as it is Shakespeare's only play about contemporary Elizabethan life. Irving Wardle, writing in *The New York Times,* May 4, 1968, reviewed a production of the play presented the night before by the Royal Shakespeare Company at Stratford-upon-Avon, England, and called it "a brilliantly funny piece of work . . . sustained by a serious intention." The director Terry Hands viewed "the play as a dialogue between patrician and middle-class values. Falstaff, the courtly hanger-on, gets a lesson in virtue from the citizens of Windsor, while they—eager to marry their children for money —get their lesson from Fenton, the only other aristocrat in the cast." The reading of the character of Falstaff as outlined above might very well fit in with this view of the meaning of the play, so long considered only as frank entertainment originally designed to amuse Queen Elizabeth.

The search for originality and freshness in characterization has caused directors and actors to seize upon the slightest indication of a new psychological trait and blow it up out of all proportion. The character of Malvolio has been particularly investigated and explored. He has been played as a social climber; as a Puritan; as a would-be executive, interested in Olivia as a means to wealth and status; as one obsessed with the need for law and order, to the verge of lunacy. He has been conceived in varying degrees of the comic, grotesque, evil. Of course the question of directorial freedom and choice arises. By changing the emotional tone of a principal character, the director may also transform the overall tone of the play: A comedy such as *Twelfth Night,* with a melancholy strain, may become pervasively serious. But in these times of change and reversal of values traditional concepts of dramatic genres are susceptible to reexamination and discovery. Traditional ways of looking at a play as a whole are being challenged, but where there is challenge there is danger.

A director may approach a play from many angles. His choice of approach may depend upon his orientation to theatre: His primary interest may be in character, production, or theme, and so on. Thematic interest seems to dominate today's innovative productions. This may be so because many of the experimentalists are social critics. They are highly influenced by the political and philosophical as well as the theatre theories of Brecht, Beckett, and Artaud. An example of an innovative production of a play usually considered a comedy is John Hancock's presentation of *A Midsummer Night's Dream* in New York. Dan Sullivan in his review asserts that the staging "sets a kind of high-water mark for avant-garde productions of Shakespeare. It also suggests why such productions don't generally work very well." He tells of the casting of a tall young man in a blond wig to play Helena; "a glow-in-the-dark codpiece registering the fitful passions of Demetrius, and a 1940 jukebox in the corner of the stage emitting the Mendelssohn score." Nevertheless, the director has a serious intention. He "has built his production around two themes present in the text but generally unstressed in performance: the grotesque side of the spirit world that governs the events of the play and the callous side of King Theseus's court." Evil pervades the world of the fairies and the court. Sullivan sums up his review by saying, "Where Shakespeare gives us light-hearted merriment, Mr. Hancock gives us heavy-hearted (sometimes heavy-handed) irony, and something close to despair. The fun of the lovers' mixup, the fun of the rude mechanicals is transmuted into empty gesture. . . . he has given us a comment on a play instead of the play itself." Evidently the director was successful in doing what he set out to do but failed to do those things "that have kept the play alive since it was written." [3]

Certainly the theme chosen by a director influences his approach to the characters if the characters are to be organic and functional. In making *A Midsummer Night's Dream* a black comedy, the humanity of the court, fairies, and mechanicals is diminished. The whole play becomes a medium for broadcasting the voice of the director rather than of the playwright. In selecting the themes of grotesquerie in the fairy world and callousness in the court, the director overlooks the predominating themes of the natural, warm humanitarianism of both groups of characters who demonstrate both weaknesses and virtues. In order to emphasize his themes the director, according to the reviewer, causes the court

---

[3] "Theater: Opium 'Dream'," *The New York Times,* July 1, 1967.

guards to set upon the rustics and throw them out after their performance of the little play presented in honor of the Duke's wedding. This is purely gratuitous and at odds with the court's and Theseus' obvious delight with the naiveté and ineptitude of the performers. Moreover, the director's choice of theme is invalidated by the end of the play in which the audience sees the reconciliation of Oberon and Titania, Oberon's intention to bless their marriage bed, and his dispatching the fairies to stray through the palace to "each several chamber bless." Puck's epilogue rounds out the author's intention to resolve the play with good humor and happiness to all—including the audience.

Another experiment with one of Shakespeare's comedies is England's National Theatre production of *As You Like It,* directed by Clifford Williams. According to Martin Esslin's review, the idea of the production is attributed to Jan Kott's essay in *Shakespeare*

Our Contemporary, in which Kott discusses sexual ambiguity in Shakespeare's comedies inasmuch as many of them present girls disguised as boys. Of course, the Elizabethan actors were boys dressed as girls and thus we have boys pretending to be girls who in the fiction of the plays pretend to be boys. As we are now in an age when boys wear shoulder-length hair and feminine-looking clothes and girls wear trousers, Esslin says, "it is often difficult to tell from a distance whether a long-haired creature is male or female." Thus, Kott argues, "we are entering an era when love itself will transcend the boundaries of sex." Though the director of this production in a note in the program denies Kott's influence, Esslin claims the idea of the production can be traced to Kott. Anyway, he says, it is "Shakespeare in Beatle-style costumes" with beat music in an abstract set made of translucent plastic; plexiglass tubes hung from the flies suggest the Forest of Arden. The sexual

The National Theatre Company of Great Britain's production of As You Like It *with an all-male cast, directed by Clifford Williams, 1967. Christopher Timothy appears as Silvius and Richard Kay as Phoebe. Photo: Dominic.*

ambiguity of the all-male cast works best, according to Esslin, with the actors who play the secondary roles of Audrey and Phoebe because their physical attributes make the one coarse and funny and the other lovely. The boys in the principal parts of Celia and Rosalind fail in their performances because they are without feminine allure and "devoid of sexuality, ambiguous or otherwise, and this robs Shakespeare of its main point, purpose and attraction." The best performance is Robert Stephens' in the role of Jaques, whom he plays "as an eccentric scholar, pedantic and introverted, with his head in the clouds, and thus he makes the old stock character a wholly believable misanthrope whom one might meet on any college campus." [4]

Esslin believes wrong casting of the principal characters invalidates in performance a valid theme. But is "sexual ambiguity" the valid theme of *As You Like It?* Is this what the play is really about? Is this what *Twelfth Night* is about? In the Elizabethan theatre it, too, had boy actors asking the audience to believe Olivia and Maria were girls and Viola a boy pretending to be a girl pretending to be a boy. Certainly "sexual ambiguity" was a part of both plays, but was it the main part? An all-male cast in a play with feminine characters in the modern theatre is certainly titillating as it was in the Elizabethan theatre—but with a difference. In the Elizabethan theatre such casting was a part of its convention and was employed for serious plays in which the audience was asked to be actively unaware of a double level of illusion. Surely the audience believed completely in the femininity of Ophelia, Juliet, and Cleopatra. Their being played by boys was a *donnée* of Shakespeare's theatricalism and not the source of sexual titillation. One can only suspect the motive of a modern director who uses a male cast for female characters. It cannot be justified on historical grounds. No intelligent director or scholar claims that a production of Shakespeare today can duplicate Elizabethan stage conditions. The physical theatre and audiences are different. The past cannot be revived. The National Theatre's production of *As You Like It* "in drag" appears to be a case of pandering to ambivalent sexual tastes or adding a "showmanship" value extraneous to the dominant tone and main dramatic values

of the play as written. Again, the director's—or the critic's—view of life is interposed between the play and the audience. Finally, it is interesting that the performance of Jaques was the most successful in the production. Even though it was contemporary in character concept it was still Shakespeare's character. Its essentials were not changed or distorted—or transmogrified. Come to think of it, why didn't the director cast a girl as Jaques? Isn't *he* as a character androgynous too?

SHAKESPEARE'S DIALOGUE AND THE ACTOR

The drama is the only form of literature that expresses itself mainly through dialogue. The novel and the poem may use dialogue, but descriptive matter usually accompanies it. A play does include descriptive detail in stage directions for the reader. Such directions vary in length and detail according to the wishes of the playwright. George Bernard Shaw, for example, can hardly be said to be laconic: His stage directions consume pages of the acting version of the play, and in case, Shaw evidently felt, there was a chance of misunderstanding about his play, he provided his now famous prefaces. Shakespeare, on the other hand, has been most parsimonious in providing stage directions, and many of them are of dubious authenticity. The various editors of the plays, preparing copy for publication, have added conjectured directions. Stage directions in modern texts, Shakespeare's and the editors', do help the reader—and the actor. The language of Shakespeare's plays does need stage directions—conjectured and authentic—a glossary for the words, and notes as well as scholarly commentary to explain difficult segments.

The modern actor usually has many qualms about tackling Shakespeare. (In the last few years, since the proliferation of repertory companies, actors have been more adventurous and have, in spite of their feelings of inadequacy, welcomed the opportunity to play Shakespeare.) The most frightening aspect of Shakespearean acting is the dialogue, its problems of meaning and its perils vocally. The actor is faced with strange words, written in an order he is unaccustomed to and in a definite meter when in verse. The prose sections of dialogue are difficult because of Shakespeare's use of words and expression of meaning. It is dialogue, in verse or prose, which sounds little like everyday conversation. And

[4] Martin Esslin, " 'As You Like It,' or Boy Meets Girl," *The New York Times,* October 15, 1967.

the actor is used to conversational, reportorial speech.

Contemporary plays, from Arthur Miller's to Harold Pinter's, approximate or at least suggest everyday conversation. The actor's ears and tongue are oriented to it in word usage and especially rhythm, which is expressive of everyday movement, gesture, and behavior as well as speech. Shakespeare's language is written to another beat. The main problem for the actor and the director revolves around the question of whether to bend the actor to Shakespeare's speech or Shakespeare to the actor's speech.

The Royal Shakespeare Company of England, under the administration of Peter Hall, from 1960 to 1969 acted Shakespeare from spring to fall at the Memorial Theatre in Stratford-upon-Avon and contemporary plays (many new) at the Aldwych in London from fall to spring. Often the repertory for the London season would include plays by Shakespeare or some other Elizabethan (originally produced at Stratford), together with those by modern playwrights. The actors would thus become flexible vocally, alternating between Shakespearean verse and modern prose from performance to performance. The scheme that permitted this was economically advantageous, guaranteeing year-round employment for the actor and box-office continuity. It was also artistically advantageous in that a company ensemble could be created; and by working together every day the company could undertake a training program, using orthodox and experimental approaches. Much attention, therefore, could be devoted to the approach to speaking Shakespeare and a style for playing him. In an article, "The Royal Shakespeare Company 1965," in *Shakespeare Survey,* John Russell Brown says the "company has been taught to scrutinize every word in a play so that they know, always, what they are saying. . . . Generalizing and debilitating resonance and overblown fullness of phrase have been rinsed away; and most individual quirks and flourishes of elocution. . . . and so a scene that is stubbornly artificial on the page achieves its illusion of psychological subtlety." However, "For moments of consideration or deep feeling . . . [the company] take everything lightly, adding an energy and comic timing which have only a quick-fading gloss of irreverence to recommend them above the older varnish of impressive 'verse speaking'." He reproaches them for making the first scene

of *The Comedy of Errors,* involving old Aegeon's arrest, funny by pushing rhetorical elaboration into comedy; and "weighting . . . dramatic implication at the cost of rhythmical and metrical coherence" in *Love's Labour's Lost.* "At other times," he asserts, "dramatic effectiveness is joined with a precise psychological realism, a fresh awareness of character and situation" which is best achieved in "verbally simple and short speeches . . ." For the sake of realism and contemporaneity the actors use everyday inflections of speech not only in short lines but in longer rhetorical passages. This manner of speaking, together with elaborate realistic behavioral detail like Polonius' continually providing Claudius with state documents, Laertes' packing books for his visit to Paris, Shylock's calculating loans on an abacus, Portia's sipping wine with Nerissa, and the use of painful and violent detail in the history plays, gives the productions modern immediacy. However, Brown feels that such business is "trivial" in contrast with "the wider implications and strong verbal statements of drama." And he urges that this "new realism must be used together with a sure and detailed response to the metrical and poetical qualities of Shakespeare's writing." He feels that Sir John Gielgud has "shown that the fusion of styles is practicable." [5] His advocacy certainly appears worthy of consideration.

In discussing the various manifestations of Shakespeare's theatricalism, the presence of the poetic with the realistic has already been noted. Thus amalgamation in production is the goal to be achieved. It is not easy to achieve in the speaking of the verse.

The actor's study of the words will lead him to observe imagery and its revelation of themes and allusions to historical persons and events. He can learn to savor verbal decorative conceits often so expressive of character. He can come to understand language as a reflection and a source of illumination of the narrational and environmental aspects of a play. He may ultimately discover the poetic texture of the language and at the same time find Shakespeare's attitude to life as it is expressed by each play. Study, of course, must be translated into speech and action. Discoveries made through study form a subtexture of images, desires, and attitudes that can serve as stimuli

---

[5] John Russell Brown, "The Royal Shakespeare Company 1965," *Shakespeare Survey,* No. 19 (Cambridge, Cambridge University Press, 1966), pp. 111–17.

for the actor's use of his emotional, vocal, and physical equipment. And, the director and actor must remember, words come alive when they are lifted from the printed page and transferred to the stage. What sometimes seems abstruse, even unintelligible, and dull in print is made vital, vibrant, and beautiful by the human voice and the human body. Cold intellectual understanding of words and themes is transmuted into warm feeling and behavior.

The director and the actor realize the viability of a text by reading it aloud. Verbalizing stimulates not only a wide variety of impulses involving images, gesture, and action but the ways and means to communicate the language of a play.

Let us examine King Henry IV's opening speech.

> So shaken as we are, so wan with care,
> Find we a time for frighted peace to pant,
> And breathe short-winded accents of new
>   broils
> To be commenced in stronds afar remote:
> No more the thirsty entrance of this soil
> Shall daub her lips with her own children's
>   blood,
> No more shall trenching war channel her fields,
> Nor bruise her flowerets with the arméd hoofs
> Of hostile paces: those opposéd eyes,
> Which, like the meteors of a troubled heaven,
> All of one nature, of one substance bred,
> Did lately meet in the intestine shock
> And furious close of civil butchery,
> Shall now, in mutual well-beseeming ranks,
> March all one way, and be no more opposed
> Against acquaintance, kindred, and allies.
> The edge of war, like an ill-sheathéd knife,
> No more shall cut his master. Therefore,
>   friends,
> As far as to the sepulchre of Christ,
> Whose soldier now, under whose blesséd cross
> We are impresséd and engaged to fight,
> Forthwith a power of English shall we levy,
> Whose arms were moulded in their mothers'
>   womb
> To chase these pagans in those holy fields
> Over whose acres walked those blesséd feet
> Which fourteen hundred years ago were nailed
> For our advantage on the bitter cross.
> But this our purpose now is twelve month old,
> And bootless 'tis to tell you we will go:
> Therefore we meet not now. Then let me hear
> Of you, my gentle cousin Westmoreland,
> What yesternight our council did decree
> In forwarding this dear expedience.
>
> (Henry IV, Part I, 1. 1)

In analyzing this speech for performance it is useful to paraphrase it and break it down into thoughts. The meaning of every word may not be clarified but the general meaning should be.

1. Even though I (we: The King speaks for his subjects as well as for himself) am weak and pale with trouble, I will take the time and breath to speak of peace.

2. With labored breath I speak of new military action to begin in foreign lands.

3. Our land will no more be soaked with our children's blood.

4. Our fields will not be turned into trenches for war.

5. Our little flowers will not be trampled by roughshod horses' hooves.

6. Men with antagonistic eyes, like stars in an angry sky, of the same essential character and of the same qualities of breeding, who recently have slaughtered one another in violent attack, shall now march together in closed ranks, no more to fight acquaintance, kinspeople, or friends.

7. War, like an unsheathed knife, will no longer cut its owner (who should control it).

8. Therefore, friends, since we are soldiers of the cross, already sworn and pledged to fight, I shall draft an English army—whose soldiers' strength was inherited from their mothers—and go to Christ's tomb to chase those pagans out of the Holy Land where fourteen hundred years ago walked the blessed feet which were nailed to the cruel cross.

9. It is useless to tell you that this is my year-old wish (to go to the Holy Land). And this is not the reason for our meeting.

10. Therefore, let me hear from you, my dear friend Westmoreland, what the council authorized last night to promote this deeply desired campaign.

The language is still somewhat formal but it is no longer elliptical, and the rhythm has been changed. If the actor will improvise the speech and bring out the ten units of thought, he will make it conversational and more meaningful for himself. The units of thought and their sequence reveal explicitly and implicitly something about the character of Henry. Each thought suggests a unit of objective—what he wants.

As to what Henry is, physically and mentally, the first line tells the actor explicitly. The whole speech sums up his mental and emotional attitude. The natural question for the actor to ask is: Why does he think and feel as he does? A knowledge of *Richard II* and *Henry IV, Parts I* and *II* is necessary to answer this question fully. However, there is enough evidence in the play in which the speech appears to learn that Henry is guilt-ridden about his causing the death of Richard II, his usurpation of the throne, and his feeling that God is punishing him with civil war and the profligate behavior of his son Prince Hal. His overall desire as revealed by this speech is to atone for his sins by going to the Holy Land to fight the infidels. Each unit of thought in its own way reflects this desire. The actor and the director must determine such a desire or objective before coming to conclusions as to how the words will be said. This approach to the language through character will support the words, meaning, and meter subjectively. An objective approach through the words, their arrangement and relationship, and meter can be helpful too.

The study of imagery in the speech will be rewarding.

> No more the thirsty entrance of this soil
> Shall daub her lips with her own children's blood,

sets forth the mental image of the soil as a thirsty mouth whose lips have been painted with blood. (The soil becomes horrifyingly human.) The soil can become dry and receptive to liquid—rain and blood. The thought of blood of human beings swallowed up by the soil also suggests the biblical prophecy that human clay will revert to dust.

> No more shall trenching war channel her fields,

furthers the image of blood being channeled through fields in trenches dug or cut by war. The cutting characteristic of war is contained in the simile

> The edge of war, like an ill-sheathéd knife,
> No more shall cut his master.

and the knife, unsheathed by its owner, will turn against him and cut him just as internecine war involves families, friends, countrymen turning against and killing one another. They

> Did lately meet in the intestine shock
> And furious close of civil butchery,

and here we have the gut ("intestine") shock of cutting like butchers in hand-to-hand ("furious close") fighting.

As the actor reads this speech he will probably find, as he keeps in mind Henry's units of objective, that the tempo, volume, and emotional intensity will speed up and build beginning with

> No more the thirsty entrance of this soil

and will reach a climax with

> No more shall cut his master.

Perhaps the actor will pause. (He will need a pause to take a new breath to support the rest of the speech.) And then he will begin slowly to build the segment of the speech beginning with

> Therefore, friends,
> As far as to the sepulchre of Christ,

and ending with

> For our advantage on the bitter cross.

This unit of dialogue has considerable force and pressure but probably not as much as that related to the theme of civil war. Of course, character interpretation will decide where emotional and vocal emphasis will be placed.

The study of imagery, insofar as the actor is concerned, should not be from an intellectual or purely literary point of view; rather, from the viewpoint of finding a sense of reality and stimuli to feed the emotions. The reduction of poetic imagery to literal descriptions and explanations helps the actor not only to understand but also to see in his mind's eye a picture of what the image represents. He sees colors, shapes, textures, lines, and so on, and responds to them. Visual stimuli may evoke other sensory stimuli also. If, for example, the actor sees the "soil" as a repulsive human being or an animal drinking human blood and smearing his lips with it, he can in his imagination smell, touch, and taste the blood. Such stimuli give the image reality and stir the mind and emotions. An actor bases his performance on a sequence of images and stimuli. And thus an individual speech consisting of images becomes a link in the sequence.

Of course Shakespeare's language is a rich source for gesture, posture, behavior, and movement. The director's interpretation and the stage setting will determine what kind and how much. The Royal Shakespeare Company production of the play in 1966 set the first scene in the King's room, which contained three outstanding elements: a bed, a wall-hanging statue of Christ on the cross, and a group of wooden or lead soldiers arranged on a map on the floor. Henry was wearing a nightgown or its equivalent. These elements of scene and costume were highly connotative, symbolic, and significant. They determined the physical behavior not only of Henry but of Westmoreland and Blunt. The scene was not that of a formal meeting but an informal one in which the King's advisers come to his bedroom to report what has happened at the council meeting and on the battlefield. Henry's first speech suggests limited walking about inasmuch as he is "shaken" and "wan with care"—unless the words indicate mostly a nervous or even neurotic condition. In this case he might pace about agitatedly and sit (on the bed) after he addresses his question to Westmoreland. The action in the speech is mental and emotional rather than large physical movement about the stage. His nervous condition would suggest small gestures and/or the handling of objects. His being "shaken" and "wan with care" must not, however, be so debilitating that he would not be able to hold a council meeting or go to war in the scenes that follow.

A speech which permits larger movement, because of the character's intense agitation emanating from maddening frustration, is Lear's (*King Lear,* 2. 4), which begins

O reason not the need! Our basest beggars
Are in the poorest things superfluous.
Allow not nature more than nature needs,

and ends with

No, I'll not weep:
I have full cause of weeping, but this heart
Shall break into a hundred thousand flaws
Or ere I'll weep. O Fool, I shall go mad!

after which he leaves with Gloucester, Kent, and the Fool. In the speech he addresses successively Regan, the "heavens," both his daughters, himself, his daughters, and finally the Fool. It is full of changes of focus, thought, and direction of movement; it is a series of starts and stops. The speech can be built to a most effective climax by Lear's turning and going toward each person addressed, turning away as though leaving, and finally departing. (This is known as "working up an exit.")

A word of caution about speech and move-ment. Too much movement while the actor is speaking will make the words and thoughts more difficult for the audience to understand. (Productions on in-the-round or thrust stages especially are prone to this difficulty.) Furthermore, excessive movement tends to break the psychological contact between actors. (Eye contact between actors is very strong psychologically for actors and audience.) The audience watches the movement and responds to the emotion of the actor but words are disadvantaged. Young, high-strung actors want to activate everything by movement. They need a director's guidance to edit out movement for movement's sake and to find the inner action of a character. *Richard III,* for example, has many speeches which demand close concentration by the audience because they are long and complex. Richard as a character moves mentally more than physically; his physical disabilities argue against much movement; he compensates mentally for lack of physical action. And his public self must always be seen in contrast with the private.

Another thing to consider is that the plot lines of *Richard III* and all the histories are difficult for modern audiences who know little English history and cannot draw upon their knowledge to fill in the gaps made by loss of words and narrative information. The large number of characters in the histories makes distinction and function a problem too. Costumes, makeup, and behavior can clarify and distinguish character to a certain extent, but words are needed for complete understanding. Unfortunately audiences today, unlike the Elizabethan, are not trained to listen, nor do they love words for their own sake. (The listening audience that was being built up by radio has been destroyed by television.) For all these reasons Shakespeare's words must be protected. The director must constantly invoke checks and balances to defend the auditory from the distraction of the visual. Too, his own familiarity with the speeches must be guarded against; it will often delude him into thinking the audience, mostly unfamiliar, will understand what the actors are saying.

In spite of the references to the performance time of Shakespeare's plays as "two hours' traffic," found in *Romeo and Juliet* and *Henry VIII,* modern audiences can count on being in the theatre usually up to three hours unless the play has been drastically truncated. These references would seem to indicate, if taken literally—and they can be taken symbolically—that the Elizabethan actors spoke and moved very rapidly, and therefore modern actors should aim for speed. They should indeed—but not at the expense of clarity. Complete understanding of the dialogue and proper stressing of words and maintenance of meter will permit the actor to speak more rapidly and communicate the meaning to the audience. The actors at Stratford, Canada, and Stratford, England, manage this, though their rapid tempo and English pronunciation, especially by the Royal Shakespeare Company, make audibility a problem for American audiences. After a few performances and critical protest in this country, these actors and members of other English companies pace their speech more slowly than for English audiences. Directors will be wise to insist that American actors speak comparatively slowly at the beginning of a play in order to give the audience a chance to attune their ears to strange voices and speech before accelerating the tempo. Speed and simplicity are guiding words. Simplicity needs special attention.

"Pear-shaped" tones and self-indulgent and ostentatious vocalizing should be avoided. Shakespeare needs no vocal gilding. And yet the actor should savor Shakespeare's words, savor them to evoke creative stimuli. He can and should be aware of the poetic and imagistic values of decorative language and speak it for these values. Sonority and beauty of language should not be destroyed but shared with the audience—and they can be if meaning is communicated. Ponderous, sepulchral speaking—evidence more of the bardolatry of the nineteenth- and early twentieth-century school of Shakespearean acting than of modern understanding and relevance—should be avoided by the actor. (Granville-Barker was an innovator in stressing clarity, speed, and simplicity of speaking in his productions in 1912.) Poetry should be intrinsic by an adherence to meter more than by false vocal coloration. Vocal variety and proper stressing of key words will give the dialogue true color.

Speech in everyday life sometimes lacks color. We tend to speak without stress for meaning, in a monotone, and with little change in volume, pitch, or tempo. Actors in many modern plays and in all of Shakespeare's plays should seek vocal variety. Changes in volume and tempo usually constitute the range of variety achieved by most actors today. Their training in or attempts to use the Stanislavski

Method possibly explains this. In America the emphasis in the acting influenced or nurtured by the Method is upon the training of the emotions. (Stanislavski advocated the training of the voice and body too.) And the emotions induce changes in speed and volume of speech. The danger in highly emotional acting lies in the loss of control. The actor then not only squeezes out his emotions in rasping, reedy tones but garbles his words and shouts. In an attempt to achieve highly emotional, even a bigger-than-life performance, the actor succeeds only in a strained, unintelligible performance. The audience tries to forgive such ineptitude and tries desperately to follow the play—for a while. Continued shouting and agonized acting will eventually alienate the audience. Some members of the audience thus cut off from the play will blame Shakespeare as well as the actors—so often do they become the victims of verbal and emotional saturation and anarchy in performances of Shakespeare. Poor voice quality and poor communication are attributable also to another cause.

The actor needs more breath for Shakespeare than for the modern realistic play, written in short and often one-line speeches. In the long speeches a great deal of breath is needed, and breathing places must be carefully discovered and designed in order to pay out breath efficiently to keep in reserve enough breath support for each unit of speech. Breath support is necessary for clear diction. Vowels and consonants require sufficient breath to assist the mouth, tongue, and resonators to articulate proper, recognizable, and communicable sounds. Only by daily exercises and practice in performance can the actor develop sufficient breath support for good and beautiful voice quality and audience audibility.

The nonverbal phase in which we find ourselves in the theatre of the 1970s, brought about partly by the teachings of Antonin Artaud and expressed in his essay "No More Masterpieces," is responsible for so little attention to Shakespeare's language in many productions. The Living Theatre, oriented toward Artaud via the socially and politically biased minds and emotions of Julian Beck and Judith Malina, has been influential in the directorial emphasis upon the body rather than the word. And though the Living Theatre itself has not produced Shakespeare but other classics, it has exercised an influence on directors who would present Shakespeare in an innovative manner. Shakespeare, no longer living to protect his rights as author and with his works in the public domain, has been fair game for the innovators who update the visual and submerge the verbal. This means the loss of a rich dramatic value: The audience is over-fed from one kind of stimulus and starved for another. Of course the emphasis on the physical and visual in such productions purposes to communicate some "relevant" social and/or political view of life. In many instances the means is more significant than the end: The medium becomes the message. The nonverbal theatre is obviously antagonistic to Shake-speare's theatricalism, which is predominantly verbal, the chief means of communication.

Granville-Barker has rightly said that "when it comes to staging the plays, the speaking of the verse must be the foundation of all study." [6] Yet, though Shakespeare's theatre is predominantly verbal, it needs the support of the physical and visual. Modern audiences in general, unlike the Elizabethan ones, will not submit to the declamation, recital, or "reading" of Shakespeare unless in a presentation like "The Ages of Man" by Sir John Gielgud, a star performer; or in a presentation like "The Hollow Crown" by outstanding English actors. And, even so, such presentations do not have wide appeal; "listening" audiences are narrowly limited. How, then, can the director meet the demands of Shakespeare and non-Elizabethan audiences? Over the years directors have attempted to do this by making him contemporary.

PROBLEMS

Basic Staging of Key Scenes

1. Select the key scenes in *Macbeth* and analyze them for their narrational and thematic dynamics; their physical demands in terms of space, entrances, and exits, and continuity of scenes; and their use of furniture. Is an upper stage or level needed and/or helpful? Is an inner stage or area needed? Place these scenes on a set designed for a proscenium stage. Then place them on a thrust stage.

2. Analyze the key scenes in *As You Like It*. Consider points in problem 1.

Continuity

The problems that follow are from *Julius Caesar*. The whole class will study the play

and be able to participate in discussions of the problems involved in the scenes.

1. Analyze the first two scenes of Act 1 for their mood values and determine ways and means to join them rhythmically and maintain continuity.

2. Study 2. 2, 3, and 4 for problems of continuity, placement, locale, mood, and rhythm. What directorial techniques would you employ to solve them? Visualize a practical setting for the play. (How would you handle the problem of Artemidorus and locale?)

3. Direct the Cinna the Poet scene, 2. 3, and join it with 4. 1, which involves Antony, Octavius, and Lepidus, who, if you follow modern editors' stage directions, will be placed seated around a table.

4. Direct the end of 5. 1, after the exit of Octavius, Antony, and their army; scenes 2 and 3 to the death of Cassius.

Combat

1. Rehearse and present *Macbeth,* 5. 2, which involves the Scottish army of Menteith, Caithness, Angus, and Lennox. The scene marks a contrast with the mood and emotional impact of Lady Macbeth's sleepwalking episode. Establish the marching character of the army under command of its leaders. Certain necessary information must be conveyed to the audience, and yet the high tension and excitement of the impending confrontation with the forces of Macbeth must also be communicated. Remember the symbolic and impressionistic character of Shakespeare's fighting forces.

2. Plan the general pattern of movement or choreography of the climactic fight between Macbeth and Macduff. Protect the dialogue from the strong attention-taking power of movement. Present the scene to the class.

3. Rehearse and present the fight between Cassio, Roderigo, and Montano in *Othello,* 2. 3. Start the scene with Cassio driving in Roderigo and end it with the entrance of Othello and Iago's "hold, for shame!"

4. Study and rehearse *Coriolanus,* 1. 4. Pattern the movement of the scene very slowly and methodically. Break the scene into units of action. Rehearse each one carefully and in sequence but do so in broad, general terms at first. Use improvisations. Refine staging in subsequent rehearsals—eliminating, adding, and polishing. Let the rhythm of the units of action gradually evolve and establish itself.

---

[6] Harley Granville-Barker, *Prefaces to Shakespeare* (Princeton, Princeton University Press, 1946), *1*, 12.

Remember to work for total impression rather than the minute details of actuality. Do not prolong any unit of action. Time each according to its narrational importance.

Ceremony

1. Visualize and plan a procession and coronation for Richard in *Richard III,* 4. 2, leading to Richard's "Stand all apart.—Cousin of Buckingham,—" Determine the participants and their order of entrance. Analyze the dramatic values of the occasion, especially the ironic ones. Rehearse and present to the class.

2. Visualize the ceremony involved in the "Hymen" scene of *As You Like It,* 5. 4. Begin with the entrance of Hymen and end with the entrance of Jaques de Bois and work out the pattern of movement, posture, behavioral detail, and the pictorial aspects of the scene and present it to the class for criticisms and suggestions. The mood of the scene is very important.

3. Plan the procession and wedding ceremony of Claudio and Hero in *Much Ado About Nothing,* 4. 1. Placement of characters and the pictorial dramatization of the event should be carefully analyzed. Rehearse and present the scene to the class. End the scene with the exit of Claudio, Don Pedro, and Don John.

4. Stage the opening of *The Merchant of Venice,* 4. 1. End the scene with the entrance of Shylock. The placement of the Duke and the visual relationship of Shylock, Antonio, Nerissa, and Portia to him are very important. The ritual and ceremony of the trial must be worked out in detail and accuracy.

Comedy

1. Name two plays you consider comedies because of their prevailing lightness of tone. Defend your choices by analyzing the comic nature of the plot, characters, and language.

2. Name two you consider "dark comedies." Discuss their thematic values.

3. Select a comic scene from a predominantly serious play. Determine its degree and kind of comedy resulting from the emotional climate of the play as a whole. Present it to the class for criticism.

4. Present a scene illustrating a character in the "grips of an attitude."

5. Present a scene whose comedy emanates primarily from situation.

6. *The Taming of the Shrew* and *Much Ado About Nothing* contain scenes which demonstrate the battle of the sexes. Two students will select and present two such scenes for class discussion. Language and situation are important interpretive and directorial considerations.

7. Direct the scene in *Twelfth Night,* 5. 1, in which Viola and Sebastian recognize each other and are reunited. Start the scene with the entrance of Sebastian and end it with Olivia's "Fetch Malvolio hither—."

8. Direct *Romeo and Juliet,* 2. 5, between the Nurse and Juliet.

9. Direct 1. 1 of *The Comedy of Errors* for comedy, though the scene taken literally is serious.

10. Direct the scene between Don Armado and Moth in *Love's Labour's Lost,* 1. 2. End the scene with the entrance of Dull, Costard, and Jaquenetta. The emphasis is on language but character and character behavior must be conceived in comic terms to communicate the comedy inherent in the language.

Shakespeare's Dialogue and the Actor

1. Study the Bastard's "commodity" speech at the end of *King John,* 2. 1. First of all, paraphrase it and learn it in this form. Break it down into units of objective. Discover an image for each unit and string the units together in sequence. Memorize the words of the speech exactly. Finally, search for and set a pattern of movement, gesture, and behavior. Try to find some object or part of the character's costume to use for dramatic purposes.

2. Follow the procedure in problem 1 in your study and presentation of each of the three characters in *King John,* 3. 1. In working on Constance's speech search for vocal variety through tone, tempo, volume, and pitch. This variety must come through images and objectives.

3. Analyze *Twelfth Night,* 2. 4, for its staging possibilities and the acting problems in Malvolio's fantasizing. Work out the vocal and behavioral pattern of his speech from his moment-to-moment objectives and images. The interjections of speech and behavior of the other characters must come during Malvolio's pauses for thought and action. Be alert to rhythmic changes and continuity of the scene. Start the scene with the entrance of Malvolio and end it with his exit.

4. Rehearse the soliloquy made by Richard III at the opening of *Richard III,* 1. 1. The speech establishes him as a character, reveals his overall objective, and gives the audi-

ence a point of view toward the play. Determine the tone of the speech as well as the physical behavior of the character.

5. Study the images in Othello's speech to the Senators in *Othello*, 1. 3, which tells of his courtship of Desdemona. The speech begins with "And, till she come, as truly as to heaven/ I do confess the vices of my blood," and ends with "Here comes the lady; let her witness it." Analyze the psychology of Othello in this appearance before his superiors in government. Look for units of objective as well as images which will bring vocal variety to the speech.

6. Analyze and rehearse the Chorus' speech which opens *King Henry V*. Pay special attention to images and the train of thought. Mood and tempo are important.

7. Study and present the speech on "degree" spoken by Ulysses in *Troilus and Cressida,* 1. 3. Work for clarity of thought in this complicated speech. Remember that Ulysses believes strongly in what he says.

8. *The Tempest,* 2. 2, is a comic scene depending upon a simple but laughable situation deriving from the attitudes and behavior of Caliban, Stephano, and Trinculo. However, audience laughter is aroused not so much by what they do but by what they express in words. Find the characters' units of objectives in their speech and actions. Stage the scene.

9. Analyze the problems of staging and orchestrating speeches in *Love's Labour's Lost,* 4. 3. Focus audience attention on the verbal gymnastics of the scene. Work for comedy and clarity of thought. The play is a verbal comedy, and the scene between the King, Biron, Longaville, and Dumain is a game, each of them trying to score points. (End the scene with the entrance of Jaquenetta and Costard.) Rehearse and present to the class.

10. As an exercise in "building" a speech, analyze, rehearse, and present Shylock's speech in *The Merchant of Venice,* 3. 1, which begins "To bait fish withal" and ends with "I will better the instruction."

Chapter V

MAKING SHAKESPEARE CONTEMPORARY

Ben Jonson said that "He was not of an age, but for all time!" The history of the productions of Shakespeare's plays, however, has been characterized by apparent doubt of the truth of this statement. Beginning with the Restoration, producers and writers have shown less than full faith in the plays' appeal to audiences living in an era other than the Elizabethan. Each era has had its own theatrical ways and means and has insisted upon Shakespeare's conforming to them to achieve contemporaneity.

Modification of Text

Sir William Davenant's and John Dryden's version of *Julius Caesar* in 1719 was Shakespeare reconstructed to conform to current literary tastes and audience satisfaction. "Davenant's 'reconstruction' of *Macbeth* was so full of songs that Pepys thought it 'one of the best plays for variety of music and dancing I ever saw.'"[1] Bent on supposedly improving *Measure for Measure* by adding more comedy, Davenant introduced the characters of Beatrice and Benedick from *Much Ado About Nothing*. Davenant, however, was only one among many who rewrote Shakespeare. Edward Howard gave *Romeo and Juliet* a happy ending. Nahum Tate's version of *King Lear* saved Cordelia from death and married her to Edgar. Colly Cibber's adaptation of *Richard III*, with over half the dialogue by Cibber and most of Shakespeare's lines used in the play taken from his other historical plays, was so successful with audiences that it was performed for more than a hundred years in preference to Shakespeare's version.[2] Although there has been a gradual return to the original texts, modern producers have, for example, combined the two parts of *Henry IV* to make a play called *Falstaff*,[3] and the three parts of *Henry VI* and *Richard III* have been edited, arranged, and performed under the general title of *The War of the Roses*.[4] It is, of course, common practice today to use one text and borrow dialogue from other texts. This may be in the interest of textual accuracy or directorial whim but most certainly of enhancing modern audience appeal.

The nineteenth century was a period outstanding for pandering to public taste by wholesale cutting, emending, and rearranging the texts for the interpolations of "tableaux, processions, dances, crowd scenes and 'panoramic illusions' ": Augustin Daly showed Theseus' barge sailing to Athens in his production of *A Midsummer Night's Dream*; Sir Beerbohm Tree staged a tableau showing the signing of the Magna Carta in *King John*, a scene depicting Antony's return to Alexandria in *Antony and Cleopatra*, an actual procession showing Bolingbroke's entry into London in *Richard II*, and Duncan, in *Macbeth*, being escorted to his chamber by harpists and singers, after which the three witches "rushed on, cackling malevolently, and executed a grotesque pas de trois."[5] Henry Irving felt that the public came to Shakespeare to see the star and opulent spectacle. Since Irving played Shylock, who does not appear in the last act of *The Merchant of Venice*, and was convinced that the audience lost interest after his exit, he cut the last act. Typical of his detailed realistic settings and his use of scores of actors was his production of *Henry VIII* at the Lyceum Theatre in 1892. Charles Kean, who established the tradition of the importance of the spectacle followed by Irving, so emphasized lavish displays that William Macready

---

[1] Norman Marshall, *The Producer and the Play* (London, Macdonald, 1957), p. 134.
[2] Marshall, pp. 134–5.

[3] American Shakespeare Festival, summer 1966.
[4] The Royal Shakespeare Company, Stratford-upon-Avon, 1964.
[5] Marshall, pp. 139–40.

described Kean's productions "as scenes annotated by the texts." [6] In 1948 at Stratford-upon-Avon "the crowd scenes, brawls, fights, processions and dances were so over-elaborated that the momentum of the play [*Romeo and Juliet*] was constantly held up by those brilliant but irrelevant displays of production which dragged out the performance for three and a quarter hours in spite of the fact that more than three hundred lines were cut out of the play." [7] Even in 1966 the Royal Shakespeare Company at Stratford was not guiltless of spectacular displays of large armies and the wheeling onstage of wagons, cannons, and other massive instruments of war which also belong in the category of overelaboration—and box-office buildup. The directors might argue for all this in the name of realism and contemporaneity, which, they allege, modern audiences demand. (The staging also emphasized the brutality of war, a thematic value of the production.)

Realism of another kind was the reason for victimizing Shakespeare. Elaborately detailed, realistic scenery required cuts and scene rearrangements to lessen the number of scene changes. Such scenery was usually not easily movable and necessitated grouping scenes of one locale to play them consecutively. When producing *The Merchant of Venice,* for example, it was for many years standard practice to play all the early Venetian scenes together and then to play the Belmont scenes. Scenes so grouped could then be played one after another and the curtain would have to be lowered only once for a change of scenery. Beerbohm Tree and Augustin Daly, both devotees of mammoth realistic scenery, were notable for their ingenious rearrangement of scenes in *Twelfth Night* to accommodate the scenery and scene changes. Of course such rearrangements played havoc with Shakespeare's dramatic effects carefully designed for the alternation of locales, plot exposition and development, variation of mood, creation of suspense, and so on. Shaw, reviewing a Shakespearean production of July 2, 1895, starts off by calling it "The piece founded by Augustin Daly on Shakespeare's 'Two Gentlemen of Verona' " though "not exactly a comic opera" nor "a serpentine dance" but "a vaudeville."

He continues by saying he cannot speak harshly

towards a gentleman who works so hard as Mr. Daly does to make Shakespeare presentable: . . . His rearrangement of the scenes of the first two acts is just like him. Shakespeare shows lucidly how Proteus lives with his father (Antonio) in Verona, and loves a lady of that city named Julia. Mr. Daly, by taking the scene in Julia's house between Julia and her maid, and the scene in Antonio's house between Antonio and Proteus, and making them into one scene, convinces the unlettered audience that Proteus and Julia live in the same house with their father Antonio. Further, Shakespeare shows us how Valentine, the other gentleman of Verona, travels from Verona to Milan, the journey being driven into our heads by a comic scene in Verona . . . followed presently by another comic scene in Milan in which the same servant is welcomed to the strange city by a fellow-servant. Mr. Daly, however, is ready for Shakespeare on this point too. He just represents the two scenes as occurring in the same place; and immediately the puzzle as to who is who is complicated by a puzzle as to where is where. Thus is the immortal William adapted to the requirements of a nineteenth-century audience. [8]

Though satisfied by sumptuously realistic scenery, the public had to suffer the extra playing time caused by long waits between scene changes. Tree's productions at Her Majesty's Theatre between 1898 and 1911 were characteristic. "Gordon Crosse (*Fifty Years of Shakespearean Playgoing,* 1940) recalls that on one occasion he timed the intervals while the sets were built up and found that forty-five minutes were lost this way . . ." [9] Usually a third of the play as written by Shakespeare was also lost. However, curtain calls between the scenes and musical interludes were presented as diversionary devices. And at least three intermissions gave the audience rest periods even if they contributed to the lateness of the hour when they arrived home.

USE OF MUSIC

Another element of production which helped subordinate Shakespeare in the interests of contemporary audience appeal was the use of music. Music was as pervasive of a production

---

[6] M. St. Clare Byrne, "Fifty Years of Shakespearian Productions: 1898–1948," *Shakespeare Survey,* No. 2 (Cambridge, Cambridge University Press, 1949), p. 2.
[7] Marshall, p. 136.

[8] George Bernard Shaw, *Dramatic Opinions and Essays* (New York, Brentano's, 1909), *1,* 160–1.
[9] Byrne, p. 5.

in the Edwardian era as it is today in the usual motion picture or television program—and as it is in some stage productions. Music was used as overtures to acts, to build up entrances, to serve as background for soliloquies, and to emotionalize love scenes, scenes of conflict, scenes of mystery and suspense, or death scenes. Shakespeare was literally accompanied by music or in some cases music was merely accompanied by Shakespeare. Sometimes the actors sang their speeches instead of speaking them. It was not uncommon for managers, unsatisfied by the number of songs Shakespeare used in a play, to borrow songs from other plays. Daly, for example, when producing *Twelfth Night,* used a chorus of villagers to welcome Sebastian and Antonio to the coast of Illyria with *The Tempest's* " 'Come unto these yellow sands.' Later in the play Olivia conveniently fell asleep in her moonlit garden so that" Orsino could come onstage accompanied by "a male-voice quartet to serenade her with 'Who is Sylvia?'—which, of course, fitted very nicely when the first line had been changed to 'Fair Olivia, who is she?' " [10]

HISTORICAL ACCURACY

The public's delight with such divertissements, regardless of the damage to the texts of Shakespeare's plays, did not prevent their insistence upon historical accuracy in stage settings. They were willing to endure strain upon their backsides waiting for scene changes but insisted upon as much realism as history and archeology could provide in canvas and paint. Their taste in painting was reflected in their demand for realism on the stage. Actor-managers such as Charles Kean, the first to advocate and practice historical accuracy in every detail of production, Beerbohm Tree, Sir Squire and Marie Bancroft, and Henry Irving obediently complied. They were rewarded with huge audiences for Shakespeare and succeeded in keeping him on the stage by making him conform to public preferences.

A review of the history of Shakespearean production would make us take note of the revolt against the reign of the actor-managers and approvingly discuss the work of William Poel and particularly of Harley Granville-Barker, who did much to rescue and restore the real Shakespeare, but our concern here is with the theatre's efforts to make Shakespeare

[10] Marshall, pp. 140–1.

Barry Jackson's modern-dress production of Hamlet, *staged by H. K. Ayliff at the Kingsway Theatre, 1925. From Norman Marshall,* The Producer and the Play, *p. 176, used by permission of Macdonald and Co., London.*

popular in any age by bending him to the prevailing theatrical conventions of each age—to make him conform to time rather than find his timelessness. One of the ways most highly favored to bring Shakespeare up-to-date is to dress his characters according to the current fashion.

SHAKESPEARE AND UPDATED DRESS

Barry Jackson's production of *Hamlet,* directed by H. K. Ayliff in modern dress at London's Kingsway Theatre in 1925, started a trend that has developed into a kind of stylistic movement. Although this particular production appeared to many as just a stunt, it convinced others of the modernity of the play. The change in costumes caused a change in character interpretation and behavior which brought to light new facets of character and new insight into the meaning of the play as a whole. Realism resulted in some benefits but it is said that the verse lost some of its beauty and magnificence. Simplicity of speaking added clarity and directness of communication enhancing the universality of Shakespeare. Yet the device of using modern costumes remains questionable for some of the plays.

Jackson's next production, a modern-dress *Macbeth,* proved to many that period clothes are essential to plays of strong historicity and rhetorical language. Later Jackson went a step further in modernizing Shakespeare by not only clothing *The Taming of the Shrew* in the prevailing fashion but also substituting modern expressions and modern furnishings and properties. This approach, of course, did not so much enhance the values of the play as make of it an anachronistic joke. Oscar Asche's production of *The Merry Wives of Windsor* was another example of using Shakespeare's plays as vehicles for adaptation to the modern mode. It was completely rearranged, cut, emended, and rewritten as a hugely successful diversion at the expense of Shakespeare. *The Shrew,* in particular, has since become fair game for any adventuresome director. Sir Tyrone Guthrie's production of the play at Stratford, Ontario, in 1954 was a brilliant exercise in comic invention and spoofing when he dressed the characters in cowboy clothes, high-button shoes, Lautrecean dresses, blue blazers, white trousers, canes, and straw hats out of the turn-of-the-century fashions. The comedy of the Keystone Kops, Mack Sennett, Charlie Chaplin, the Marx brothers, *Annie Get Your Gun,* and *Hellzapoppin* was grist for his mill. No other director has yet managed to be so wildly eclectic, irreverent, or dazzlingly funny in manhandling the play. But it was Guthrie's *Taming of the Shrew,* with only incidental help from Shakespeare. It was also a case of shrewdly tailoring Shakespeare to audience taste—the pun is intended.

Experiments with Shakespeare in England influenced American productions. The first and one of the most successful modern-dress productions in the United States was Orson Welles's and John Houseman's *Julius Caesar* in 1938. With characters dressed in the black shirts of Fascist Italy, audiences saw the parallel between Rome's Caesar of 44 B.C. and Rome's Mussolini of A.D. 1938. The political and emotional climate of the nation conditioned public response and made Shakespeare a "modern" playwright. Maurice Evans' production of *Hamlet* immediately after World War II was in nineteenth-century military and court dress and gave the play a kind of timeliness. It emphasized plot over character, but the production ran for 147 performances on Broadway and had an extended tour of the country. Guthrie's production of the play during the first season of the Guthrie Theater in Minneapolis also utilized nineteenth-century dress. The use of pistols, flashlights, and other modern properties updated the production further than Evans'. This incongruity called attention to them and made the production appear tricky. Guthrie has often been taken to task for this sort of thing.

T. C. Worsley, drama critic of *The New Statesman,* wrote a book called *The Fugitive Art.* In it his review of Tyrone Guthrie's production of *Henry VIII* starts off by saying:

> There are two Tyrone Guthries, as there are at least two of most of us. There is Mr. Tyrone Guthrie, one of our leading producers, an original artist with a most imaginative mind, a great feeling for the visual, a highly developed sense of theatre. Then there is his *alter ego,* Master Tony Guthrie, let us call him, an inky urchin, with a fourth-form sense of humour and a violent self-destructive streak; the kind of urchin who, having completed a lovely neat fair copy, can never resist the fleeting impulse to spatter it with blobs of ink. . . . [Master G.] is the leader of what we may call the "Wouldn't-it-be fun (just for a change)" School.[11]

Although his *Hamlet* was brilliantly conceived and produced, it jarred its critics' sensibilities. Evans' and Guthrie's productions, however, managed to draw *Hamlet* closer to the audience and gave its subject immediacy. Less successful than these two was the 1964 Gielgud-Burton *Hamlet* in rehearsal and street clothes. Fault was found with the absence of a strong directorial point of view and with much of the acting. The production failed to achieve complete theatrical viability and modernity.

The American Shakespeare Festival has updated several plays with varying degrees of success. In *The Directorial Image* I have discussed two of them, *Measure for Measure* in 1956 and *Troilus and Cressida* in 1961, to point out that their modern-dress productions resulted in changes in dramatic values that went counter to the plays as written. The first was an out-and-out spoof of the play and the second, in American Civil War dress, became a game devoted to scoring points of parallels between Greeks and Trojans on the one hand and the Confederate and Union soldiers on the other. A reviewer of another production said, "The American Shakespeare Festival at Stratford opened its new season yesterday afternoon with a gay Victorian pastel fashioned around 'Twelfth Night.'" Pointing out that Katharine Hepburn who played Viola and Rouben Ter-Arutunian, who designed the settings and costumes, dominated the production, he said the play "as arranged . . . is full of brisk attractions and bright conceits— an operetta-like adventure in sentiment." In

---

[11] T. C. Worsley, *The Fugitive Art* (London, John Lehmann, 1952), pp. 87–8.

Twelfth Night *as produced by the American Shakespeare Festival Theatre, Stratford, Connecticut, 1960. Directed by Jack Landau; designed by Rouben Ter-Arutunian. Photo: Martha Holmes.*

fact it all looked like *The Pirates of Penzance* or *H.M.S. Pinafore*. It should at least have been funny but, as the reviewer put it, "The promise of a constant rollick is there. But as played yesterday . . . the seaside zephyr is more puff than steady breeze. The eye is amused and the mind is almost becalmed." [12] The Spanish-American costumes in a new version of *Much Ado About Nothing* met with Brooks Atkinson's general approval. He thought "the acting has a lightness of touch and an idiomatic flow" and the play "an example of Shakespeare's literary opportunism and professional untidiness. It combines realistic comedy with the artificial story-telling of the Middle Ages, and it need not be taken reverently." [13]

The Stratford, Ontario, Shakespearean Festi-

val, whose production of *The Taming of the Shrew* has already been cited for its successful irreverence—and irrelevance—to that text, was forcefully taken to task for its 1963 production of *Timon of Athens* in *The New York Times* Sunday article, "On Going Modern: Perils of Shakespeare in Up-to-Date Garb," by Howard Taubman. In the mind of this critic, "The only valid test" involved is "whether an updated production serves the play." Calling *Timon* "a weak play, simpleminded in structure and development," he asks, "Can a modern-dress approach help to shore up the play's disabilities? Probably not. The Canadian production merely diverts one's attention to other things. For it is replete with ingenious inventions." Modern costumes, bits of business, and character behavior were used to stand in contrast with the audience's view of ancient Athens, and once again they were asked to play a game of "Look out for what they will think of next."

[12] R. J. Leeney, *The New Haven Register,* June 3, 1960.
[13] Brooks Atkinson, "They Have a Style," *The New York Times,* August 18, 1957.

Timon of Athens in a modern-dress production at the Stratford Shakespearean Festival, Ontario, Canada, directed by Michael Langham, 1963. Designed by Brian Jackson. Photo: Peter Smith.

Apemantus, the churlish philosopher, is got up like a cynical newspaperman . . . A contemporary cliché is invoked but casts no new light on character and merely becomes a conceit that doesn't come off. . . . Allowing for theatrical license, one finds it difficult to accommodate one's mind to frequent contrasts between look and language. Glimpsing Timon as modern fashion-plate, one cannot easily adjust to words like this: "Mine honest friend, I prithee, but repair to me next morning." There is also something startling when, after a trumpet's sound, a servant announces, " 'Tis Alcibiades, and some twenty horse, all of companionship," and Alcibiades in a smart modern uniform strides forth as if he had stepped out of a command car . . . Once you commit yourself to modern-dress Shakespeare, you are likely to be tempted into literalisms, which can be ludicrous as well as anachronistic.

The audience on opening night of the production, however, responded with "bursts of applause for each bright, modern touch," even though "These responses came occasionally in the midst of speeches, often fragmenting lines

and phrases." The danger of "going modern," he concludes, "is that the clever, modern correspondence, rather than the play, becomes the thing." [14]

MODIFICATIONS OF EXTERNAL ELEMENTS AFFECT INTERNAL

In trying to make Shakespeare contemporary other dramatists have changed the form and structure of his plays, and directors have experimented with various aspects of physical production. The approach has been external for the most part. Yet the modifications of the external elements have affected the internal. That is, the characters and the meanings of the plays have undergone changes. And this was to be expected when the plays were reconstructed. The means of performance have been equally responsible for such changes. Modern costumes, for example, must affect character movement and general behavior, and characterization takes on different coloration. The clothes make the man. Audiences gen-

[14] *The New York Times,* September 8, 1963.

erally find that modern psychology is immediately discernible when no longer hidden under strange clothes and behavior. This is so because the director and the actors in preparing the productions were forced to visualize the characters as people of today rather than of some world remote from the present. Conventional movement, gestures, makeup, and stage business had to be abandoned in favor of the convincingly realistic. Perhaps most important of all, modern dress demanded modern speech —or, at least, speech less romantic or declamatory and more underplayed vocally and emotionally. Thus the content of Shakespeare's plays tends to be seen, heard, and felt more realistically and is experienced with more immediacy and applicability. But this is true only if the externals of production do not dominate the play. We have already seen that certain of Shakespeare's plays respond to modern productional restatements whereas others do not. The crux of the problem lies in a play's meaning and purpose as written by Shakespeare and a communication of the play which will bridge the centuries between the age for which it was written and the age for which it is being produced.

The modern and enlightened director in his experimentations has demonstrated an awareness of the problem. The modern-dress productions by such a director have evolved from a true desire to capture the universal qualities of Shakespeare by examining the plays for their contemporaneity. Norman Marshall points out that Barry Jackson, whose "Hamlet in Plus Fours" succeeded in revealing the modernity of *Hamlet,* decided to produce *Timon of Athens* in modern dress at the Birmingham Repertory Theatre because "The play had a good deal in common with contemporary Birmingham." [15] The topicality of *Troilus and Cressida* was underscored by its modern-dress production directed by Michael Macowan when it opened in London the day after the announcement of the Munich pact. Guthrie pointed up the contemporary in his 1956 production of the same play by finding "the modern equivalent for many of Shakespeare's models" and transferring "the play to a period approximately fifty years ago when wars were still regarded as romantic and heroic." [16] Though the means of production may stand out because of their novelty they are,

when successful, dependent upon valid interpretations.

INTERPRETATION REPLACES THEATRICAL DEVICES

In the last several years interpretation, rather than novel theatrical devices, has become the main stepping-stone to Shakespearean production. And the purpose of interpretation is usually to find a play's essential reality and its viable truth for the present time. Martin Esslin, in his introduction to Jan Kott's *Shakespeare Our Contemporary,* says that "Great works of art have an autonomous existence, independent of the intention and personality of their creators and independent also of the circumstances of the time of their creation, that is the mark of their greatness. The tragedies of Aeschylus, the paintings of El Greco, the poems of John Donne have a significance to twentieth-century man of which the contemporaries of their creation could not have had the remotest notion." He goes on to explain that poetry and plays take on new and deeper meanings when seen in the light of psychoanalysis, expressionism, and the poetry of Rainer Rilke or Ezra Pound. The writing of history and literary criticism must be understood in terms of the past which illuminates the present. Therefore Shakespeare speaks to each age differently. He was by turns different to Samuel Johnson, Coleridge, William Hazlitt, Georg Brandes, and Granville-Barker, and is different to us today. "And likewise," Esslin says, "the angle of vision changes with the place, as well as the time, from which the great, the autonomous work of art is seen." He finds the point of view of Jan Kott, a product of post–World War II Poland, victimized by destruction, concentration camps, and the ideologies of both Hitlerian Germany and Stalinist Russia, most revelatory of modern correspondences and equivalencies in Shakespeare. The histories and the great archetypal tragedies create a world which the Polish philosopher and critic Kott found familiar. Filled as they are with war, conspiracy, brutality, and indifference to human suffering, they parallel the life of mid–twentieth-century Poland and Eastern Europe. He found that they were "akin in their ultimate sense to the contemporary Theatre of the Absurd." And Esslin believes that "if the Theatre of the Absurd can be regarded as being particularly of our time, then the particular impact of Shakespeare on our time must spring from a deep

---

[15] Marshall, pp. 179–80.
[16] Marshall, p. 188.

inner connection between the themes of Beckett or Ionesco and Shakespeare's subject matter." [17]

SHAKESPEARE AND THE THEATRE OF THE ABSURD

The Theatre of the Absurd has been widely accepted as the voice and philosophy suitable for the world of today. Its influence has been readily acknowledged by playwrights. The leading ones include Harold Pinter and N. F. Simpson in England and Edward Albee and Jack Gelber in America. Playwrights in the rest of the world have also felt the impact of this new theatre. They all seem to feel and express a similar disorientation with a society in which nothing is certain, reasonable, logical, or sacred. They have lost faith in the old established values of life because they have tested them and found them wanting: Religious faith gave way to faith in a better way of life, nationalism, and various political ideologies only to have this faith destroyed by the real war and the cold world of the cold war. "Cut off from religious, metaphysical, and transcendental roots, man is lost; all his actions become senseless, absurd, useless," [18] Ionesco has declared. This is the theme which dominates the thinking of such playwrights.

In order to find a unity between this view of life and a form of expression, playwrights have rejected order and the openly comprehensible in favor of no story or plot in the conventional sense; allegorical, archetypal, or puppetlike characters, without subtlety or motivation; non-sensical and non-sequitur speech, fragmented and incoherent; and vague, inferentially stated themes presented in a special world of dreams and nightmares. A world in chaos is presented without argumentative theory or suggestions for ameliorative solutions. The *presentation* of such a world is all that matters. The world *is,* and the audience must accept its existence—and so the absurdist play.

Without logical or, at least, conventional form, recognizable characters, intelligible dialogue, or a precisely enunciated or demonstrated theme, the plays can be felt and understood only by an audience which can escape from its traditional and conditioning critical standards and learn to play the game of theatregoing in a different way. On the other hand, the audience schooled in the conventional theatre finds itself frustrated, confused, irritated, and outraged without its frame of reference and aesthetic security. Obviously such an audience protects itself by remaining objective and emotionally uninvolved in what it sees and hears on the stage. Its experience may include laughter out of lack of understanding and frustration, but empathy is firmly rejected. Fleeting images, consciously or unconsciously recognized, may be part of the experience. Grotesquely ironic parallels between life and the fiction of the absurdist play may flash through the minds of the audience. And, if so, the play is being communicated. The audience finds "concrete stage images of the absurdity of existence . . . In Ionesco's *The Chairs,* for example, the poetic content of a powerfully poetic play does not lie in the banal words that are uttered but in the fact that they are spoken to an ever growing number of empty chairs." [19] This kind of theatre naturally makes new demands upon playwrights, actors, and directors as well as audiences.

Playwrights, particularly those most disillusioned and sensitively contemplative and philosophical about life, responded with enthusiasm to this new theatre. They not only subscribed to the view of the human condition but to the mode of expressing it. Naturally, the directors of their plays, if they were to understand them and communicate them to audiences, had to be sympathetic or at least open to the absurdist view of life and the techniques of expressing it. These techniques are actually not novel; they derive from various traditional kinds of theatre. The novelty of the Theatre of the Absurd results from the eclectic combination of techniques borrowed from the past.

Abandoning language as the main medium of communication, dominant in the realistic conventions, the Theatre of the Absurd leans heavily upon ritualistic or stylized movement, pantomime, the use of properties, and sound to create visual imagery for the expression of metaphysical meaning. The use of clowns and jesters in mime and double-talk dialogue serves to juxtapose most vividly the grotesque and the logical. The influence of the ancient mime, the commedia dell'arte, the English music hall,

---

[17] Martin Esslin, Introduction to Jan Kott, *Shakespeare Our Contemporary* (Anchor Books ed. Garden City, N.Y., Doubleday, 1966), pp. xi–xx.

[18] Martin Esslin, *The Theatre of the Absurd* (Anchor Books ed. Garden City, N.Y., Doubleday, 1961), p. xix.

[19] Esslin, pp. xx–xxi.

American vaudeville, the Keystone Kops, Charlie Chaplin, and the Marx brothers is clearly seen in the comic tones of the Theatre of the Absurd. And the theatricality of the plays is obviously derived from expressionism, surrealism, dadaism, and the epic drama of Bertolt Brecht, which project the allegorical content of the world of dreams, mental aberrations, and fantasy. All those forebears have characteristics in common: They are forms of commentary which when comic are satirical and when serious are ironic; they present archetypal characters in episodes which are associational rather than organized; and they keep the audience outside, superior, and unempathic with the personages and events onstage.

The directorial and productional techniques demanded for such drama are highly theatricalist. Improvisation to create comic behavior and business and significant detail is a strong medium of expression. Out of improvisation usually comes a profusion of movement and often great physical exuberance. In general, the visual takes precedence over the aural. Directorial communication is thus largely based upon concrete stage images calculated to impress the audience consciously or subconsciously. Abstraction rather than realistic representation is the operative rationale, and the director is free to reject the unifying force of a single established style in directing the play. The directed play thus becomes a kind of theatrical collage. The director, like the absurdist playwright, may select and combine whatever techniques he wishes.

English directors, in particular, have adopted the view of the Theatre of the Absurd and applied it in interpreting Shakespeare. The most notably successful example is Peter Brook's *King Lear* production with actors from the Royal Shakespeare Company. First

Peter Brook's production of King Lear, *with Paul Scofield and the Royal Shakespeare Company, Stratford-upon-Avon, 1964. Designed by Peter Brook.*

presented in London, it came to New York in May 1964. Brook has acknowledged his indebtedness to Jan Kott's essay on the play, "King Lear or Endgame," in which Kott has tried to show the parallels between the two plays. Kott sees both plays as allegorical accounts of the "decay and fall of the world."[20] Brook shows Kott's influence in a variety of ways. The setting for his production, for example, was stark, simple, and elemental. He used two enormous gray rectangular panels which acted as an inner portal to frame an unornamented gray wall in the background. In some scenes he lowered rectangular, copper-looking sheets of metal and used roughhewn fences and large rough tables. Otherwise, the stage was "like a vast, empty, heartless earth."[21] As Kott said, "In *King Lear* the stage is empty throughout: There is nothing except the cruel earth, where man goes on his journey from the cradle to the grave."[22] Taubman in his review of the production says that "Brook has composed his scenes in the framework of the open spaces of his deep stage so that man, though often in the foreground, is a small figure against the thick rotundity of the world. Mr. Scofield as the mad, spent Lear and the blind Gloucester of John Laurie, consoling each other, form a sculptured pietà in an unfeeling plain."[23] Here is allegorical theme projected by a concrete stage image. Kott noticed that an instance of influence from the Theatre of the Absurd was the use of shoes in various scenes. In the opening scene, as directed by Peter Brook, court figures put on their boots, and in the scene when Lear returned from hunting, servants helped him take off his boots, and he rubbed his foot; and when, in a later scene, Gloucester met the mad Lear, he took Lear's boots off, hugged them to him, and kissed them. As the curtain goes up on *Waiting for Godot* a pair of shoes lies near the footlights. Later, shoes are incorporated into the action of the play.[24] Kott also points out that "The first three acts" of *Lear* "almost belong to epic theatre. There are few objects, but every one of them is real and means something: the orb and the sword, the map drawn on leather, old Gloucester's

astrolabe, stocks, even the chain-spoon carried by Oswald as the court steward."[25] Walter Kerr in reviewing the production in New York mentions the sparseness and meaningful nature of objects used by the director: "A crown, a riding crop, and a few other leftovers of a lost universe lie loosely gathered, for occasional use, on a spare table. Torches have no flames in them. . . . Thunderclouds fail to darken the stage: a man running from the storm merely writhes against one screen and Lear goes mad in endless, blinding light."[26] This is, of course, Brechtian theatre and one of the aspects of the tradition of the Theatre of the Absurd.

SHAKESPEARE AND BRECHT

It can be seen, then, that the staging of Brook's *Lear* followed Kott's *Lear-Endgame* concepts in a general way without being slavish to them. Kott's thoughts were seminal. Brook rethought them in terms of the stage, actors, and productional possibilities. The details of character interpretation, as worked out by Brook and the actors, contributed to the general theme of the play conceived by Kott. And such interpretation also reflected Kott's study of certain critical scenes of the play, such as the Gloucester-Edgar scene at Dover and the handling of the Fool-Edgar-Gloucester-Lear scene on the heath. Lear's acceptance of madness and of himself as fool or clown was absurdist and vivid in Paul Scofield's performance guided by Brook. What was the overall impact of this approach to the play? Though the human condition was presented in all its grotesqueries, the audience response was seldom emotional. Brechtian "alienation" or "distantiation" cooled sympathy for Lear and Gloucester but seared the mind with their predicament—and Everyman's condition imposed by some inexorable "mechanism." This contemporaneity was still another example of Brecht's influence. Indeed, Brecht as playwright and director has proven a rich source of ideas for producers of Shakespeare. Some directors have used him more appropriately than others.

William Gaskill's production of *Macbeth* in London in the fall of 1966 was also Brecht based. Gaskill used a bare, stark stage illuminated by unchanging brilliant light. The cos-

[20] Kott, p. 152.
[21] Howard Taubman, "Theater: 'Lear', a Team Achievement," *The New York Times,* May 19, 1964, p. 43.
[22] Kott, pp. 146–7.
[23] Taubman, *ibid.*
[24] Kott, pp. 365–6.

[25] Kott, p. 364.
[26] Walter Kerr, "King Lear from England," *New York Herald Tribune,* May 17, 1964, p. 12.

tumes were designed with simplicity of line and detail and subdued colors in such a way as to suggest a degree of modernity of dress. The acting, with Sir Alec Guiness and Simone Signoret in the leading roles, was calculated to "distance" audience response. One critic, on the side of the majority, who considered Gaskill's production of *Macbeth* a failure, condemned the use of the Brechtian "touches," which he said "may be *echt* Brecht but they warp the play, drawing our attention too often to W. Gaskill and away from W. Shakespeare. Whether or not they seem idiatic, they might have worked to the play's gain had it been possible to discern a purpose behind them other than the ingenious application of alienating shock. Question: Did we acquire by their means a better understanding of ambition, temptation, tyranny? Answer: We didn't." To this critic, "The point at issue is whether seemingly perverse innovations can be justified in the cause of experiment if they impede understanding." [27] In the case of Brook's absurdist-Brechtian production of *King Lear,* experimentation was more successful because the purpose behind it was discernible. It was discernible because of the brilliance of the director and the leading actor Paul Scofield, who caught in his characterization of Lear the inherent tragedy in an old man victimized by the absurd and wanton circumstances surrounding him. The text of the play lent itself to the interpretation and directorial means chosen for the production. Lear is unable to alter the circumstances of his life regardless of his attempts to will them to change. Macbeth, on the other hand, could have willed a different course in his life. Determinism is ineffectual in the one play and is possible in the other because Shakespeare wrote the two plays accordingly. The absurdity of life is patent in *Lear* and is not in *Macbeth.* Brook emphasized a dramatic value intrinsic in the text. Gaskill superimposed a value extrinsic to *Macbeth.* Consequently one director and his actors revealed the play in a new and justifiable light whereas the other went counter to his material and obscured its inherent meaning. Moreover, the latter borrowed Brechtian techniques and used them literally when they were not literally applicable, and Brook used them when their purpose was consistent with the motivating forces behind them, and used them in modification.

[27] Jeremy Kingston, "Theatre," *Punch,* November 2, 1966.

In tracing Brecht's influence, it is interesting to cite the 1966 repertoire of Shakespearean productions at Stratford-upon-Avon. First of all, it is to be noted that the Royal Shakespeare Company at Stratford was under the general direction of Peter Brook, Peter Hall, and Paul Scofield. They were united by an approach to Shakespeare which stresses the contemporaneity of the plays. In operating both the theatre at Stratford and the Aldwych in London they used the Royal Shakespeare Company of actors at the Memorial Theatre mainly for Shakespeare and at the Aldwych primarily for modern works. The 1966 program for the plays states that in performing modern plays at the Aldwych "a bridge is built between Shakespeare and the modern theatre so that each reflects something of the other's attitudes and techniques." Under such an arrangement the company can work "constantly together in varied repertoire" to create "a flexible ensemble with a distinctive character." Peter Hall and his colleagues in their productions of *Hamlet, Henry IV, Parts I and II, Henry V,* and *Twelfth Night* vividly demonstrated their philosophy.

As expressions of directorial concepts, the settings for all the plays were marked by simplicity, functionalism, and dynamism. The furniture and other properties—carefully selected for symbolic values—were placed in position by actors as they were needed and were set up during the scene and light changes; or both settings and furnishings were "tracked" and flown in by mechanical means. They were undeniably theatrical in their magical appearances and disappearances. In effect, they became other "actors" in the total performance. Scenic animation, with its connotative and symbolical qualities, was an essential part of the directorial approach to most of the plays.

Hamlet and the *Henrys* were served by two black, shiny metallic-looking thick walls which slid in a track and related to one another at different angles. Often they suggested the back wall and one side wall of a room. In this relationship the two walls would sometimes separate and create a large opening with tremendous dramatic effect. A specific example of scenic animation was the entrance of Claudius, Gertrude, Hamlet, and Polonius seated on a bench upstage of and attached to a council table. This platform and furniture unit rolled from upstage center downstage toward the audience and gave the effect of a close-up in films. The image of Hamlet wedged in or trapped among his adversaries was a memorable moment. The choice of scenic properties seemed determined by their audience recognition and symbolic associational value. In *Henry IV, Part I* a bed, toy soldiers on the floor, and a crucifix on the back wall were highly suggestive in introducing the ailing soldier-king Henry IV, who was obsessed with thoughts of guilt and the need for expiation by a pilgrimage to the Holy Land. Hal, in the next scene, was placed at one side of a room filled with a diamond-shaped table whose top looked like burnished metal. In fact, it reminded one of a shield with the inscription "Henry IV" hammered out in the center. Hal, in association with this shield-table with his father's name upon it, was in an excellent stage position for his soliloquy dealing with his prodigal way of life and his future royal responsibilities. The visual image was noticeably impressive and emblematic. And sound created its special images.

Auditory stimuli of various kinds were used as active instruments of theatrical communication to change the mood of the audience suddenly and sharply. For example, the stillness, quietness, and mystery of the first scene in *Hamlet* were abruptly shattered by the loud scraping and metallic sound made by the unexpected opening of a large and heavy door onto the battlements. This was an effect well planned to jar audience sensibilities and enhance mystery and suspense. Characteristically, changes in sound were not made to allow audience members to accommodate themselves gradually and with ease but to jolt them into quick and new accommodations. The deafening roar of cannon, the sharp and strident sound of a trumpet, or the dry shocking boom-boom of drums in the *Henrys* are other examples of the galvanic nature of sound.

This activistic approach to setting and sound was applied to lighting too. Contrast of color, shape, and intensity of light is dramatic. The

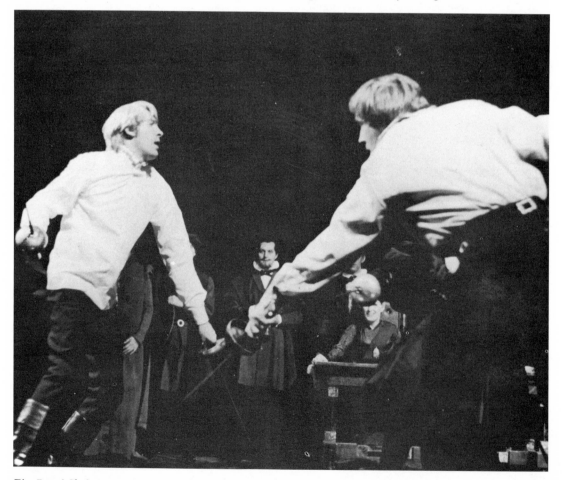

The Royal Shakespeare Company's Hamlet *at Stratford-upon-Avon, 1966. Directed by Peter Hall. Designed by John Bury.*

The Royal Shakespeare Company's Twelfth Night, *directed by Clifford Williams, 1966. Designer: Sally Jacobs.*

greater and more abrupt the contrast, the more dramatic—if it is integrated into the overall concept of the play's production. Sometimes the lighting at Stratford was intrinsic and did not call attention to itself. Its extrinsic use, however, was more characteristic of the directors' approach. Each light change became a theatrical effect. The "shock" value was intended. One of the most memorable effects was achieved in the scene between Hamlet and the Ghost. First of all, the large black walls of the set separated and created an impressive opening for the Ghost to come through in "unfamiliar guise" as an enormous floating figure. When Hamlet accepted the Ghost as his father he turned to him with his back to the audience, leaned heavily against him, and extended his arms upward on his chest, his white hands and yellow hair in highlight against the blackness. They were embraced with a circle of golden light. This moment not only communicated a sense of reunion between

father and son but symbolized much more. It signalized absolute fealty to the father and served as a motive force for all of Hamlet's subsequent behavior and action. It was a startling and unforgettable visual premise for the rest of the play. Hamlet's doubt about the truthfulness of the ghost or devil never thereafter became more than transient.

Certain costumes were designed specifically for their calculated effect to astonish and overwhelm the sight. Pistol in *Henry IV, Part II* appeared in a costume recalling the motorcycle-riding "hood," complete with black leather jacket adorned with raised silver metal pieces and leather fringe. A pistol, slung Western-style around his waist and handled cowboylike, further provoked audience recognition. Elizabethan tights and oversized boots served both history and modern times. The comic and the realistic were thus wedded in astonishing fashion. Falstaff's figure in both *Henrys* was padded to gargantuan proportions. In profile

Henry IV, Part I, *by the Royal Shakespeare Company, directed by John Barton, Trevor Nunn, and Clifford Williams, 1966. Designer: John Bury.*

he was hilariously funny and all in all undeniably a ton—or two—of flesh. He was a lumbering, waddling source of wit—exaggerated and intensified out of truth to life but congruent to the directors' basic concept of the play and its production. Ophelia in her mad scene was bedraggled and dirty and looked as though she came straight from bedlam, but she strummed her guitarlike musical instrument and sang in modern folksong fashion in an Elizabethan version of Joan Baez in rags. Bardolph in the *Henrys* had a bald head atop a costume which gave him a zombie look. His behavior emanated from his appearance: He was a heavy-footed and mentally retarded automaton out of Boris Karloff's repertoire of horror characters.

Nearly all of the characters in the plays at Stratford had a new and fresh (though not always convincing) look. The most sensational and most successful characterization, from the viewpoint of box office, was David Warner's "cool" Hamlet. Long, lean—all flopping hands, arms, and elbows, and skinny legs continually folding and unfolding—here was no

"soldier" or "gentleman" Hamlet but possibly the beatnik-scholar-poet Hamlet. Casting Warner for his physical characteristics and the general image he creates for youth everywhere was the basis for the director's interpretation not only of the role of the central character but of the entire play. He evidently saw a parallel between the dilemma of Hamlet and that of youth today. (This search for modern relevance is an overruling preoccupation of all the directors at Stratford.) And all of us, struggling with thoughts of war, death, destruction, and ever changing values, can see the parallel in terms of personal uncertainty, doubt, indecisiveness, and even melancholy. Warner's natural look of bewilderment and futile gestures helped to dramatize this. Yet his "cool" Hamlet left many of the audience cold. A tortured, agonizing Hamlet he was, but so intense and self-centered that he seemed to be truly mad and in need of psychiatric help. Here was no Hamlet putting on "an antic disposition." As a "personality" with "presence" onstage he had undeniable fascination, but he had little warmth and sympathetic attractiveness for many of the audience. (The college boys and girls scattered through the audience and standing behind the orchestra rail found him amusing, endearing, and totally sympathetic. In fact, they saw him as they saw themselves.) Although he had the mannerisms of the modern intense Greenwich Village poet, there was little poetry in his performance. The director and the actor evidently decided to seek novelty of verbal expression as well as of behavior, and thus poetry became conversation, lyricism became clinical hysteria, beauty and warmth became ugly and cold. It could be argued that just this effect was calculated: It was necessary to present man's human condition through an Everyman-Hamlet who had just stepped off the front pages—or stepped in from the street. So newsworthy, so up-to-date, so recognizable, and so faddish was this Hamlet that it was valid in terms of the directorial concept.

The character of Pistol in *Henry IV, Part II* has already been referred to. His costume was the foundation for his character. (Whether the designer thought of it first or whether the director did makes no difference because the director accepted it and evidently approved it as an expression of his own integrating concept.) Another novel character in the *Henrys*, played by the same actor in the two plays in accordance with all characters in both plays, was Prince Hal. He was presented from the outset as a studious, calculating prince, knowing full well that he was destined for kingship. He was thus capable of playing the part of the good-time boyhood friend of Falstaff in *Part I* and that of the responsible king who did not hesitate to cast off Falstaff in *Part II*. This interpretation solved the thorny problem of unifying the characterization for both plays. When the character appeared in the production of *Henry V* he was the same practical, unidealistic man of the world who knew the hard facts of living without illusions. The play thus emerged as a modern treatise on hardheaded opportunism, practical politics, and fact-facing rather than a paean of praise for nationalism and the divine right of kings. Here again the unity of interpretation and the centrality of the character in all three plays created a lack of the usual warmth and sympathy for him. The warm emotional impact conventionally generated by these histories was absent and replaced by cold intellectualism. The resultant aesthetic distancing of Hal and Henry achieved audience perspective and ob-

jectification evidently desired by the directors and instanced another example of their Brechtian-absurdist theatre philosophy.

The behavior of the characters cited and others was appropriate to the directors' novel and provocative interpretations. It was not surprising for Pistol to stand legs apart and twirl his pistol in the best Hollywood Western tradition. A few shots fired at the right moment to impress his friends or enemies pleasantly fulfilled audience expectation. The dry, gutteral cackle of Bardolph signified a sense of humor natural to the outlook of a robot. His slow, heavy movement when walking, sitting, or gesturing was mechanical rather than spontaneous. When Pistol poured sack over his large egghead, he did not respond but allowed it to drip off at will, to the delight of the audience. When Francis, the befuddled waiter, stepped into a large bucket of sack and withdrew a dripping foot, it was behavior in keeping with his character established in an earlier scene in which Hal and Peto turned him into a puppet by calling "Francis" from all directions. The splashing of the contents of the bucket about the stage appropriately increased in accordance with the farcical behavior of the rowdy company and recalled the behavior of the Keystone Kops and the Marx brothers. If the liquid stuff happened to splash on the members of the audience sitting near the apron of the stage—and it did frequently—it was just another way of provocatively activating the audience: Bystanders were turned into participants. Another instance of this brand of aesthetics may be demonstrated by the battle scenes in the *Henrys*. The soldiers fired cannons, muskets, and pistols and filled the stage with smoke. It was not surprising that the smoke blew into the auditorium, choked some of the audience, and started them coughing. The appearance of bloody hands and bloody wounds simulated by actual red liquid had for the audience a certain realistic shock value at climactic moments of hand-to-hand conflict between two principal characters. But after the initial reaction of momentary belief there was always a counterreaction of disbelief and a break in illusion. This is another technique consciously employed to activate the audience—even if illusion is replaced by objectivity. In fact, changing the audience's aesthetic relationship to the stage, whether through actual physical involvement or active rejection of simulated reality, is an integral part of this new look at

Coriolanus *by the Berliner Ensemble with Helene Weigel as Volumnia and Ekkehard Schall as Coriolanus, directed by Manfred Wekwerth/Joachim Tenschert, 1966. Photo: Vera Tenschert.*

Shakespeare. Consistency of aesthetic attitude has long been a convention, if not a law, of theatre. Conventions and laws are being challenged and broken, and the audience is being asked to expect and accept a different kind of dramatic experience.

Still another example of novelty of dramatic experience was the occasion of Gertrude's drinking from the cup of poisoned wine in the last scene of *Hamlet* and actually spewing forth the contents as vomit. Again there was momentary shock and then disbelief *and then* disgust. Needless to say, illusion was shattered, and alienation momentarily occurred, but then almost immediately the audience was drawn back into the illusion of a life-and-death struggle between Hamlet and Claudius by the accumulated emotional impact of the action, suspense, and partisanship of sympathy. Yet the surprise and the verisimilitude of Gertrude's vomiting onstage was so revolting and so dominates the memory of the last scene of the play that this secondary character and the act acquire an importance not rightfully theirs. Even

during the performance, when the focus of attention was shifted from her to Hamlet and Claudius, the memory of the moment was not completely eradicated. This shocking and repugnant incident served to distort the dramatic values of this section of the play. Its validity can therefore be seriously questioned. This appears to be a matter of directorial caprice rather than artistic responsibility.

On the other hand, such examples of frontal attack on audience sensibilities are so characteristic in the new approach to Shakespeare that they must be considered intentional and calculated. Obviously, certain aspects of this approach show a Brechtian influence. Much of his philosophy and his technique are exemplified in his version of Shakespeare's *Coriolanus* as directed by Manfred Wekwerth and Joachim Tenschert and presented by the Berliner Ensemble at the International Theatre Festival in Venice September 17 to October 10, 1966. (It is assumed that the regisseurs Wekwerth and Tenschert were faithful to Brecht in all aspects of the production.)

The physical aspects were simple and stark, in keeping with Brecht's theatrical philosophy. The stage was used as pure space—undecorated and unenclosed. Environment was suggested only by a towerlike structure upstage center. In the middle of this tower was an archway, suggesting the gate to Rome or, when turned around to reveal the other side, the entrance to Corioli. The Roman side of the unit was white and, though rough in texture, subtly reminded one of a marble arch. The other side looked as though it were made of tree trunks and roughhewn lumber. A primitive ladder led to a balcony above the opening below. This connoted the Volscian locales. A revolving stage made the changes from Rome to Corioli. A white, sheetlike curtain, strung on a wire, spanned the proscenium opening and was drawn to reveal a new scene and closed to indicate a scene change. The half curtain, of course, only partially hid the backstage area and scene changes. Chairs, benches, and other furnishings essential to the action were placed in position behind the curtain. Bright, hard, white light from hanging instruments plainly visible to the audience illuminated the stage in a continuous brilliant glare.

This scheme of production made little concession to realism and actually called attention to the fact that this was a world of make-believe and theatricalism that in many ways suggested the Elizabethan stage conditions.

The audience was asked to piece out the imperfections with their imaginations.

The physical behavior of the actors in Brecht's *Coriolanus* was often highly stylized in simultaneous group reactions. When, for example, the citizens listened to Menenius' "tale of the belly," they adjusted their body positions and turned to him as though they were a group of robots and shifted their positions to adjust to any change of position by Menenius. There was no individual byplay, detail of movement, or individualistic action or reaction. Each individual became unified with the group and symbolized a unit of mob behavior. The complete immobility of the citizens established between group movements was a formalistic, stylized device. The battle scenes were also symbolic in their meticulous and beautiful choreography reminiscent of the Kabuki theatre. They became ritualistic dances of conflict and death. Martial music set the tempo and established the mood.

Music was used throughout the production, mostly for satirical and shock effect. It was heavy with brass instruments and tympani which abruptly changed the tempo and mood. Strident, clashing, dissonant sounds characterized the score, especially composed for the production by Paul Dessau. The music had great dramatic value, utilized to comment upon the dialogue, a character, or a situation. Often the comment was made by the antimodal nature of the music, which said the opposite to what the dialogue said. Even music which came out of the situation, like that for the triumphal entrance of Coriolanus into Rome, for example, was not without mocking overtones which served to belittle the pomp, ceremony, grandeur, and joyous celebration of the moment. The music spoke a language clearly communicated to the audience. The theatre sound engineers in control of the transmission of the music during the performance had several cues to increase volume suddenly or gradually in order to enhance the dramatic moment. The source or direction of sound was also used to heighten a moment. Particularly effective dramatically were those instances in which the audience was surrounded by sound; it broke through the proscenium arch and filled the auditorium, coming from all sides of the theatre. The audience felt itself to be in the very middle of the dramatic action. Here was direct physical involvement rather than alienation.

The basic costumes were modern for the citizens and a combination of everyday dress and accessories of a historical nature for the principal characters. The symbolic was thus emphasized over the realistic. The costumes and the director's techniques applied to the actors were not the kinds usually associated with the production of Shakespeare to induce the audience to sympathize with the characters. Rather, the Brechtianisms forced the audience to objectivity and nonparticipation; they were alienation devices.

They were consciously used in Brecht's characteristic intention to "teach" the audience in a "learning" theatre. As director, he did not attempt to make the audience sympathize with Coriolanus but tried to present an indictment against him.

Of all of Shakespeare's plays, *Coriolanus* lends itself most readily to Brecht's political and theatrical ideology. Yet he was not the first to use the play for political purposes. A French production presented during the German occupation made Coriolanus a Fascist tyrant and the people innocent victims. And since then there have been a number of English-language productions in the United States, Canada, and England which have followed a similar line of interpretation. However, the French- and English-language productions adhered for the most part to Shakespeare's text and did not include rewritten or new scenes, tailored to fit the anti-Fascist theme. Brecht's version of the play, aside from cuts and changes in the dialogue, was unfaithful to Shakespeare, particularly in the last scene. This scene is really an epilogue which, like the last scenes of many of Brecht's own plays—and Shakespeare's—presents the moral of the story.

None of the directors at Stratford-upon-Avon changed the texts of Shakespeare's plays so drastically. Faithfulness to the texts is expected of the twentieth-century director in England. The English directors allow the plays to stand as written but project their modern interpretations by directorial emphases. And Brechtian principles of staging and acting are helpful in expressing such emphases.

In comparing the productions at Stratford with Brecht's production of *Coriolanus*, one finds definite close similarities in the approach to settings, costumes, and the use of music and sound. Differences, however, are numerous. Except for Brook's and Gaskill's avowed Brechtian productions of *Lear* and *Macbeth*, lighting was used at the Memorial Theatre for its emotionalizing and full theatrical effects.

The productions of *Hamlet,* the *Henrys,* and *Twelfth Night* underscored character psychology and detail though characterization was not naturalistic in complexity. The acting relied on coolness and understatement of emotions—though not in the manner found in *Coriolanus.* Brecht satirized his characters into one-dimensional mouthpieces. His look at them was cool, but they behaved with exaggerated and phony emotionalism. Brechtian staging of group scenes emphasized simultaneous unit movement and elimination of individualizing behavior which ended in frozen pictorial compositions. Group scenes in *Hamlet* and the *Henrys* were directed more freely and realistically, although formality and ritual were often pointed up. The *Coriolanus* battle scenes were totally dissimilar to those in the *Henrys.* Carefully controlled stylized choreography characterized those in the one production and a definite degree of realistic behavior those in the others.

Another difference between the Brecht and the English productions is the means used to achieve audience alienation—and both achieved it. It might be said that, whereas Brecht employed stylization, the English directors used extreme naturalism which resulted in a shock effect on the audience. The shock techniques no doubt evolved artistically from the discoveries made from the Royal Shakespeare Company's experimental productions of the Jacobean antecedents of Shakespearean drama, Thomas Middleton's *Women Beware Women,* Christopher Marlowe's *Jew of Malta,* and John Webster's *The Duchess of Malfi*—all blood-soaked and macabre—and its studio work in the methods of the Theatre of Cruelty. The texts of Shakespeare's plays are also the sources for the discovery of values most vividly expressed by shock techniques. The histories show the power structure, the brutality, the cheapness of life, and the horrors of war; and the tragedies, especially *Hamlet* and *King Lear,* demonstrate the absurdity of the human condition meaningful to modern audiences as a reflection of the world they live in. This modernity in Shakespeare awakens and vivifies a view of life readily acceptable to the directors of the Royal Shakespeare Company and the English youths whom they attract to the Memorial Theatre as audiences. Weary from the malaise created by the disillusionment which set in after the last world war, whose years of sacrifice produced no reward, they have turned upon the social order

with savagery. Horrified by the moral stench of Auschwitz, revolted by the continued struggle for power current in the cold war, and outraged over the war in Vietnam, they have adopted the absurdist philosophy of life. Blood, terror, and man's inhumanity to man are all a part of the world insane asylum. A theatre of shock and cruelty is a natural medium for communicating the contemporary. Shock which is organic to the play and not interpolated as a sensation-getting gimmick is achieved by the responsible artist-director of taste and integrity. He balances terror with absurdity and points the way to exciting theatricalism. Shock is a jolting and bruising assault upon audience sensibilities to create a dramatic event with Shakespeare holding the mirror up to his age and our own as well.

We see, then, that making Shakespeare contemporary since the Restoration has meant cutting, rearranging, emending, and rewriting the texts to conform to the dramaturgic conventions of each age and to the prevailing physical conditions of the stage. However, beginning with Barry Jackson's production of "Hamlet in Plus Fours," it was discernible to many that modern dress tended to illuminate character values and opened Shakespeare's plays to contemporary audience responses. Clothes and furnishings created a modern environment which highlighted psychological, social, and political parallels with the Elizabethan age. The influences of the absurdist and Brechtian theatres on the techniques of production for Shakespeare gave him contemporaneity theatrically as well as productionally. Anger, cruelty, brutality, and violence have been key words to be expressed in emotional and physical terms to produce the shock necessary to alert audiences to a more active participation in the theatrical experiences. Thus there has been a reversion from arbitrary conformity to stage *conventions* and *conditions* to emphasis upon Shakespearean *interpretation.*

DIRECTORIAL CONCEPTS

Propelling this development is the seminal theatre philosophy of Antonin Artaud. Rebelling against the Comédie Française' ossified productions of Molière, Corneille, and Racine, he seemingly calls for a complete liberation from classical Western dramatic literature. In "No More Masterpieces" he says: "Masterpieces of the past are good for the past: They are not good for us. We have a right to say what has been said and even what has not been said in a way that belongs to us, a way that is immediate and direct, corresponding to present modes of feeling, and understandable to everyone." [28] He then proceeds to attack the way of language in Sophocles' *Oedipus*—language too refined for our age. He maintains that words once spoken are dead and communicate only at the moment uttered. They are fixed in a form that no longer answers the needs of the world we live in. Literary masterpieces erect a formal screen between themselves and the public.

If, as Artaud maintains, people are discouraged from going to the theatre, it is because the theatre has fostered the false and the illusory. We have become used to "a purely descriptive and narrative theatre—story telling psychology . . ." The public no longer is shown itself "but the mirror of itself." Shakespeare himself is responsible for this because he is preoccupied with psychology.[29] This amounts to art for art's sake, and Shakespeare and his imitators are responsible. It is detached art "which creates nothing and produces nothing." This literary poetry is personal and involves only the man who created it at the moment.

"We must get rid of our superstitious valuation of texts and *written* poetry." He calls for the poetry beneath the text, "without form and without text. . . . I propose then a theatre in which violent physical images crush and hypnotize the sensibility of the spectator seized by the theatre as by a whirlwind of higher forces." With the spectator in the center of the theatrical spectacle these physical images would be created by the subtextual poetry comprised of sensory responses to "sounds, noises, cries which are chosen first for their vibratory quality" and "then for what they represent." [30] In addition to sound he would use light for its suggestive qualities. Above all, underneath the words of the playwright would be the dynamism of action communicating with the inner forces of energy. "A violent and concentrated action," Artaud says, "is a kind of lyricism: it summons up supernatural images, a bloodstream of images, a bleeding spurt of images in the poet's head and in the spectator's as well." [31]

A scene from Joseph Papp's production of Hamlet *suggesting Denmark as a police state, 1967. Photo: George E. Joseph.*

In insisting upon putting an end to the subjugation of the theatre to the text and creating a "unique language halfway between gesture and thought," he suggests the replacement of the playwright by the director, who will become "a sort of unique Creator upon whom will devolve the double responsibility of the spectacle and the plot." [32]

This authority, so influential in the thinking about a New Theatre, has given the director unprecedented power. The use of this power has, of course, varied with the talent, taste, knowledge, intelligence, and imagination of the director. Today's director of Shakespeare therefore often feels free to rework his plays—or give his plays a working over. An example is Joseph Papp's 1967 production of *Hamlet* at the New York Shakespeare Festival Public Theater in Lafayette Street.

Clive Barnes, critic for *The New York Times,* titles his review "Theatre: Slings and Arrows of Outrageous Papp." And subtitles it "Director Throws Bard to the Philistines."

[28] Antonin Artaud, *The Theatre and Its Double* (New York, Grove Press, 1958), p. 74.
[29] Pp. 76–7.
[30] Pp. 78–81.
[31] P. 82.

[32] Pp. 89, 94.

Arguing that Papp was heavily influenced by Jan Kott's arguments in his *Shakespeare Our Contemporary* that "to understand Shakespeare today it is essential to relate the playwright to our own times," he says the director does not produce a *Hamlet* for our times but a "fundamentally aimless Hamlet for Philistines who wish to be confirmed in their opinion that the Bard is for the birds." As the critic describes the production as "an almost pitiful attempt at avant-garde theatrical devices" and Papp's "directorial tic of wherever possible having some lines spoken directly at individual members of the audience—down to crazy undergraduate excesses," it can be argued that Papp has been influenced not only by Kott but by the philosophy of Artaud as it applies to "No More Masterpieces." [33]

Evidently Richard Schechner, then editor of *The Drama Review,* in a letter to *The New York Times* had adopted some Artaudian theories and saw them exemplified in this production of *Hamlet.* He alleged that it, like Brook's *Marat/Sade* and the work of Jerzy Grotowski, "points to emerging and liberating forces within the theatre." Echoing Artaud's rejection of bardolatry, he claimed that "our reverence for it puts it clear out of consciousness. As much as anything in theatre literature, *Hamlet* is 'the classic.' We have learned to stand away from it, daring only to 'reinterpret' this or that nuance." He goes on to say the production "went beyond interpretation toward confrontation." [34] The dialogue and scenes were rearranged, lines interpolated, and the text used as Artaud urged: "as the point of departure for all theatrical creation." [35] Moreover, exemplifying another Artaud tenet, the production by its "disunity brought into play an interchange between production and audience that is all too infrequent in our theatre." However, though the "vertical spaces" of the theatre were "used to stretch meaning and to make new connections between otherwise tired dialogue," Schechner complains that the director didn't involve the audience enough. He would drive "the farce terror of this 'Hamlet' . . . into the audience's consciousness." He thought the "most liberating was the double-edged knife of debunking and opening new views of 'Hamlet'. Certain scenes—and certain stances in our theatre—have become all too classic . . . They struck at the heart of an old and nearly meaningless 'Hamlet': while probing into the stuff out of which our own 'Hamlet' can be made." [36] He thus marries Artaud and Kott in his handmade scheme of theatre architects.

Obviously the two points of view of Clive Barnes and Richard Schechner raise a fundamental question about the approach of today's director to yesterday's drama, especially Shakespeare's: How can he present the past to illuminate the present? Sharing Artaud's concern about our tendency to be subjugated to masterpieces and to memorialize art, the director must surely liberate the plays from museums and libraries in order to communicate the living force of their drama to modern audiences. Does this mean, in the words of a well-known critic who advanced the notion tentatively, that there is no "way out of our present dilemma unless we are willing to approach classical works with complete freedom, even if this means adapting them into a modern idiom"? [37]

As a teacher of dramatic literature, Brustein had heretofore felt that a great play of the past spoke to the present because of the universality of its dramatic values and aspects of character. As a critic he had "cried out against the mutilation of the classics, either through updating, bowdlerizing, or adapting them to the musical stage." And he asserts that he still objects to some of these approaches. However, he like Schechner finds that familiarity breeds contempt. They say we have read, studied, and seen the principal plays of Shakespeare so often that they no longer have much dramatic viability for us. And awe and reverence for them have entombed them. It can be argued, on the other hand, that they speak as critics and scholars—specialists—and not as average members of audiences who have a very limited acquaintance with the classics, by Shakespeare or anyone else. Anyway, can two or three viewings of the best-known plays like *Hamlet, Macbeth, Othello,* and *King Lear* ever neutralize their drama? Can you exhaust the powers of a great symphony by hearing it a few times? Of course Beethoven's "Fifth" is overly familiar to music critics and some students of music, but must it be adapted to a

---

[33] Clive Barnes, *The New York Times,* December 28, 1967.
[34] *The New York Times,* January 28, 1968.
[35] Artaud, p. 94.

[36] Schechner.
[37] Robert Brustein, "No More Masterpieces," *yale/theatre,* No. 1 (Spring 1968), p. 11.

modern idiom to justify its inclusion in a concert?

Adaptation of one kind or another has been common in the history of literature. Among the Greeks themselves the various myths were the common bases for plays by different authors. The Electra story was turned into plays by Aeschylus, Sophocles, and Euripides. And in modern times Jean Anouilh, Jean Cocteau, Jean Giraudoux, T. S. Eliot, and Eugene O'Neill have used the Greek originals to formulate their plays. Of course, one of the most frequent justifications for adapting Shakespeare is the fact that Shakespeare borrowed from the works of Plutarch, Raphael Holinshed, and others to form his plays for his own special needs—for the Elizabethan stage and Elizabethan audiences. And, as has been illustrated above, his plays have been transformed by others to suit the tastes and conventions of theatres of the seventeenth, eighteenth, and nineteenth centuries. The twentieth century has found Shakespearean drama a veritable golden egg for hatching musicals and plays. *Your Own Thing* and *Rosencrantz and Guildenstern Are Dead,* based on *Twelfth Night* and *Hamlet,* proved two of the outstanding successes of the 1968 theatrical season. The musical version of *Two Gentlemen of Verona* was a happy and successful theatrical event of 1972. *The Boys from Syracuse* and *Kiss Me Kate* were earlier triumphs heavily indebted to Shakespeare. There can be little objection to these modernizations because they achieved distinction on their own merits.

Adaptation of Shakespeare's plays "into a modern idiom" can take more questionable forms when the director reshapes them, interpolates contemporary dialogue, and distorts characters and meaning to conform to directorial self-indulgence in the name of modernity. These adaptations retaining Shakespeare's titles often are no more than parodies of the original. They cannot, in all honesty and artistic integrity, pretend to be Shakespeare. They are "adaptations" and should be advertised as such. The attempt to find modern parallels, correspondences, and equivalences through interpretive and productional means can be justifiable, however. The integrity of the text can, except for cutting, be maintained by a change in emphasis in dramatic values. Brook's *King Lear* has already been cited as an example. Its modernity was conceptual and communicative.

The director's attempt to find a modern metaphor for the classics can lead him into private excursions in interpretation and production. His concepts and allusions can be of questionable validity if he fails to create recognizable and communicable images and symbols for his audience. He must make his reference points clear, and the facts of the play must be projected in terms of his conceptual guidelines. Jonathan Miller's production of Robert Lowell's *Prometheus* at Yale in 1967 can be seen as a case in point. Eschewing a Greek setting and Greek costumes, he chose, he said, to set the play "in some institution that represents tyranny." The time was not specific, "but some sort of decaying seventeenth-century culture that has gone bad. The characters are prisoners, they put on the play in this eternal imprisonment as entertainment."[38] As Brustein said in writing about the production: ". . . in performance, it proved to be much more vague, blurry, and imprecise." This was true because the audience could not apprehend these reference points from the dialogue or action of the play —or from its direction. The director's concept or metaphor remained private and has been made public only by a critic's reportage.

Whereas Miller decided to dispense with conventional and recognizable gods, Ocean was presented as a selfish, wheedling old man, Hermes as a "Heil Hitler"–saluting Nazi, and Hephaestus as a wooden-legged Negro who hummed while he worked at enchaining Prometheus. These modern equivalences were counterpointed by the crumbling, aged brick structure going upward and downward out of sight. And high above the actors hovered the statues of Greek gods tucked into niches. This was the director's concession to specific analogy. The modernity of the characters assumed by the gods was easily discernible by the audience but the ancient and contemporary parallels in time and place and tyrannical power were not so immediately apparent.

These and other directorial images for characters and production were doubtless stimulating to Miller and his actors in the daily work of rehearsal but it is questionable that they were sufficiently specific and apprehensible for the audiences in general. "Miller was anxious to let the action resonate in the minds of the auditors without allowing them to decide on any single interpretation."[39] If "to

---

[38] Brustein, p. 17.
[39] Brustein, p. 18.

resonate" means, according to the dictionary, "to vibrate sympathetically with some source of sound," and in this case the sound of words tumbling out of the mouths of the actors in Lowell's *Prometheus,* most members of the audience could not decide upon any interpretation at all. The resonances (in the poetic and metaphorical sense) of the production oscillated, for the most part, only in the inner ear of the director.

In citing this example of an attempt to find contemporary analogies in an ancient myth turned into a modern play, one must agree with Brustein when he says that "The dangers of this line of attack are obvious: Everything depends upon the tact, taste, and talent of the director. If new values are not unearthed by a new approach, then the whole effort is worthless; and if these new values are merely eccentric or irresponsible, then it is careerism rather than art that has been served." [40] Few can quarrel with this responsible statement except to specify that "the talent of the director" should include his ability to make his directorial work communicable and apprehensible to and by the audience. Moreover, this should mean avoidance of the self-indulgent and esoteric, understood only by a like-minded coterie audience. The problem of the director in finding modern relevance in a classic is not the same as that of the scholar-critic, who can build up thematic hypotheses for the reader who will have the printed word at his command—the printed word which can be pondered in the privacy of the study. The members of the audience in a theatre have little time to ponder the word or the visual signs created by a production.

The private vision of the interpreter, be he critic or director—and I say that interpretation for the former is often not valid and practical for the latter because of the differences of communication to the reader on the one hand and the members of the audience on the other —must be communicable and immediately perceptible in terms of sight and sound. A moment of movement, gesture, actor grouping, and aural phenomena must be selective, emphatic, mentally or sensorily associational, and capable of conscious or unconscious integration and comprehension by the audience. This means that directorial bits and pieces must form a meaningful mosaic. The parts must be organic to the whole. The whole, in

A scene from Michael Kahn's NOW production of Love's Labour's Lost *by the American Shakespeare Festival Theatre, Stratford, Connecticut, 1968. Set: Will Steven Armstrong; costumes: Jane Greenwood. Photo: Friedman-Abeles.*

all the aspects of production, must be based on an interpretation which is also organic and not superimposed by a highly individualistic angle of vision derived from reactions to disconnected and isolated aspects of the play which illustrate some particular social, political, psychological, or aesthetic point of view.

Such a point of view is often derived from the discovery of modern relevance in terms of parallels or correspondences suggested by literal similarities, images, similes, or metaphors. For example, Michael Kahn, in his 1968 production of *Love's Labour's Lost* by the American Shakespeare Festival, evidently saw the play in terms of a present-day hippie love-in. Berowne, Longaville, and Dumaine represent the far-out though idealistic youth of today—possibly more particularly the Beatles—who go off, not to the King of Navarre's court, which would be "a little academe," to war against their affections "And the huge army of the world's desire—" but to an Indian guru's pad. The other characters are made to fit into the scheme; Don Armado is, of course, right at home in a psychedelic

---

[40] *Ibid.*

environment—he is truly "turned on." During the course of the performance each of the three principal young men picks up a floor microphone and sings his love soliloquy to the miniskirted young ladies of France, accompanied by pulsating rock music. All of this adds up to a funny, relevantly modern version of the play. Naturally, the character, plot, and language values of the original become changed and distorted. Thematic values are brought up-to-date and the tone of the play is completely transformed. This version is comic, but comic in terms of period difference and gimmickry. The satire is no longer so much aimed at the characters as at Shakespeare. The production is actually a parody of the play Shakespeare wrote. As a dramatic work it has been diluted into a fashionable entertainment without its original insight into character and wit of dialogue. And, importantly, it has lost its universality of theme: a gentle derision of youthful delusions and pretensions. The follies of human nature have been transformed into irresponsible waywardness.

The director, it must be admitted, clearly and unmistakably communicated to the audience a view of timely and recognizable visual and aural phenomena of modern life. Yet the view was superficial—an image without profundity or originality. He replaced literature with journalism. He mistook gimmickry for creativity.

In comparison, Peter Brook's production of *Love's Labour's Lost* at the Shakespeare Memorial Theatre, Stratford-upon-Avon, in 1946 presented a vision of youthful whims and illusions dramatized in a pastoral never-never land. In settings and costumes based upon the prints of Jean Watteau, the scenes of the play unfolded with all the charming artificiality, pretentiousness, languid and overgenteel posturing of narcissism necessary to comment on the characters amiably but satirically. Beautifully composed in a series of pictures, the actors played out the incidents of plot with joy and playfulness of behavior and language. The Watteau costumes emphasized the gentle satirical elements in the play; their design in line and color, and the use of velvet, silk, and satin enhanced the soft, luxurious, slightly unreal world of the play. This directorial treatment of *Love's Labour's Lost* gave the audience sufficient perspective to see the characters and events in a comic light which pointed up Shakespeare's ridicule tempered with human understanding. The follies and foibles of

youth were smiled upon indulgently. Berowne, Dumaine, Longaville, the King of Navarre, Don Armado, and all the rest were not ideographs cartooned by the director but human beings suffering transitory delusions—just like ourselves and our neighbors who daily become entrapped in wishful thinking, whims, and fantasies only to be rescued by human nature and common sense. Everything the director did was organic and served the inherent dramatic values, tone, and style of the play. (Even the arrival of Arcade announcing the death of the King of France made dramatic sense in Brook's production, whereas it did not in Kahn's.) His interpretation was not arbitrarily superimposed but grew out of the text. The characters were not disrupted and twisted to suit a fashionable or political concept of life, yet they were freshly perceived and vigorously communicated. Their behavior and vocal mannerisms retained the truth and conviction of the original while jumping the historical gap from the Elizabethan era to our modern one.

In order to stress present-day obsession with business, the contemporaneity of *The Merchant of Venice* was dramatized by the British National Theatre production in 1970 when the director Jonathan Miller moved the

Jonathan Miller's production of The Merchant of Venice *by the National Theatre Company of Great Britain, 1970. Anthony Nicholls appears as Antonio and Laurence Olivier as Shylock. Photo: Anthony Crickmay.*

play from its traditional Renaissance humanist environment and placed it in the late nineteenth century when Britain was the center of world trade. The Victorian setting with its ornate furniture provided the appropriate ambience for richly upholstered characters who spoke Shakespeare's verse in the clipped and dry tones of big business. In Miller's interpretation not only Shylock and his loan-shark friends but Christian merchants, genteel ladies, and young lovers were motivated by profit and loss in life's daily transactions. Moonlit poetry and romance were shortchanged and the magic and beauty of Belmont were devalued in a world where everything is bought and sold.

Shylock, the gold merchant of Venice, dominates this world of the play and takes possession of the drama. As played by Sir Laurence Olivier, Shylock is the center of attention. His Jew is a Victorian gentleman with top hat, Prince Albert coat, cane, and gloves. He has come up from the ghetto and now moves in nouveaux riches circles. Yet under his top hat

he wears a yarmulke and when the veneer of Gentile society is peeled off by the shocking court defeats, Shylock the Jew reverts to the rough habits of speech and animal outrage of a race cruelly frustrated and despairing since the beginning of time. When he leaves the stage there is a pause which is finally shattered by a chilling shriek of lamentation. Shylock the merchant learns a lesson in human justice and mercy and is caught in the fine print of a business contract of his own devising—hoist by his own petard!

A play is like putty in the hands of the director. It can be pushed in here and pulled out there, and in the process its shape is changed. As an object it communicates certain impressions and has certain connotations. In the production of *The Merry Wives of Windsor* referred to earlier in the section on "Comedy" and in *The Merchant of Venice* just cited, the directors emphasized elements of the play and production to focus attention on specific thematic values pertinent to our society. In both cases the central characters

The French forces in Henry V *as conceived and staged by Michael Kahn for the American Shakespeare Festival Theatre at Stratford, Connecticut, 1969. Set: Karl Eigsti; costumes: Jean Button. Photo: Martha Swope.*

were presented in new colors and dimensions which affected the entire dramatic organisms. The physical productions created the environments, and emotional and intellectual climates helped in projecting the thematic choices. The period dress and architectural features of the settings—the visual elements—chosen by the director tend to strongly influence audience reactions. They can be so impressive as to be distracting from the language, characters, and narrative of the play. The Victorian milieu and clothes for *The Merchant of Venice* were intensely appealing visual stimuli but their interpretational validity was established by their social and historical connotations which projected the characters' prepossession with materialism. The productional elements thus expressed the people and theme intrinsic to the play. They were not gratuitously superimposed on the material. The visual and productional side of directing can become an end in itself. The director can be carried away with the excitement of personal visual expressivity.

Director Michael Kahn's production of *Henry V* in the summer of 1969 at the American Shakespeare Festival Theater might illustrate this. There is no question of Michael Kahn's ability as an imaginative and resourceful director. His production was memorable for its bold and arresting visual images created to enforce their Brechtian didacticism. Selecting the metaphor that war is a game, he introduced a prologue of improvisatory activity on a stage bare of furnishings except for a jungle gym and swing. As the audience took their seats before a curtainless stage they saw boys and girls dressed in sweatshirts, dungarees, football jerseys, sweaters, and T-shirts dribbling a basketball, riding bicycles, wrestling, shadowboxing in an urban playground. An East Side/West Side rumble develops—and a game turns into a war. With the piercing sound of a whistle the improvisation ended and the actor to play Henry was given a cape and a crown, and the swing became his throne. (Incidentally, the King's crown was made available to him by a contraption of steel mesh and odd wheels—a kind of "war machine.") Then Shakespeare's play began.

A dungareed chorus, destined to be present throughout the play, with apelike grunts and scratching, scrambled over the jungle gym as Henry declared war against the French. The killing of prisoners was mimed by guards with pikes, and the victims froze into grotesque postures. The French were costumed like gargantuan hockey players, the King and the Dauphin elevated by cothurni. They gave the false impression of invincibility, dispelled by the siege of Harfleur when the cardboard castle with paper walls was easily ripped to shreds. These are strong and even poetic images. But when the director has Shakespeare's dialogue spoken by the French translated into French and retranslated back into English by United Nations–style interpreters with microphones, the cleverness of the director takes precedence over the play. Fearful lest some members of the audience will fail to understand that the play is being presented as an antiwar tract, the director uses lines of his own devising which are spoken by the production's stage manager or interlocutor, reminiscent of Brecht's narrative captions projected on screens above the play's action. Thus we are told that the scene we are about to witness illustrates "The War Machine" or "The Propaganda Machine." Before the St. Crispin's Day speech we are told that "The Machine Creates the Believable Lie." The delightful courting scene with Henry and Kate is prefaced by the caption, "The Deal." In addition, a masked, bloodied Chorus of the Dead hovers in the background of the scene. This same chorus had represented the dead when the roll call of the missing was read on the battlefield and they rose to stand in a solid line facing the audience. Henry and Kate are married with Death as the chief wedding guest, and *Henry V* becomes a play which mocks heroism and patriotism and makes war man's chief enemy. Obviously this is not what Shakespeare's play has always been thought to be about. It has been considered a patriotic play showing the growth of a leader to be admired by his countrymen.

This is an example of a production animated by the choice of a subsidiary theme by a director bent upon exploiting a play for its timely overtones rather than its timeless melody. He would capitalize upon a prevailing climate of audience opinion against war. But what is to be gained from a sermon against sin when the audience is already converted? Does the minister preach the sermon because he likes the sound of his own voice and enjoys a flamboyant display of homiletics? Is this production a valid attempt to make Shakespeare contemporary through responsible and cogent interpretation or an exercise in gimmickry and directorial exhibitionism?

Under the provocative influence of Antonin

Artaud, who conceives of the director as the dominant artist in the theatre, some directors have exploited Shakespeare to show off their private points of view. They feel absolutely free to cut, change, rearrange, restructure, and adapt a play in any way to suit their purposes. Directorial and productional aspects are calculated to assist in conveying their point of view. Shakespeare simply provides a convenient warehouse of plots, characters, themes, locales, and dialogue for the would-be overall creator: playwright-director-actor-designer. Sometimes his "creative" efforts consist of patchwork rewriting and reorganization, and at other times the dominant director works more deeply with his source material and devises something entirely different and new and his own rather than Shakespeare's.

Charles Morowitz, an American critic and director based in London for several years and noted mainly for his experimental work with Peter Brook in their performances in London of what they, influenced by Artaud, called "Theatre of Cruelty," wrote and produced *Hamlet: A Collage.* Admitting his contempt for Hamlet as a character, he moved the original lines about to try to communicate his feelings to the audience. In a lengthy introduction to the published version of his collage he explains why he has such a low opinion of Hamlet, but the disruption of the speeches and their allotment to characters for whom they were not originally intended do not achieve his intention but evoke laughter. The whole undertaking resembles a parody created by a rather clever and self-satisfied sophomore to be performed by the college literary club at one of their "smokers."

In March 1973 Ellis Rabb brought his production of *The Merchant of Venice* to The Repertory Theater of Lincoln Center stage and got five favorable, three mixed, and three negative reviews. The production evidently evolved from Rabb's vision of the play rather than Shakespeare's. Rabb's dialogue is superimposed on Shakespeare's to project an unflattering view of *dolce vita* Christians—sensual, decadent, hedonistic. This eclectic view of the play focuses on a man (Antonio) in love with a man (Bassanio) who is torn between his love for a man (Antonio) and a woman (Portia). Shylock turns out to be the one truly admirable character in the play. At the end of the play Antonio is left alone onstage as he watches the couples leave him in the moonlight. Apparently the staging, acting, setting, and costumes are deftly and imaginatively shaped to create theatre of an estimable artistry, though Shakespeare's writing and dramatic values are, in the minds of some, nevertheless to be preferred to Rabb's.

A. J. Antoon's production of *Much Ado About Nothing* for the New York Shakespeare Festival, which opened in the summer of 1972 and was later moved to Broadway, proved once again that play's resilience to contemporary directorial treatment.

In 1957 the American Shakespeare Festival at Stratford, Connecticut, presented a vastly amusing version of the play set in the Spanish-American Southwest circa the middle 1800s, with a ranch house as the locale for the action and colorful Spanish costumes for the characters. The production starred Katharine Hepburn and Alfred Drake as Beatrice and Benedick. They played with wit, Latin temperament, and verve. Virgil Thompson furnished a lively score interspersed with music reminiscent of the popular "Lone Ranger" radio series together with charmingly romantic interludes. The directors John Houseman and Jack Landau had a bright productional concept which worked for a modern audience. Even the Don John scenes and the Hero "death" scene fitted into the framework. The Dogberry low-comedy scenes, however, stubbornly refused to be updated and transplanted out of their Elizabethan milieu. They, therefore, were a jarring note in an otherwise very successful presentation which stretched the texture of the play but did no damage to its basic tone and meaning.

In 1965 Franco Zefferelli set London's National Theatre production of *Much Ado* in a nineteenth-century Sicilian village with twinkling lights glowing in fiesta colors. A brass band started the festivities by crossing the stage and bringing on the heroes in comic-opera uniforms and pillbox hats. The girls wore tacky wigs and homespun finery. Peanut vendors and other sidewalk merchants peddled their wares. Don John's villainy was adulterated by spoiled-child petulance, and his plotting and scheming posed little threat but served as a necessary complication to keep Hero and Claudio from solemnizing their marriage and ultimately to bring Beatrice and Benedick together in a common cause. Close to burlesque, the characters were kept in continuous action, sometimes with dizzying velocity. Movement was the chief staging device. Not only were the characters in perpetual motion but parts of the scenery were animated: Stone mermaids nodded their heads in approval or disapproval, and a statue in armor standing on his plinth abandoned his sword momentarily to hold an umbrella for the sorely vexed watchman. Needless to say, the language of the play often took second place to action. There were numerous textual revisions contributed by the poet Robert Graves in the interest of modernization. Though there was a weak outcry by academe against this Mafia onslaught on the play, the production was hailed by the nontraditionalists and it overwhelmed the audience with laughter.

Antoon's vision of the play was a considerably less strain on the text. Like Zefferelli, he used a brass band to bring onstage Benedick, Claudio, Don John, and the others, heroes of the Spanish-American war in turn-of-the-century uniforms. The girls in dress of the period applauded, shrieked with joy, and tossed flowers at the returning soldiers. A large gazebo in the background and lattice-work supporting flowers everywhere suggested a summertime celebration in an ambience for virginal love and short-lived, unserious quarrels and capricious misunderstandings. Period-

flavored music, which included Dixieland tunes, tied the scenes together and enhanced the varying moods of the scenes. While gentle spoofing was the director's approach and signaled to the audience the desired attitude to the production, tampering with the text was minimal. Everything was calculated to evoke belief in the characters and concern for their problems consonant with a pleasurable theatrical experience. The director served the play for the most part, while opening it up for the full enjoyment of today's audience.

The most masterful demonstration of Shakespeare's relevance to the contemporary world was Peter Brook's production of *King Lear*. Second to this was his production of *A Midsummer Night's Dream,* which was the peak of success for the Royal Shakespeare Company in 1970. In both productions the director-innovator Brook was apparently putting into practice certain theories of Artaud in his approach to theatre masterpieces, of Brecht in his production techniques (and of Vsevolod Meyerhold), and of Jan Kott in his "Endgame" interpretation of *King Lear*. In his iconoclastic production of *A Midsummer Night's Dream* he seems to have been influenced by some of Kott's ideas, especially the

A. J. Antoon's production of Much Ado About Nothing *for the New York Shakespeare Festival, 1972. Designed by Ming Cho Lee. Photo: George E. Joseph.*

view of the bestiality of love. However, Brook shaped this view toward his own purpose, which, in my opinion, emphasized the humor and charm of the play and reconciled passion with rationality, dream with reality. The darker implications of a bewildering dream experienced by the young lovers, Titania, and Bottom were present in performance but took second place to the lighthearted knockabout comedy and charm of the play. Puck was more the trickster than the devil Kott saw. He was stage manager–clown. In his first appearance he came swinging onstage on a circus-like trapeze and was dressed in a clown's yellow, billowy, baggy trousers. He spread confusion among the lovers and played practical jokes on Titania and Bottom, but in the epilogue of the play he asked for pardon and referred to himself as "an honest Puck."

To achieve a tone of warm humor and lightness and to project his interpretation, the director recognized the necessity of integrating the fantasy world of the fairies and the realistic world of the court and the mechanicals. One device to accomplish this was his use of one actor to play Theseus and Oberon, and one actress to play Hippolyta and Titania. And the actor who plays Puck also plays Philostrate. To what extent the audience was aware of the effect this doubling had on the meaning of the play is a matter of conjecture. (Latecomers who had little opportunity to consult their programs may not even have been aware of the doubling.) Such casting by the director helps to create a double vision of the characters showing their contrasting attitudes toward love. (Bottom and company present a third vision of love.)

Evidences of Brecht's and Meyerhold's theories were apparent in the productional means used to convey the director's interpretation of the play. First was the high-walled white set brilliantly lit with Brechtian white light, unchanged during the performance. The side walls and the down-right and -left front walls inside the proscenium had metal-runged ladders leading to a black catwalk at the tops of the side and back walls. Musicians and actors used the catwalk for mounting trapezes, awaiting cues, watching the action below, and suspending silver coils of wire which represented the briars and brambles of the wood. Two doors were in the center of the back wall. The floor, without benefit of furnishings, was the circus theatre of Meyerhold's empty

space. Gone were the Corinthian pillars and steps representing the court, a hut for the mechanicals, and trees and flowering banks for the lovers and fairies. The audience was allowed to use its imagination uninhibited.

The imagination of an audience permitted free play will respond favorably to the unexpected and oscillate between fact and fantasy. Tired of the cloying prettiness and cuteness of traditional fairies dressed in stiff white tutus, they gleefully accepted hippie-looking young men in slacks, sweaters, and sweat shirts in attendance upon Titania and singing Titania to sleep with tunes reminiscent of the music of the Beatles. The spinning disks handed from Puck to Oberon as they sat airborne on circus trapezes created a delightful magic spell for audience and characters. Light flowing and billowing costumes for fairies and kimonolike costumes for the court personages enhanced fantasy and simple formality associated with the oriental theatre.

Not the least important element was the tapping of hollow wood and musicalized noises which tied the scenes together and created the dream world of the play where images of brutally expressed eroticism can melt effortlessly with sacred love, and order can replace anarchy, where night turns into day and wakefulness.

Here was a production which did not disrupt or transform the text or neglect the poetic language but emphasized the poet's vision beheld from a fresh angle by a director aware of Shakespeare's universality and contemporaneity.

A case can be made for directorial probing and valid experimenting to find the means to reveal Shakespeare in his universality by contemporary interpretive and productional allusions. The past can speak to the present by liberating it from the transient particularities of history and focusing on timeless and recognizable generalities. The message need not be sacrificed or transmitted into the medium which, in many productions seeking Shakespeare's modernity, becomes the message. In such instances the creative work of the director and the productional group can take precedence over the creativity of the playwright. It seems characteristic of the New Theatre that the plays presented by them appear to be written by the director rather than by the playwright. Does this not bring up the problem of preserving dramatic literature as part of our cultural heritage? This heritage is a civilizing influence needed urgently in our violent society. Throughout the years Shakespeare, in spite of the adapter, actor-manager, or director, has spoken to man in every age in more timely terms than the transient innovations of theatrical production: His insight into human nature, the beauty of its expression, and the depth of his thoughts have survived theatrical vagaries. However, the current emphasis upon Artaudian physical language, cries, sounds, noises, pyramidal compositions of bodies, and efforts to physically involve the audience at the expense of the playwright's words, plot, character, and theme can ultimately destroy the original work of art and prevent its survival from generation to generation. Is it possible to control the use of these techniques to enhance and illuminate Shakespeare's text? Can the search for relevant modern metaphors for Shakespeare deepen the director's and the audience's awareness and response to his plays? These questions must be answered by today's director of Shakespeare. He must make decisions and choices. And they must be made in terms of audience communication and enlightenment if the plays of Shakespeare are to be as vital and dynamic as they were when the Elizabethans responded to them.

PROBLEMS

1. Evolve a production concept for *As You Like It* by visualizing the Forest of Arden as a site for a commune or utopia for refugees from court (Establishment). How does such a concept affect character interpretation and behavior? Must the costumes necessarily be modern ("hippie" or "mod")?

2. Study *Othello* as a play about black and white relationships.

3. Develop contemporary relevance in an analysis of *Macbeth* as a play in an Asiatic country.

4. Try to conceive of the Capulets and the Montagues as two rival Mafia families of present-day Sicily. Visualize scenery, costumes, and the directorial approach.

5. Develop a Brechtian production of *Richard III* as a study in the rise and fall of a Hitler archetype.

6. Translate *Twelfth Night* into a commedia dell'arte play with rock music.

7. Plan a production of *Troilus and Cressida* as a reading emphasizing the ironies of war.

A SELECTED BIBLIOGRAPHY

Adams, J. C. *The Globe Playhouse*. 2d ed. Cambridge, Mass., Harvard University Press, 1942.

Artaud, Antonin. *The Theatre and Its Double*. New York, Grove Press, 1958.

Beckerman, Bernard. *Shakespeare at the Globe*. New York, Macmillan, 1962.

Bergson, Henri. *Laughter*. Tr. C. Brereton and F. Rothwell. New York, Macmillan, 1911.

Bethel, S. L. *Shakespeare and the Popular Tradition*. Westminster, P. S. King and Staples, 1944.

Bradbrook, Muriel. *Themes and Conventions of Elizabethan Tragedy*. Cambridge, The University Press, 1935.

Bradley, A. C. *Shakespearean Tragedy*. London, Macmillan, 1904.

Brook, Peter. *The Empty Space*. New York, Atheneum, 1968.

Brooks, Cleanth and Robert B. Heilman. *Understanding Drama*. New York, Henry Holt, 1948.

Brown, John Russell. "The Royal Shakespeare Company 1965," *Shakespeare Survey*, No. 19. Cambridge, Cambridge University Press, 1966.

————. *Shakespeare's Plays in Performance*. New York, St. Martin's Press, 1967.

Byrne, M. St. Clare. *Elizabethan Life in Town and Country*. Rev. ed. London, Methuen, 1950.

————. "Fifty Years of Shakespearian Productions: 1898–1948," *Shakespeare Survey*, No. 2. Cambridge, Cambridge University Press, 1949.

Chute, Marchette. *Shakespeare of London*. New York, Dutton, 1949.

———— and Ernestine Perrie. *Worlds of Shakespeare*. New York, Dutton, 1963.

Coghill, Nevill. *Shakespeare's Professional Skill*. Cambridge, The University Press, 1964.

Crosse, G. *Shakespearean Playgoing: 1890–1952*. London, A. R. Mowbray, 1953.

Esslin, Martin. *The Theatre of the Absurd*. Anchor Books ed. Garden City, N.Y., Doubleday, 1961.

Fluchère, Henri. *Shakespeare and the Elizabethans*. New York, Hill & Wang, 1956.

Granville-Barker, Harley. *Prefaces to Shakespeare*. Princeton, Princeton University Press, 1946. 2 vols.

Harbage, Alfred. *Shakespeare's Audience*. New York, Columbia University Press, 1941.

Heilman, Robert B. *This Great Stage: Image and Structure in* King Lear. Baton Rouge, Louisiana State University Press, 1948.

Hodges, C. W. *The Globe Restored*. 2d ed. New York, Coward-McCann, 1968.

Hunt, Hugh. *Old Vic Prefaces: Shakespeare and the Producer*. London, Routledge & Kegan Paul, 1954.

Johnson, Samuel. "Preface to Shakespeare," in D. Nichol Smith, ed., *Shakespeare Criticism*. London, Oxford University Press, 1936.

Joseph, B. L. *Acting Shakespeare*. New York, Theatre Arts Books, 1960.

Kermode, Frank, ed. *Four Centuries of Shakespearean Criticism*. New York, Avon Books, 1965.

Kitchin, Laurence. *Drama in the Sixties: Form and Interpretation*. London, Faber and Faber, 1966.

Knight, G. Wilson. *The Wheel of Fire*. London, Methuen, 1949.

Kott, Jan. *Shakespeare Our Contemporary*. Anchor Books ed. Garden City, N.Y., Doubleday, 1966.

Marshall, Norman. *The Producer and the Play*. London, Macdonald, 1957.

Nagler, A. M. *Shakespeare's Stage*. New Haven and London, Yale University Press, 1958.

Parrott, Thomas Marc. *William Shakespeare: A Handbook*. New York, Charles Scribner's Sons, 1934.

Ribner, Irving. *William Shakespeare: An Introduction to His Life, Times, and Theatre*. Waltham, Mass., Blaisdell Publ. Co., 1969.

Shakespeare, William. *Mr. William Shakespeares Comedies, Histories, & Tragedies* [the First Folio]. A facsimile edition prepared by Helge Kökeritz, with an Introduction by Charles Tyler Prouty. New Haven, Yale University Press, 1954.

Southern, Richard. *The Open Stage*. New York, Theatre Arts Books, 1959.

Sprague, A. C. *Shakespeare and the Actors: The Stage Business in His Plays (1660–1905)*. Cambridge, Mass., Harvard University Press, 1944.

———— and J. C. Trewin. *Shakespeare's Plays Today*. Columbia, S.C., University of South Carolina, 1971.

Spurgeon, Caroline F. E. *Shakespeare's Imagery and What It Tells Us*. Cambridge, The University Press, 1935.

Sterne, R. L. *John Gielgud Directs Richard Burton in* Hamlet: *A Journal of Rehearsals*. New York, Random House, 1967.

Stewart, J. I. M. *Character and Motive in Shakespeare*. London and New York, Longmans, Green, 1949.

Stoll, E. E. *Art and Artifice in Shakespeare*. New York, Barnes & Noble, 1951.

Styan, J. L. *Shakespeare's Stagecraft*. Cambridge, Cambridge University Press, 1967.

Tillyard, E. M. W. *The Elizabethan World Picture*. London, Chatto and Windus, 1943.

Trewin, J. C. *Shakespeare on the English Stage, 1900–1964*. London, Barrie and Rockliff, 1964.

Webster, Margaret. *Shakespeare without Tears*. New York, McGraw-Hill, 1942.

Willett, J. *Brecht on Theatre*. New York, Hill & Wang, 1964.

172

INDEX